The Future of Leadership

The Future of Leadership

Today's Top Leadership Thinkers Speak to Tomorrow's Leaders

Warren Bennis

Gretchen M. Spreitzer

Thomas G. Cummings

Editors

 JOSSEY-BASS
A Wiley Company
San Francisco

Published by

JOSSEY-BASS
A Wiley Company
350 Sansome St.
San Francisco, CA 94104

www.josseybass.com

Jossey-Bass books and products are available through most bookstores. To contact Jossey-Bass
directly, call (888) 378-2537, fax to (800) 605-2665, or visit our website at www.josseybass.com.

Substantial discounts on bulk quantities of Jossey-Bass books are available to corporations,
professional associations, and other organizations. For details and discount information,
contact the special sales department at Jossey-Bass.

Library of Congress Cataloging-in-Publication Data
Bennis, Warren G.
 The future of leadership : today's top leadership thinkers
speak to tomorrow's leaders / by Warren Bennis, Gretchen M.
Spreitzer, and Thomas G. Cummings.
   p. cm.
Includes bibliographical references and index.
 ISBN 0-7879-5567-1 (alk. paper)
 1. Leadership. 2. Organizational effectiveness. 3.
Organizational change. 4. Management. I. Spreitzer, Gretchen M.
II. Cummings, Thomas G. III. Title.
 HD57.7 .B4577 2001
 658.4'092—dc21   2001000575

FIRST EDITION
HB Printing   10 9 8 7 6 5 4 3 2 1

Contents

Preface

This book is the result of an extraordinary event celebrating the distinguished life and career of Warren Bennis. Called a *festschrift,* a German term for a volume of essays contributed by colleagues as a tribute to a scholar, this event was hosted by the Department of Management and Organization at the Marshall School of Business at the University of Southern California. The festschrift took place in May 2000 and started with a day-long conference attended by over two hundred of Bennis's friends and colleagues; it concluded with a banquet with almost twice that number attending. The conference honored Bennis's many contributions to the management field and also looked ahead to address his current passion about the future of leadership.

In organizing the conference, we asked Bennis to reveal the important questions that keep him awake at night and challenge his intellect and curiosity. He responded with a series of thought-provoking issues that tomorrow's leaders will need to understand and resolve if they are to succeed. These are presented in Chapter One. We used these questions to frame the conference and to choose presenters who could provide key insights for future leaders. Many of the presenters are Bennis's longtime colleagues; others are more recent friends. Together, they form a remarkable group of scholars and practitioners including many of the leading thinkers in management today and some of the newest crop of young leaders. We asked them to address particular issues in their presentations; we encouraged them to push the envelope and to address the really important challenges for tomorrow's leaders. The chapters in this volume represent their collective wisdom and keen speculations about the future of leadership.

Audience

This book presents valuable insights about the challenges leaders are likely to face as the new millennium unfolds. It identifies the emerging environmental and organizational conditions that tomorrow's leaders are likely to face, and shows what they need to do to succeed in those situations. Executives and administrators, whether in the public or private sector, whether new or experienced, will find this book stimulating and useful for their own understanding and development. The book also offers important knowledge and ideas for human resources professionals, organizational consultants, and organization development practitioners who seek to understand the future and help leaders adapt to it. Academics and researchers who study organizations and leadership will also find the book a rich source of issues for future inquiry and a confirmation or challenge to their own speculations about the future of leadership.

Overview of the Contents

Part One of this book sets the stage for the future that leaders are likely to encounter. In Chapter One, Warren Bennis provides a general introduction to the future of leadership. He identifies twelve challenging issues that leaders will need to understand and learn how to resolve if they are to succeed in tomorrow's organizations. Chapter Two, by Edward E. Lawler III, identifies key technological, political, and economic changes that have combined to make human capital a critical and universally acknowledged element in the effectiveness of most organizations. It shows how human capital can be a source of competitive advantage, and what leaders can do to promote the acquisition, development, and retention of human capital.

Part Two describes the organization of the future that tomorrow's leaders will probably inhabit. In Chapter Three, Charles Handy characterizes this organizational landscape as consisting of large, efficiency-driven firms (called *elephants*) and small, innovative start-ups and professional firms (called *fleas*). He argues that flea organizations will proliferate and grow in importance; they will provide new challenges for leadership at all levels in society.

He describes the characteristics of successful flea organizations, the kind of leadership they require, and how those skills can be developed.

Chapter Four, by Thomas H. Davenport, suggests that tomorrow's organizations will increasingly be populated with knowledge workers who require a different kind of organization and leadership from what works for traditional industrial workers. It outlines the characteristics of knowledge work and shows how leadership will need to change to support and develop it. This includes building knowledge-work communities and supportive cultures where knowledge workers can thrive and grow.

In Chapter Five, Steven Kerr argues that organizations of the future will increasingly face problems of differentiation among their employees, customers, products, and competitive environments. He describes how boundaryless organizations can help to organize this diversity by moving money, people, and information across internal and external boundaries. He uses his own experience in General Electric to illustrate how boundaryless organizations work and the challenges they provide for leadership.

Chapter Six, by Thomas A. Stewart, suggests that future organizations will be more like networks than like hierarchies. They will rely less on formal mechanisms for coordination, direction, and control and more on trust among members. It shows that networked organizations need specific supports to create and reinforce trust, and presents tools that leaders can apply to facilitate trust among members.

Part Three describes the leader of the future. It shows what leaders will need to know and do if they are to succeed in the organizations and environments characterized in Parts One and Two of this book.

In Chapter Seven, James M. Kouzes and Barry Z. Posner make a strong case that certain leadership lessons from the past will continue to guide successful leaders in the future. They present four enduring principles of leadership and apply them to leading tomorrow's organizations.

Chapter Eight, by Karl E. Weick, argues that because the future will be more unpredictable and unknowable than the past, sensemaking rather than decision making will become the central issue for twenty-first-century leaders. It shows how leaders can help organization members make sense out of their world. This provides members with a common sense of direction and helps them stay in touch with a constantly changing and evolving context.

In Chapter Nine, Philip Slater suggests that in tomorrow's flatter, more fluid organizations, leaders will need to function more flexibly and democratically. This will require a deep knowledge of self and an ability to manage one's personality so that it does not unwittingly thwart effective leadership behavior.

Chapter Ten, by Mihaly Csikszentmihalyi, suggests that for an organization to survive in a competitive environment that requires constant adjustments to changing conditions, leaders must create a context for creativity. They do not necessarily have to be creative themselves but must choose the best people, provide the best information, and recognize and support the best ideas.

In Chapter Eleven, Jean Lipman-Blumen argues that in an age of uncertainty and change, organization members are especially vulnerable to bad leaders who provide them a false sense of security. She describes how members can be freed from this external dependence by discovering their more heroic selves, the leader within, thus providing more leadership talent throughout the organization.

Chapter Twelve, by Cathy L. Greenberg-Walt and Alastair G. Robertson, summarizes the work of the Executive Leadership Research Team at the Accenture Institute for Strategic Change. The team's long-term study of the evolving role of leadership shows that future leaders will need to share leadership with others, to lead across different generations of employees, and to meet the demands of a global environment.

In Chapter Thirteen, James O'Toole suggests that leadership can be an institutional capacity, not solely an individual trait. Based on a multicompany study of leadership and organization effectiveness, he shows how organizations can build leadership tasks and responsibilities into their systems, practices, and cultures. This greatly expands leadership capabilities in the organization and makes it less dependent on a single great leader.

Part Four addresses how leaders stay on top of their game; how they continue to renew, energize, and develop themselves. Chapter Fourteen, by Tom Peters, provides a highly personal account of what keeps him fresh, motivated, and curious. It identifies a number of personal traits and motives that drive him forward and account for his remarkable staying power in the leadership field.

In Chapter Fifteen, Jeffrey Sonnenfeld argues that the sustaining power of leaders should be measured by how they respond to adversity and not simply by how they handle success. He describes how leaders can be resilient in the face of adversity—how they can turn tragedy into triumph and grow and develop from such experiences.

Part Five provides insights about the future of leadership from young leaders who will be our next generation of top executives. Chapter Sixteen, by Tara Church, recommends that the best way to secure a healthy future for our rapidly changing business, political, and social institutions is to engage youth directly in the dialogue and practice of leadership. It draws on her experience in creating the Tree Musketeers to show how to support young community activists and, in turn, to empower them as leaders of social and environmental change.

In Chapter Seventeen, Edward W. Headington argues that leadership must be considered from a generational perspective. He shows how Generation Xers are developing a servant model of leadership that emphasizes involvement and change at the community level.

Part Six presents closing thoughts on leadership. Chapter Eighteen, by Gretchen M. Spreitzer and Thomas G. Cummings, examines the contributions in this book and the implications of their insights for the future of leadership. In the closing Postlude, Warren Bennis presents a personal memoir of his career, recounting the experiences that shaped his life and fueled his passion for understanding and practicing leadership.

Acknowledgments

We would like to express our appreciation for all of those who made this book possible. Arvind Bhambri, Judith Blumenthal, and Larry Greiner helped us in designing the conference part of the festschrift and in recruiting the remarkable presenters whose contributions appear in this book. Laura Bristow, Marie Christian,

Kimberly Hopkins Perttula, and Luminita Voinescu provided excellent administrative support for the festschrift, while Barbara Myers guided our fundraising and Kim Jaussi administered the process of editing this book. We are particularly grateful to the staff at Jossey-Bass, especially Cedric Crocker and Susan William, who provided generous financial support for the festschrift and helped us to conceive and bring this book to life.

Los Angeles, California　　　　　　　　Thomas G. Cummings
March 2001　　　　　　　　　　　　　Gretchen M. Spreitzer

The Future of Leadership

Part One

Setting the Stage for the Future

Chapter One

The Future Has No Shelf Life

Warren Bennis

> *In my room, the world is*
> *beyond my understanding;*
> *But when I walk I see that it*
> *Consists of three or four hills,*
> *and a cloud.*
> —WALLACE STEVENS

In his *Report to Greco,* Nikos Kazantzakis tells us of an ancient Chinese imprecation, "I curse you; may you live in an important age." So we are all damned, encumbered, and burdened as well as charmed, exhilarated, and fascinated by this curse. What a time! Tom Friedman in his book *The Lexus and the Olive Tree* tells us that the world is ten years old and what he means by that is that the Berlin Wall fell a little over ten years ago, November 9, 1989, marking the end of the Cold War. The symbol of the Cold War, he wrote, was the Wall; the symbol of our "important age" is the Web; the former, an armed fortress and the latter, a boundaryless world.

The world is just over ten years old when you consider that all of the old foundations of success are gone; for example, controlling natural resources, land, gold, and oil. Now it's information and, as Bill Gates said, "The only factory asset we have is human imagination." I think he can say that without being accused of hyperbole. (At last count, Microsoft's market capitalization is $470 billion; I suspect that the factory assets don't add up to more than 1 percent or 2 percent of that.) And just consider:

- Ten years ago there were maybe four hundred people who understood the power of the Web and today there are countless millions.
- Ten years ago there was virtually no e-commerce and according to Forrester Research there will be $1.3 trillion in 2003. I think it's going to be closer to $2 trillion.
- Ten years ago Japan was riding high and we were entering a recession.
- Ten years ago AT&T was moribund and now it's an agile giant betting its future on cable TV as much as fiber optics.
- Ten years ago, the top ten growth stocks would have been a combination of energy, banking, and manufacturing companies; today the top ten are all information technology firms—Dell Computer, Cisco Systems, Sun Microsystems, QualComm, EMC, and so on down to #10, Intel.
- Ten years ago Amazon was a river in Brazil . . . and today it's a verb, as in, we've been "amazoned."
- Ten years ago thirty-five was young and sixty was old.
- Ten years ago eBay didn't exist; it is now a partner with Butterfield & Butterfield, the third-largest and one of the classiest auction houses.

And what CEOs are worrying about today and keeps them awake after midnight are such nontrivial issues as keeping their best talent, disruptive technologies, new channels of distribution, being dis-intermediated out of business, overcapacity and hyper-competition, phantom competitors (dramatized by two boys in a garage coming up with a new Great App), internal communication (not new but more problematical), grow or be taken prisoner, having to cannibalize their best-selling product.

So the world we occupy today is a vastly different world from the world of just ten years ago, vastly different from the world of fifty years ago when I started work for my Ph.D., or forty years ago when Benne, Chin, and I ingenuously put together *The Planning of Change*. Of course, we Americans have always lived on the fast track but today's hyperturbulent, spastic, volatile, uncertain, vertiginous—I promise you I won't run out of descriptors—is qualitatively different, more *chasmatic*, to coin a word, more consequential, affecting more of our life-space than other tectonic changes we've experienced, even the introduction of electricity or the turbine engine.

I can only assert that, of course, not prove it. But it seems entirely plausible to me because my old prophet's rod has failed me and when I wander from my room, I seem unable to see over the three or four hills and the cloud Wallace Stevens saw when he wandered from his room. No, the future has no shelf life these days, but it certainly poses a number of questions that we scholars and teachers and students of human organizations should be thinking about.

I'd like to raise a few of these difficult questions here, both because of their pressing urgency and because they are questions that will enliven our discourse.

1. Playing with the idea that the world is only ten years old, what will the world of organizations look like on its twentieth birthday, in 2010? Will the pattern resemble the huge megamergers of GE, Time-Warner, PB-Amoco-Arco, Viacom, and Intel—or will it look like a smallish, ramshackle Hollywood model, where groups from diverse disciplines gather together for short periods of time, develop or finish a product, and then after a spell, regroup? Or will there be some kind of combination, a hybrid of Great Groups working rather independently under some large, decentralized behemoth?

2. And what about the New Leaders? When the world is twenty, will they look like C. Michael Armstrong, Andy Grove, Jack Welch—or will they resemble Carly Fiorina, Scott McNealy, Tim Koogle, and Jeff Bezos, the under-forties? Will the New Leaders have the same competencies as the over-sixty crowd?

3. What about the future of "high involvement" organizations? American democracy, as de Tocqueville told us long ago, is not always and in all ways the very best kind of thing. It often goes too far, he thought, and when it does it has a tendency to pervert the very values it tries to foster. How does this relate to contemporary organizations, to so-called *empowered organizations,* where workers are demanding and getting more autonomy, more say in decision making, and where self-managed teams are becoming less exceptional? Will modern organizations turn into parliamentary

democracies where leaders are chosen by the led, where employee-owned management companies, like United Airlines, will have board members who are employees calling the shots?

·4. Another dilemma of democracy and one we tend to duck (I do it myself) is what we do with disparities in talent? Not to sound Nietzschean, but what do we do with—or do we admit to—superior and inferior talent? Is it Hitler's Ghost, the fear of the *Übermensch,* that blocks the view to that question? The future is here, but as someone said, it's distributed unequally. So is talent. This raises at least two pertinent questions for us: As far as organizations go, can everyone be a leader? Should everyone want to be a leader? Burt Nanus and I argued strongly for yes to the first question and ducked the second. Don't people vary a great deal with respect to intelligence, whether it's emotional or cognitive? Don't certain neurosurgeons, cello players, tennis players, and yes, leaders, have the "touch"? How many Agassi's and YoYo Ma's or Welch's do we have in any given population sample?

The second question is more complex, but must be asked. The increasing chasm of income between the top quintile and the bottom quintile—along with the obscene differential between the average CEO and the average worker ($419 to $1 at last count)—is a serious issue. It's important to note that nearly 90 percent of stocks are owned by only 10 percent of the population with the top 1 percent owning 51.4 percent. Add to that the disparities in education and family background. Should we not be worrying about the "Brazilification" of our society? Do we have any responsibility for that or ways of doing something about those achingly stubborn inequalities?

5. What about the important demographic changes that are now upon us? I'm thinking specifically about ageism, both young and old ageism. It came to mind recently when I was invited to speak at a conference called TED (Technology, Entertainment, and Design). Richard Wurman, the founder of this highly successful confab, told me that in the Y2K conference, the invited speakers would either be in their thirties and under or seventies and older. Interesting, I thought—but it brought more sharply into relief in the *New York Times* I read this morning, as I was writing this (September 12, 1999). The headline was "Andreessen Steps Down

from AOL." The story went on to say that Andreessen's successor, a fifty-three-year-old former professor, may be more suited to the ways of America Online (where executives tend to be in their late thirties and forties) than the twenty-eight-year-old cofounder of Netscape. I recalled that Andreessen was only twenty-three when he helped found the Internet browser.

Now put that together with the other side of the equation, the sixty-and-older crowd who are not only living longer and living healthier but according to all reports wanting to work way beyond sixty or sixty-five. In fact a recent study by Civic Ventures reports that 50 percent of older Americans (however that's defined) are working for pay in their "retirement" and another 40 percent do volunteer work. The golden years are dead, the report claims.

Think of this: As recently as 1960, according to a recent *Economist,* "men could expect to spend 50 of their 68 years of life in paid work. Today, they are likely to work for only 38 of their 76 years." So what do we do with these old duffers who have their energy and health and hopefully their marbles? What should organizations do to retain the wisdom without forestalling the futures of the coming generations? And what about the bored twenty-something millionaires: will they have to suffer a long life starting up start-ups as Andreessen wants to do? Or will they become philanthropizers?

The policy issues these demographics raise have serious implications. Just to take one: if workers continue to take early retirement (and the average age of retirement seems to be declining to the early sixties in the United States; much lower in all the European countries), and with the boomers in massive numbers hitting retirement in the near future, there won't be enough wage earners to support the retirement of the boomer spike.

6. What about the social contract between employers and employees, that hallowed implicit contract that usually offered some form of loyalty and responsibility to both parties? Roughly 25 percent of the U.S. workforce has been dumped since 1985 and even at present, when the unemployment rate is the lowest in over thirty years, you can figure on a half to three-quarters of a million employees in flux every year. What's interesting is that in 1998, about 750,000 workers were laid off or quit or retired, and of those,

92 percent found jobs that paid either more or were equal to
what they had been getting. A recent survey reported in the *Wall
Street Journal* revealed that four out of ten of employees were less
than three years in their job, only a third of the workforce works
in an old-fashioned 9-to-5 job, and the quit rate this year is 14.5 percent. It was about 3 percent ten years ago. I figure that the *churn*
of the workforce at any given time is between 20 percent and
25 percent; that is, the number of workers who are temporarily
out of work or looking for new opportunities is roughly that
figure.

I'd like to put a more "human face" on those numbers. I was
fascinated to read in Peter Capelli's new book the *explicit* social contract at Apple.

> Here's the deal Apple will give you; Here's what we want from
> you. We're going to give you a really neat trip while you're here.
> We're going to teach you stuff you couldn't learn anywhere else.
> In return . . . we expect you to work like hell, buy the vision as long
> as you're here. . . . We're not interested in employing you for a
> lifetime, but that's not the way we are thinking about this. It's a
> good opportunity for both of us that is probably finite.[1]

Along these lines, John Sculley told me that one of the reasons
he found the culture of Apple difficult (after Pepsi) was what he
considered a total lack of loyalty when he was there. Groups of people would abruptly leave, empty their desks in the middle of the
night and set up a new business before the next workday was over.
And not long ago, I was having dinner with a faculty colleague and
his parents. His father was in his late eighties and had been an
extremely successful banker. In passing he told me that when he
was running his business, he would never—"I mean *never*"—
he proclaimed, hire anyone who had held more than three jobs.
"Because I have to assume they're either disloyal or incompetent."
Considering today's serial monogamy of the workforce, where the
average worker may have five to eight jobs in a lifetime, I thought
his statement was rather quaint.

So what about the social contract in our Temporary Society,
in our Free Agency Society, where the new contract seems to
resemble Apple's: "We're not interested in employing you for a
lifetime . . . that's not the way we're thinking about this. It's a good

opportunity for the both of us that is probably finite." Is it all going to be one neat, finite trip?

7. Do we have or need *a* theory of organizational change? There has been much good work on leading change, on major interventions of change management, from a variety of researchers and consultants—but is there any consensus around the major strategic variables that can lead to sustainable change or a paradigmatic model of organizational change? Are complex human institutions too diverse in history, product, demography, and markets to have one monolithic model?

When I think of the prevalent business models today, it appears as if two extremes paradoxically coexist. On one hand, in this Internet Era, we have the Silicon Valley model: three people under twenty-five with a hot idea. Small is beautiful. Sound familiar? At the same time, we can cite another bromide: Size matters. Mergers are on the rise; is it quixotic to think we can come up with *the* theory of organizational change?

And by the way, are these megamergers—let's call them by their real name: takeovers—do they perform well and are they good or bad for the consumer? I've got my doubts, especially with the recent creation of the media monoliths, Viacom being the most recent example. The potential for the bureaucratization of imagination—to say nothing of the conflict issues, for example, CBS reviewing a Paramount film or a Simon & Schuster book and pretending it's objective reporting—should concern all of us.

8. Since writing *Organizing Genius,* a book about Great Groups, I've been concerned about a puzzling moral and ethical issue, one we ignored in the book, which continues to haunt me—and has no name. I can illustrate my question with examples more easily than I can describe it, let alone understand, it. The paradigmatic Great Group in the book was the Manhattan Project under the leadership of the distinguished physicist J. Robert Oppenheimer. Beginning in January 1943, that small group of scientists designed a nuclear device that brought an end to World War II. Exactly a year earlier, another group met, this time in Wannsee, a suburb of Berlin and ironically a district where (before the War) many wealthy Jews had lived. That group, under the leadership of the Chief of Nazi Security, Reinhard Heydrich, assisted by Adolf Eichmann, his secretary, was brought together to design the Final Solution, a plan to

exterminate all of Europe's remaining Jews. Another Great Group which formed itself during the last quarter of the eighteenth century was made up of six men, under the leadership of George Washington, and designed and implemented a plan to establish a new republic.

In a way, all these groups were "great" using the criteria ordinarily used in the literature to describe "high-performing systems." They all had exemplary leadership and a high degree of commitment, alignment, and trust; they all developed innovative solutions and carried them out successfully. What's wrong with that picture? Are there any important differences between groups and organizations that on one hand leave a scar on history and on the other hand, create one of the most significant social inventions of all time, the first modern, democratic nation? Should we consult for HMOs that are not doing right by the patients or a tobacco company that sells a product that kills? I could go on and on, but I'm not quite sure how to pose the question any more than I can get my nervous conceptual arms around it.

9.   One of the most frequently asked questions I get on the lecture circuit is about "balance." By balance, the questioner usually means: Can I make it at work and at home? Can I have fun and a marvelous home life *and* get a terrific bonus? My first impulse is to respond, "You're asking the wrong guy." I resist that. My second impulse is, "Brother, can you spare a nanosecond?" I resist that, too.

First of all I should make clear that balance is a mechanical term implying an equilibrium; the first definition of balance in my *Oxford English Dictionary* is a "weighing instrument." Somehow I believe that the search for balance, though deeply felt and not to be dismissed, is chimerical. We just don't do one thing at a time anymore. We multitask in the car, with a latte, with a phone, a fax machine . . . and we floss. It's interesting to note a new fraction has worked its way into our vocabulary, *24/7* as an abbreviation for everything running all the time, like our computers, twenty-four hours a day, seven days a week.

I do have a few friends who tell me they've done this; you know, a second home in Aspen, no phone calls on Sunday, four weeks with the kids on a bike trip in the Apennines. Funny, their cell phone line is always busy and when I do manage to get through, I hear their fax machine chirping away in the background. And it was Sunday! I wonder if any thirty- or forty-something who is try-ing to make it at their e-company with two children plus another one on the way or a thirty-year-old assistant professor with a work-ing spouse and a child or two and going for tenure can have bal-ance in this rat-a-tat world where the only thing we have time for is a three-minute egg. This sounds more like an editorial than a question, but tell me: Do you know anyone who has reached that state of nirvana called "balance"?

Before letting go of this question, I do think that Charles Handy is right and that we are all "hungry spirits" and that work should contain more meaning than stock options. Recently, I spoke before an audience of software executives, average age twenty-nine, average compensation, $2.5 million. They were not especially happy campers; all seemed to have a certain malaise about, yes, meaning, a kind of "is-this-all-there-is" type of question. A bad case of "affluenza," I called it. Maybe balance qua meaning can be found at work because I don't think the world is slowing down. As the historian Stephen Kern remarked, "Human Beings have never opted for slower."

10. About twenty years ago I wrote an article with the poignance of a flower child titled, "Where Have all the Leaders Gone?" What I wonder about today is where will the leaders come from? Not too long ago, I did some pro bono consulting for an out-standing research center with a small research faculty with a gazil-lion Nobel Laureates on staff. Over the last few years, they've had a lot of difficulty with their leadership. The problem was simple and also seemed intractable. Anybody who was good enough to pass the rigorous scientific criteria of the search committee didn't want the job. They wanted to do science. Having served on dozens of search committees for academic deans and presidents, I know the same problem always presents itself. There is a genuine dearth of people who are accomplished in their disciplines and want to do leadership and are competent at it. So every other year, the afore-mentioned research institute, after a long, drawn-out process, hires some reluctant soul who, after a year or so, finds out he really wants to go back to his lab and the search starts again. *Ad infinitum.*

More recently, a large financial house in New York asked if I would partner with them in developing a leadership develop-ment program. After interviewing a few of their senior partners, I decided against it because most of them were more interested in trading or doing investment banking than they were managing and leading. By the way, they didn't seem to have the foggiest notion of what leadership is, nor did they care. On top of that, many of the partners felt that doing management was somewhat beneath them, if not demeaning, certainly not worth their time. In a way, I can't fault them. They loved what they were doing, trading millions of dollars a day seemed to have more of an edge to it than worrying about the supply chain or whatever. The problem is, How do they get someone to "manage Asia"? Beats me. But perhaps that's why I should have accepted their invitation.

Now what's interesting about all this is that more and more of our workers are, to use Peter Drucker's twenty-five-year-old phrase, "knowledge workers." And today, I should add that more and more of the workforce are "investor workers," bringing their own profitable ideas into the company. Most organizations will soon resemble that research institute and the modern research university and that New York financial house. And then what: Where will the leaders come from to run this new economy?

11. Is the high rate of CEO churn we see today necessary in this business environment? There's been a lot of interest recently on the revolving doors for CEOs. A recent Harvard Business School study shows that boards are 30 percent more likely to oust a CEO than they were ten years ago. Doubtless, a number of complex factors are involved in the diminishing half-life of executive tenure: hypercompetition, Internet volatility, turbo-globalism, trillion-dollar mergers—you can round up the usual suspects. Reflecting this interest, *Fortune* ran a cover story recently with ten notable CEOs who had been axed by their Boards.

Both Morgan McCall and Dan Goleman have written seminal books on the social and emotional dramas that often lead to executive derailing. Jim O'Toole and I have written an article based on our belief that boards of directors have an enormous and not fully understood impact on executive failure. I've been intensely curious about how leaders sustain creativity, keep their juices flowing, and I think a lot of Gary Hamel's powerful question: "Are we learning as fast as the world is changing?"

How do we keep our eyes and ears open to nascent and potentially disruptive inflection points? How much does sheer luck play a part or are executives just not up to the warp speed nature of change and if so, why? Or why is it that we're witnessing this tsunami of senior executive churning?

12. Now for my final and inevitable question, and mercifully the shortest to state. What is the role of business education for the next generation? Do we continue to do what we have been doing, with just a little fine-tuning and tweaking? We *are* doing fairly well as it is, or so it seems. Certainly in terms of prestige and importance and yes, endowments. I would wager that over the last decade more business schools have been *named* and given major bucks than the combined decades preceding the 1990s. So why fix what ain't broke?

But what inflection points are we ignoring or not paying attention to? Are we providing an education that will provide the cognitive, emotional, interpersonal, and leadership competencies that will be required for sustained success in the New Economy? Is there space in our clogged curriculum for the philosophy, the metaphysics, the critical thinking of the enterprise? Are we giving our students a passion for continual learning, a refined, discerning ear for the moral and ethical consequences of their actions, and for an understanding of the purposes of work and human organizations? My greatest wish is that our students and alumni don't end up like some of those twenty-nine-year-old software millionaires, with their cell phones buzzing in their second homes in Aspen, suffering from a new kind of bug that causes affluenza and who wonder, when they retire, "Is this all there is?"

Chapter Two

The Era of Human Capital Has Finally Arrived

Edward E. Lawler III

Why did the era of human capital take so long to arrive and why is it happening now? There is no single reason why it has finally happened, but it is possible to identify some key technological, political, and economic changes that have combined to make human capital a critical and nearly universally acknowledged element in the effectiveness of organizations. The growth rate in scientific and technological knowledge is one key driver that has contributed to the growing importance of human capital. The growth of knowledge continues to accelerate; it has changed the very nature of what organizations need to do, the type of products they produce, and how they produce them. A striking example of the rapid evolution of technology is the Internet. In just a few years, it has created a host of new businesses that serve customers in new and different ways and it has created organizations that are very different in their structure, operations, and performance from anything the world has seen before.

Because of the growth in knowledge and the ways it is used by organizations, the nature of individual work has changed as well. Increasingly, work in developed countries is knowledge work in which people manage information, deal in abstract concepts, and are valued for their ability to think, analyze, and problem solve. Fewer and fewer people are doing the mind-numbing, repetitive manual tasks that used to dominate the work scene. These are being done by machines, or in some cases, sent to low-wage economies.

With the recent fall of communist and totalitarian regimes around the world, more and more of the world's economies are open to competition and free trade. This has had two profound effects: first, it has raised the level of competition in a number of industries because new competitors have entered the market. Many of these new competitors have advantages that range from geography to high-skill, relatively low-wage workforces. Second, it has opened new markets to existing organizations and challenged firms to deal with global markets and consumers. Overall, change has created a world in which what used to be good enough often is no longer good enough when it comes to organizational performance.

The combined effects of the growth in scientific knowledge, the changes in the nature of work, and the creation of a highly competitive global economy present organizations with a fundamental challenge: finding competitive advantage in a world in which many of the old sources of competitive advantage are no longer winners. Historically, organizations could often gain competitive advantage by obtaining and allocating low-cost financial capital and physical assets or by capturing critical supplies of raw materials. They could also gain competitive advantage by dominating a national market where they were protected from competition by the government or geography. The problem with these traditional sources of competitive advantage is that they are no longer effective because, in many cases, they are easily duplicated or overcome. Thus, organizations must look for new sources of competitive advantage.

Competitive Advantage

What are the sources of competitive advantage that can produce winning organizations in the future? I see three major sources that when combined can produce organizations that are likely to be winners (Lawler, 1996, 1998). The three are all concerned with the human side of business: human capital, organizational capabilities, and core competencies. These three go together in the sense that organizational capabilities and core competencies require the right kind of human capital in order to be created and sustained by corporations. Organizational capabilities and core competencies, however, clearly rest on the talent of the individuals in an organization—but they require more than simply talented labor. They require the right organizational systems and management styles. Given this, it is hardly surprising that there is an increasing emphasis on human capital and a dramatic increase in organizations competing for talented human capital.

Before I discuss the implications of the "big three"—the primary sources of competitive advantage—I need to briefly distinguish between organizational capabilities and core competencies. Core competencies have been written about extensively in the strategy literature, originally by Prahalad and Hamel (1990). They are the technical capabilities that allow an organization to design and produce products and services that allow it to win in the marketplace. Typical core competencies include Honda's ability to design and manufacture gasoline engines, DuPont's understanding of chemical processes, and Intel's understanding of microelectronics. Organizational capabilities refer to the ability of an organization to perform in ways that deliver products and services that provide distinctive and superior value to the customer. Organizational capabilities include Cisco's ability to manage acquisitions, Motorola's quality processes, and Southwest Airlines' ability to operate a low-cost, customer-focused service.

Implications for Organizations

The new business environment and the importance of core competencies, organizational capabilities, and human capital have a number of implications for how organizations need to be designed in order to be effective—and, of course, for how people interface with organizations. The most obvious is that we finally need to put to rest the traditional hierarchical, job-based, and bureaucratic model of organization that has dominated business thinking for so long.

Democracy is inevitable, even in the workplace, and the evidence suggests that this is more and more becoming a reality (Lawler, 1998). Hierarchical organizations are simply too inflexible and rigid to compete effectively in today's business environment. They fail to attract the right human capital and to produce the right core competencies and organizational capabilities. As a result, they need to be replaced by lateral forms of organization that rely heavily on teams, information technology, networks, shared leadership, and involved employees.

It is beyond the scope of this chapter to discuss in detail what these new organizational forms look like. There is room, however, to note that they will have flat, agile structures, open information, power that moves to expertise, and systems that create knowledgeable employees throughout the organization. Because they will have these characteristics, their human capital will be much more valuable and will require different treatment than has been true of the human capital in traditional organizations. This different treatment needs to start with solutions to the significant challenge of attracting high-talent individuals to join the organization, or perhaps more appropriately, to be affiliated with it. Organizations need to think of themselves as having a brand as an employer. This brand can be a single dominant brand in which all employees are treated the same and offered rewards that are attractive to the type of employees the organization wants to attract and retain. Alternatively, organizations can develop individualized work relationships and multiple brands in order to attract the diversity of employees they need.

The key strategic issue concerns what type of human capital organizations need to attract and retain. A second issue concerns how long they want to retain their human capital. A final issue concerns what types of rewards will attract and retain the right kind of human capital. Once these three issues have been dealt with, organizations need to identify what type of employment deal (or deals) is best for attracting and retaining the employees they need. It may be a single set of practices that treats most employees the same or it may be an approach such as the one often used with retail products, where a wide range of variations of the same product are offered. My guess is that most organizations will go to a multiple-employment-relationship brand simply because it has the greatest chance of attracting individuals from diverse backgrounds, but it is not always the right choice. For example, in certain customer service organizations where the organization wants to have a single face to the customer, it may make sense to strongly emphasize a particular kind of employment relationship. Southwest Airlines has done this well by hiring only those employees who have a particular style and offering only a single employment brand to most of its employees.

Whatever approach organizations take, it is clear that they need to move away from job-based approaches to managing people and toward knowledge- and skill-based approaches (Lawler, 1996). The bureaucratic model is built on the idea of jobs. Jobs are the basic molecule of the organization upon which the other elements are built. Individuals are assigned certain tasks and responsibilities, and are held accountable for performing them. They are also selected based on the nature of a job that needs to be filled, and of course, compensated based on how important or large the job is and on how adequately they perform it.

There are a number of problems with the job-based approach, all of which stem from the fact that it fails to give sufficient importance to human capital. In many respects, the job-based approach is a leftover from the Scientific Management period, in which jobs were designed to be simple and therefore doable by most individuals. A far superior approach, given the needs of today's organizations, is to focus on the knowledge and skill needs of an organization and to make this the basic molecule of the organization. Instead of job descriptions, organizations need person descriptions that outline what individuals need to do in order to perform the tasks that need to be performed. These person descriptions need to be used as the basis for selecting employees as well as for training and developing them. Finally, they should be used to reward individuals according to what they can do and how well individuals with the similar skills are paid in the external labor market (Lawler, 2000).

The switch to person descriptions from job descriptions represents the fundamental acknowledgment that human capital is critical to the effectiveness of an organization and should be the major focus of the management systems of an organization. Without this, the bureaucratic structure remains the major focus of an organization and creates a world in which people are seen as simply filling jobs rather than providing competitive advantage.

Because of the increasing importance of human capital, the relationship between employees, customers, and bosses is undergoing a fundamental change. Historically, the typical employee has held third place with respect to importance, often ending up far behind customers and managers. Employees have been evaluated on how they performed their job, but managers have rarely been evaluated with respect to how they treated their employees. Similarly, customers have been asked about their satisfaction with how employees served them, but employees have not been asked about their satisfaction in dealing with particular customers.

In the era of human capital, employees should be elevated in importance so that they are at least equal to their managers. They should be asked to evaluate their bosses, and organizations should fire bosses who do not attract or retain the best employees. To a lesser degree, the same phenomenon needs to occur with respect to customers. Organizations need to fire customers who make life intolerable for employees, and customers need to be sought based on their ability to provide challenging and satisfying work. Customers need to be looked at from a cost-benefit perspective just like products. If they cost more than they deliver, then they may not be worth having. In doing the cost-benefit analysis, of course, it is critical to look beyond just the direct costs of serving customers and to look at indirect costs such as causing employees to leave.

Impact on Individuals

Increasingly, individuals own the method of production that their organizations depend on. They deliver services, solve problems, write software, and develop products. Once they leave, it is not simply a matter of bringing another operator in to run a piece of equipment but a matter of finding an individual who can play a key role in producing a product or service. As a result of employees owning the method of production, they are much more important and valuable than they were in the era of technology-based production methods in which the physical assets of organizations were the highest value-added parts of the production process. This change from the employees' facilitating production to owning the method of production is a fundamental one in terms of its implications for how individuals will be treated as the era of human capital continues. It is likely to lead to individuals' getting a much higher rate of return on their capital. Since their human capital is mobile and can easily move to other organizations and situations that offer higher returns, the bargaining power of individuals is significantly higher. The impact of this is already apparent in organizations based on the Web. Individuals throughout these organizations are earning unprecedented returns on their skills. They are able to earn at these levels because they are in high demand and have a tremendous ability to influence the financial success of the business.

One of the major reasons why employees in Web-based businesses are earning a higher rate on their human capital than employees traditionally have is because they have an ownership stake in their organizations. In most cases, this has come in the form of stock options, which have in several respects become the basic currency of the technology world. There is every reason to believe that the growth in employee ownership that this is causing is likely to continue. Increasingly, organizations are distributing stock options to all employees and also encouraging them to buy stock. This has a number of potential advantages for organizations and individuals. If the organization is successful, it can increase the return that individuals get on their human capital. From an organizational point of view, it can provide an important substitute for the traditional loyalty relationship that existed between organizations and individuals. That it can act as a retention device, helping lock in employees and their valuable human capital for the long term, is something that is badly needed in an era in which there is a tremendous amount of competition for human capital and few employees are committed to a career with a single employer.

There are some very interesting long-term implications of employees' increasingly owning stock in the corporations they work for. For example, it could lead to a much greater role for employees in corporate governance. Historically, employees have not had seats on corporate boards simply because, in most countries, it is not required and they have not been major stockholders. With the increased use of stock options and other stock plans to retain and motivate employees, it is possible that employees will increasingly own a significant amount of stock in the corporations they work for, and as stockholders they could demand and win seats on the board. This could lead to a significant new voice in the boardroom, one that argues for greater consideration of the impact of board decisions on the workforce.

Perhaps the most fundamental change that the era of human capital is likely to create for individuals is the generation of more and more options concerning work. Options that will include who people work for, where they work, how long they work for a particular organization, and of course, what work they do. Indeed, the employment options that individuals will have are likely to be limited only by their imagination and skills. If an employee wants to constantly move from organization to organization around the world, this will be possible. Similarly, the individual who wants to work from home over the Web will have this option. And of course, the individual who wants a traditional job that involves going to a work location will also have this option.

For individuals to successfully navigate the many options they will have, they will need to become sophisticated managers of their own careers. In the era of human capital, organizations are less likely to worry about helping individuals develop their human capital and more likely to worry about the organizational capabilities they have. They, for example, are increasingly likely to hire critical human capital from outside rather than develop it, and much less likely to be loyal to people when their skills are no longer needed.

Individuals need to respond to this new world by becoming sophisticated managers of their own careers and human capital. This means they need to know the market value of their skills and the demand for different skills, and, of course, they need to constantly invest in developing skills that keep them at the state of the art. For many individuals, the best approach will be to develop a personal brand, which rests on their skills, knowledge, and work history. To do this, they will need to focus on developing credentials and visible work products and accomplishments. In the absence of good career management and developing a personal brand, individuals will increasingly be at the mercy of organizations that are not committed to them and technologies that are rapidly changing.

Societal Implications

The increasing importance and mobility of human capital has a number of significant implications for countries. Perhaps the most fundamental one is that in order to have competitive businesses, countries need to facilitate individual mobility with respect to both personal skills and work locations. When technology and the business landscape are changing rapidly, people need to change if old organizations are to effectively change and successful new organizations are to develop. In many cases, change means individuals learning new skills and physically relocating to different parts of the country or different parts of the world.

In the United States, physical mobility has been somewhat of a tradition and is often not a major problem for individuals. On the other hand, careers that involve multiple companies sometimes are a problem. Individuals who move from company to company often lose retirement benefits, medical coverage, and other financial benefits that are essential to their economic well-being. It is critical that countries create economic structures that allow individuals to work for multiple companies during their career. It is also critical that societies provide the kind of training that allows individuals to remain current in their skills and to shift their skill sets when it is needed.

It is increasingly likely that individuals will have multiple careers in the sense that they will switch their areas of technical expertise several times during their work lives. This is a virtual necessity given the rapid change in technology and the importance of individuals' staying in tune with current organizational capabilities and core competencies. Clearly, organizations should and will provide some of the training support that is needed to develop competencies and capabilities that will give them a competitive advantage, but they cannot be counted upon to do all the necessary training and development. Schools and other institutions also need to offer development opportunities for individuals who wish to switch careers or update their knowledge and skills. Clearly in the era of human capital, lifelong learning needs to be a reality and needs to be supported by companies, governments, and individuals.

Future Challenges

The era of human capital brings with it a number of major challenges. Rather than review all of them, I would like to focus on three: human capital information systems, leadership talent, and the people left behind.

The information systems in most organizations are clearly focused on the reporting and allocation of financial and physical assets. They provide almost no information about the human capital in an organization. This is particularly true with respect to the public reporting that corporations are required to do.

Simply reporting on the physical and financial assets of a corporation is no longer sufficient. Managers, society, and investors need to get regular information on the condition of the organization as a performing entity and its human capital. There are a number of major obstacles to doing this but that is not an adequate excuse for failing to push ahead in this area. With respect to public reporting, at the very least corporations can begin to report on some of their personnel data such as their investments in training, their turnover rate, and the employee satisfaction data that they collect. Without information on the human capital of an organization, it is virtually impossible for investors to make wise investments, and for organizations to effectively regulate the way corporations are managed and run. Thus moving human capital onto the balance sheet of corporations should be a high priority in all developed countries that are in or are approaching the era of human capital.

Perhaps even more important than the public reporting of human capital information is improving the internal information systems that organizations have with respect to human capital. To effectively develop a business strategy and operate an organization, it is increasingly important that organizations have a good inventory of their human capital. In essence, they need to have individual profiles of all their employees' skills, knowledge, and experience. In essence, they need to know how well individuals fit the person descriptions that are created to replace the job descriptions of the past. With the new information technology, these can be stored and individuals at any level of the organization can find what talents currently exist in the workforce and decide who might be the best individuals to do particular kinds of work. The potential exists to move from a world in which there is a lot of knowledge about the jobs in an organization but little knowledge about the skills and knowledge of individuals to a world in which there is plentiful knowledge about the skills and knowledge of all employees—knowledge that is available for planning, strategy development, and work assignment purposes.

The era of human capital requires new thinking with respect to the entire area of leadership and leadership talent. As Jim O'Toole eloquently argues in Chapter Thirteen and much of Warren Bennis's research argues as well, we need to move to an era in which leadership is an organizational capability and not an individual characteristic that a few individuals at the top of an organization have. Leadership only at the top is acceptable in the old economy and in the traditional bureaucratic organization. Indeed, it is the hallmark of many effective traditional bureaucracies, but it is not the right approach for the human capital era.

In the era of human capital, individuals throughout the organization need to self-manage because they are the ones who best understand the projects they are working on, and thus are in the best position to lead others who are contributing to these projects. Indeed, individuals often need to move from being leaders to being followers and back to being leaders as the projects they are working on change and different individuals have the knowledge and skills that are needed to provide leadership.

For their part, organizations need to focus on broadening their leadership talent by not just targeting leadership development activities to a few individuals who have the potential to be senior corporate executives. If leadership is to become a true organizational capability, it needs to be diffused throughout the organization, and that means training and development in this important area of human capital as well as in areas of technical expertise and knowledge. The failure to develop leadership talent throughout an organization is a sure prescription for creating an organization that is heavy on technical talent but weak on direction and focus.

I would be remiss if I didn't point out that in the era of human capital there is likely to be a significant group of individuals who are left behind. For a variety of reasons, these individuals will not have the technical knowledge and leadership skills to be valued and to be treated as important human capital. In essence, these people will still be treated and valued in the same way individuals have been for decades, and thus will constitute an abandoned but significant minority in developed countries that have moved into the era of human capital. The existence of this group should be a concern to everyone. They represent a potentially disenfranchised population, and there is likely to be an increasing gap between them and individuals who have high human capital.

The problem of the people left behind can be partially mitigated by creating educational opportunities for them to increase their human capital. However, this is unlikely to solve the problem and as a result other kinds of government action are likely to be needed. Specifically, governments may need to provide meaningful safety nets concerning health care, retirement, and stronger requirements that companies pay a living wage. In the absence of these structures, the era of human capital runs the risk of being a polarized era in which some, probably the majority, flourish at the expense of others. This clearly is not a situation that is likely to lead to a stable or desirable society.

Conclusion

The era of human capital that we have just entered shows great promise. It is very likely to lead to the widespread acceptance of many things that Bennis has advocated for decades. It will be clearly marked by leadership, teams, and learning being more important. This means, of course, that Bennis's many books will continue to be relevant, and something everyone should have. It also means that Bennis will need to continue to provide us with his wisdom and guidance. Organizations are taking new forms, individuals are entering into new types of employment relationships, and new leaders are emerging. They all need the thoughtful analysis that Bennis can give them and the guiding hand that he has provided for so many years.

Part Two

The Organization of the Future

Chapter Three

A World of Fleas and Elephants

Charles Handy

The world of organizations is fast dividing itself into fleas and elephants. The elephants are the large organizations of business and government; the fleas are the technological start-ups and the new dot-coms, they are the small consultancies and professional firms, the self-employed experts and the specialty suppliers that service the elephants. On a humbler scale the fleas include the little businesses that pepper our main streets with restaurants, family-run stores, hairdressing salons, and real estate agencies, not to mention the hundreds of thousands of small not-for-profit organizations, as well as all our local schools and churches.

The elephants get all the attention, from academics as well as from the press, but most people have always worked in the fleas. The elephants consolidate, but the new ideas mostly come from the fleas. The elephants matter, particularly the multinational, global ones—they fertilize the world with their ideas and their technology, they amass the piles of resources that are necessary to develop oilfields, build aircraft, research new drugs, or spread their brands around the world. They apply the advantages of scale and the clout of size to promoting efficiency and to reducing the costs to the final consumer. To an elephant, in fact, size is crucial. In pursuit of ever greater size, we have, in recent years, seen elephants swallowing elephants or, as they would no doubt prefer to put it, marrying elephants in what they call strategic mergers.

Once married or swallowed, the elephants go on a slimming diet, shedding jobs by the thousand in pursuit of a necessary efficiency. They are addicted to a productivity formula of $\frac{1}{2} \times 2 \times 3$, or an objective of having half as many people employed in, say, five years' time, working twice as hard and producing three times as much. Fine for the stockholders, no doubt, but not so good for the half a workforce that gets offloaded. Don't, therefore, look to the elephants for the new jobs; they have to come from the fleas. This is a lesson that America learned long ago, one that Europe is only slowly coming to terms with.

Nor should we look to the elephants for imaginative new ideas. Efficiency is, in many ways, the enemy of creativity. Efficiency abhors waste, is uneasy with experiments that might go wrong, finds nonconformity uncomfortable, and prefers predictability to risk. Elephants prefer to pick up innovations once they have been proved to work. They can then develop them, give them scale and mass, promote them and deliver them at an acceptable price. The new ideas, in short, come from fleas, often from fleas that arrive out of a clear blue sky, from outside the industry altogether, the Amazon.coms of our new world. The trouble is that fleas tend to live on the backs of elephants, not inside their bodies. When elephants buy up the product of a flea to develop it, they will spit out the original flea as soon as they can.

Fleas, therefore, provide the new challenges for leadership, at all levels in society. What sort of leadership does a flea organization require, particularly an innovative flea? What are the characteristics of successful flea organizations? Can they, should they grow into elephants? How can elephants grow fleas, or at least encourage them, tolerate their irritation, and make use of their creativity? What makes an innovative flea individual, how are they educated, can they be trained, or is it all a matter of genes and luck?

Fleas are currently fashionable. The First Tuesday meetings, started in London and now operating in fifty cities around the world, are fashionable flea markets, attracting up to three thousand young would-be dot-com fleas of an evening. Students are leaving MBA courses before they finish to join a fledgling flea, suddenly conscious, perhaps, that business schools are the finishing schools of the elephants. Is that what business schools should be? Or should they be flea nurseries? Can they be both, or are business schools elephants themselves, temperamentally incapable of harboring fleas?

The pressures of a global world, which demands an increased degree of scale, added to an unprecedented pace of innovation, requiring constant invention and reinvention, means that every society needs a mixture of both inventive fleas and efficient elephants. The questions that are listed here are, therefore, of some urgency if we are all going to benefit from the new frontiers opened up to us by technology.

The Leadership of Fleas

At the heart of every flea organization, at least at its beginnings, lies a creative individual. In 1999, the author and his wife, a portrait photographer, conducted a study of twenty-nine such individuals in London, England, individuals they called the "New Alchemists," meaning that they had created something from nothing, or from the metaphorical equivalent of base metal. The flea organizations that they had created or transformed ranged from businesses of various sorts to arts or community ventures, including a school and a church. The study is reported fully in *The New Alchemists* by Charles and Elizabeth Handy (London: Hutchinson, 1999).

The sample was small and could not therefore be definitive, but it did provide some clues to the nature of these leaders and the organizations that they had created, all of which were successful in their own terms. The one defining and common characteristic was *passion*. These individuals were passionate about what they were doing, whether they were building new airlines (Richard Branson), new eateries in New York and London (Terence Conran), new theater companies (Declan Donnellan with Cheek by Jowl), Britain's first and only private Anorexic Clinic (Dee Dawson), or Britain's first Healthy Living Center (built around a rundown church in the East End of London by Andrew Mawson). If the venture was a business, money was the outcome of success but was not the reason for the passion. Richard Branson says that he turns his frustrations as a customer into businesses to "improve a bit of the world."

This passion for what they did enabled them to endure anything—the long hours necessitated by starting a venture, the failures and mistakes that inevitably occur, and that they speak of as
"lessons learned" rather than failures, and even the relative poverty
that many experienced until the venture started to develop. The
passion was often neither logical nor reasonable. Business plans
would have looked wildly optimistic at the beginning, but none of
them relied on outside financing at the start. Passion, not reason,
provided the driving force. These individuals were mavericks, they
were different and were determined to make a difference. That
determination fueled their energy. Dedication, difference, and
doggedness, therefore, were the hallmarks of the alchemists.

Their passion infected their organizations. By recruiting like-
minded enthusiasts, albeit with diverse talents, the leader created
a family in his or her own image. These families were "chaordic,"
to use Dee Hock's description of the mixture of chaos and order
that seems to be characteristic of the new, fast-moving businesses.
Because they were small and like-minded they could rely on empathy for much of their communication, a sense of "what would
Richard (or Lucy) do?" governed their lives. Meetings were frequent but snappy. One alchemist had his boardroom table made
five feet high to ensure that all meetings took place standing up.
Success was shared, either by formal profit-sharing schemes or by
joint celebrations in the case of the nonprofits.

They keep the cores of their organizations tiny, so as to reinforce the sense of empathy at the center and to create trust.
Richard Branson operates out of a private house in London, still
looking very much like his home (which it used to be), relying on
a tiny core staff of six or seven. Being dyslexic he dislikes reading
reports and formal documents, relying on his lieutenants to do the
reading and preferring himself to listen and talk—to as many as
he can meet. His very personal style reinforces an atmosphere of
trust and empathy. Terence Conran lives above his design studios
in London, and has built a workshop employing some thirty people in the grounds of his country home. Andrew Mawson's Center,
now employing over seventy people with some 120 projects on the
go, is based around his church, where he is still the pastor. In these
ways they continue to emphasize the personal nature of the orga-

nizations they started. Their organizations are all mirrors and extensions of themselves.

With the exception of Dee Dawson, none of the alchemists in the study had been anywhere near a business school. Many had left formal education as soon as they could. Being different, they chafed at rules and regulations and found examinations irrelevant even when they came easily. They had little time for reading, therefore their management theories were all homemade and very personal, derived from experience. One of them (Julian Richer, the founder of hi-fi retailer Richer Sounds) had actually written two best-selling books extolling his principles of management. This all helped to emphasize the personal nature of their organizations. Cash flow and recruitment were the things they kept a close personal eye on. Otherwise they encouraged experiment and initiative as long as they knew what was going on. Good personal communication was, therefore, critical—and they all spent a lot of time talking, listening, and walking around.

In many respects, therefore, they were typical of a family firm, only it was their colleagues who were the family. They were not interested in creating a dynasty or a way of life for their heirs. Their passion was to make a difference to the world—as quickly as they could. It was what gave their organizations energy and excitement, the sense of being on a shared voyage of discovery. What was unclear was where the voyage would end up. Would the organizations turn into elephants themselves, or would they die when the founder left?

Can Fleas Become Elephants?

Elephants were all fleas once, just as oaks start from acorns, but the reverse is not necessarily true—not all acorns become oaks and most fleas do not develop into elephants. Acorns and fleas both seem subject to nature's law of abundance, there are so many of them that enough survive even if most fail. In Britain last year there were almost as many small business failures as there were new start-ups.

To move from flea to elephant requires a change of style. Infection and empathy are no longer enough when an organization becomes large and geographically dispersed. In most cases the change of style means a change of leader. Jim Clark, the founder of Silicon Graphics, Netscape, and Healtheon—and supreme among business alchemists—could never adjust to running the businesses he created. Michael Lewis, in his book *The New New Thing*, talks of the Serious American Executive who would move in to run the operations that Clark had created but could not manage.

As often as not, once the new business reaches a significant size it is bought by an existing elephant who then, immediately or in due course, gets rid of the pioneering flea-master. The elephant then takes the flea firmly in its trunk and introduces the techniques of efficiency, growing the business but in the process probably destroying much of the original excitement.

The organizations studied in *The New Alchemists* seem unlikely to either outlast the departure of their founder or to become large enough and cohesive enough to be classed as elephants. Richard Branson's Virgin Group consists of fifty separate companies, ranging from airline and railroad businesses across financial services to holiday and leisure. The only thing holding them together is Branson's enthusiasms and his Virgin brand, with its reputation for putting the customer's concerns first. On his departure it seems probable that the conglomerate he has built up will be divided into its several pieces. Conran's restaurant and design business, likewise, although large, is really a collection of individual businesses held together by the Conran philosophy and brand, a brand that may not survive the departure of its philosopher king.

Only the book empire built up by Tim Waterstone and still bearing his name seems likely to make it to the elephant category. That is partly due to the injection of finance and management expertise from the EMI group, who financed the merger of Waterstones, Dillons (a rival bookstore chain), and HMV (music stores). The result has been a perceptible change in the atmosphere of the Waterstone stores now that the founder has departed to higher regions and the chain handed over to professional retailers. Efficiency not empathy is now the watchword, Tim Waterstone himself is rarely seen and many of the original staff are leaving. Some might say that the magic has gone, others would argue that the business has grown up. What is clear is that the atmosphere in an elephant is very different from that of a flea.

What is less clear is why most alchemists or flea-masters in Britain seem uninterested in becoming the leaders of global elephants, unlike their equivalents in America. It may be that they are less ambitious, or perhaps less interested in the power that comes from the control of a large organization. It may also be that they are unwilling to exchange the family organization for something less personal. Perhaps they don't know how to do it. Does this matter? Italy has built a successful economy on the back of a long list of family firms with world-famous brand names but still flealike in the number of their employees and in their leadership style. Germany, too, has a tradition of the Mittelstander firms, small and medium-size family firms specializing in particular unspectacular niches.

The Mittelstander, however, are beginning to sell out to the elephants now that the third generation of the family has taken over and much of the personal passion of the founders has gone. When it is just a business and no longer a passion it is best to trade empathy and enthusiasm for efficiency. Italy, too, may find that its family firms cannot easily maintain a global reach with a personal style of leadership. Europe will need its elephants if it is to keep pace with the giants elsewhere, which is why, for instance, BP has been aggressively mating with other elephants such as Amoco and Burmah Oil to create the world's second-largest oil company, and Vodaphone with Mannesman to build the world's largest mobile phone company.

Nonetheless, when fleas become elephants something is lost, even though much may be gained economically. The mood of the talented young favors the flea. Elephants have a hard job recruiting all the talent that they need, or in keeping those whom they do recruit. The question, therefore, for the leaders of the elephants is whether they can learn from the fleas and whether they can themselves grow fleas. As the chairman of one Anglo-Dutch multinational put it, "My problem is that I am not sure why any young person would want to work for a company like mine today with all the other opportunities around." If he's right, it is a serious dilemma because inefficient or sickly elephants could be catastrophic for an economy.

Can Elephants Harbor Fleas?

What is clear is that personality is as important to the leadership of an elephant as it is in a flea. Jack Welch will be remembered as much for the way he expressed the purpose of GE in his own behavior and passion as for the strategic choices that he made. Percy Barnevik, when CEO of ABB, managed to infect that huge federal organization with his own enthusiasm and zeal. One CEO of a multinational described his job as a mixture of missionary and teacher, endlessly communicating his message to his people.

Yet it is not enough for the leaders at the top to forget themselves in their function. That delight, that sense of vocation or passion, must be possible right through the organization. That requires space, space to express oneself in one's work, space to experiment, space to fail—and enough space to correct the failures before too much damage is done or too many people notice. It won't be possible to create those spaces in an excessively tidy organization. Elephants have to be loose-limbed if there is to be room for fleas other than at the top.

One answer lies in federalism. Federalism was conceived as a way of combining the collective and the independent, of being both big and small, the same but different. Americans and Germans, Australians and Canadians, Spaniards and Swiss have all got federal constitutions, designed to allow independence within a union, but even these do not always see the sense in applying the same principles to their businesses. To the British, federalism is the F word, a dirty word, one that implies a loss of control to the center. This serious misunderstanding of the principles of federalism will be a handicap in the future development of both their constitution and their economy.

This is not the place for a detailed discussion of federalism. The principles are spelled out in an article for the *Harvard Business Review,* "Balancing Corporate Power: A New Federalist Paper" (Reprint No. 92604).

Suffice it here to say that federalism is a mixture of both centralization and decentralization, centralizing only those things that everyone agrees it would be crazy not to centralize, and leaving as much autonomy as possible to the various states or business groups—the space for the fleas.

Federalism is messy, and political. There are disputes over the allocation of resources. Information is guarded when it should flow freely. There are boundary disputes, necessary compromises, competing lines of accountability. To make it work requires an active understanding of "twin citizenship"—the idea that one can have at least two loyalties, to one's own group and to the larger collective, one can be both a Texan and an American. The lesser loyalty is easy, it is the larger one that requires work, because without it compromise is hard to obtain—why give up on local priorities for the greater good if you have no interest in that greater good? Hence the critical importance of the talk of *vision* and *values* and the necessity for the top leader to accentuate these in every word and action. Some distribution of the spoils of success from the center to the states also helps to reinforce the idea of a common good.

Properly done, however, federalism allows room for the fleas inside the elephant. ABB tries to restrict the size of its business groups to fifty persons so as to recreate that sense of a small enterprise, personally led and motivated. In a world of Hi-Tech, Hi-Touch (to use Ronald Naisbit's evocative terms) can easily be neglected, yet fleas rely a lot on trust, trust in those they work with, and trust needs touch to be truly trust. Technology communicates facts but not feelings. Fleas need both for trust to flourish, and few of us can know more than fifty people well enough to gauge their feelings or to know whether they can be relied upon.

The alchemists instinctively know this, which is one reason why they are reluctant to grow too big. Federalism offers a way forward, but it is neither easy nor tidy. Small wonder, perhaps, that many leaders of elephants shrink from it.

There are alternatives. One way is to run an internal venture capital bank, backing innovative proposals, either from internal groups or from individuals who want to move outside. Gary Hamel ("Bringing Silicon Valley Inside," *HBR* September-October 1999) describes one experiment of this type. In London, a young woman called Eva Pascoe was e-commerce director for Arcadia, a fashion retailer. A typical flea, she became irritated by the restrictions of the elephant and decided that she wanted to start her own Internet fashion store, Zoom.com. Arcadia agreed to back her, taking 60 percent of the shares—thereby ensuring access, not only to any appreciation in the shares, but, more important, to her innovations.

Some prefer to cultivate their own private flea gardens, a la Xerox PARC. Although the fleas often thrive in such corporate gardens there is a problem in bringing them or their ideas back into the mainstream. History is littered with examples of good ideas ignored by the same elephants who paid for them to be cultivated. It is simpler, perhaps, to go flea hunting, buying up innovative companies once they have proved themselves, dumping the bad or irritating bits and keeping the essential intellectual property.

Can Fleas Be Developed? Or Is It Luck?

The stories of the London alchemists provide some clues to the way fleas grow. Clearly genes have some part to play, but passion, self-confidence, and self-awareness, all critical to successful alchemy, can be grown in each one of us.

Early environment played a part in these people. They all benefited from *second child syndrome.* Two-thirds of the sample were second or third in the birth order of their family, but even the firstborn tended to be treated by their parents in the more relaxed way that second or third children experience. Parental expectations and inexperience are often loaded onto the firstborn with the result that the child can end up as high-achieving but also conformist and with a strong sense of duty. The pressure is often lifted for subsequent siblings. They are allowed to be more experimental, to explore a wider array of avenues for development, to experience failure without trauma and to express themselves in their own way.

These practices are not universal, of course. The point is that a child who is allowed space to experiment will soon learn that mistakes are not fatal, that self-expression is satisfying, and that confidence grows through successive experiences of success. Self-confident parents reinforce the message that we are in control of our own lives and are free to shape events as much as we are shaped by them.

Most of the alchemists in the study *The Group* were then fortunate enough to receive what Freud called "The Golden Seed." At some stage in their formative years someone somewhere told them that they had a special talent. It was often a teacher, sometimes a first boss, once a priest, occasionally a relative, sometimes a mother, but only once a father. They tucked this private nugget away in their heart but, in times of doubt or uncertainty, they pulled it out to reassure themselves. Dee Dawson did not shine academically at school, but she enjoyed biology classes. When she took her national examinations at the age of eighteen, as one does in Britain, her teacher told her afterwards that she had got the best grades in the whole region for biology. "Then I knew that I was clever," she said, and later, faced with going to medical school in her thirties she was undaunted—"You see, I know that I am clever," she said.

They were also fortunate in that they discovered their vocation or their passion early on. Terence Conran fell in love with design at the age of fifteen, influenced by his mother and his teachers at that time. Ozwald Boateng, one of Britain's fashionable young tailors, discovered his talent for tailoring by accident when helping his then girlfriend to produce a fashion show. For Julian Richer it was the thrill of doing business, a thrill he discovered when buying and selling hi-fi equipment to his schoolmates. For Declan Donnellan, theater was always his fascination once he discovered it during his schooldays. For Tim Waterstone it was marketing that fascinated him, along with books. Combine the two and you find a passion for bookselling.

None of them were conventional learners, even though a few did quite well at school. They learned by experiment and experience, helped in most cases by an early mentor, someone who had backed them financially or psychologically and whom they could rely on to tell them the truth about themselves, someone also who acted as an early model for their own work and career. With the exception of Dee Dawson, it occurred to none of them that formal education might help, although the tailor Ozwald Boateng did take some evening courses in business after his first bankruptcy at the age of twenty. Most of them preferred to compensate for their lack of expertise in some areas by hiring the expertise that they lacked rather than by studying it themselves.

This has profound implications for education at all levels, but particularly for those who would like to claim that they are developing future leaders at professional schools. It is clear that classroom study will not be adequate, indeed may be damaging to would-be alchemists. Even those whose destiny it is to lead the elephants or parts of elephants need to have a feel for the way alchemists think and for how fleas are born. This won't happen by rational analysis of case studies, it needs real-life experience.

Perhaps the time is right to rediscover the merits of what the French call *formation* and the British "professional development," in which guided experience is mixed with classroom exposition and discussion. All the older professions in Europe—medicine, law, architecture, even accountancy—combine periods of apprenticeship or "articles" with formal classroom teaching. Why should leadership, a practical art if ever there was one, be any different?

Apprenticeship by itself can be a way of embalming the past in the present. It needs the challenge of intellectual analysis to keep it relevant and contemporary, just as the classroom needs the test of practice to keep it real. To misquote Wordsworth's definition of poetry: "Education is experience understood in tranquillity." Too often, in the past, the experience and the understanding have been unconnected. Unless we can find new ways to reconnect them the business schools will remain the finishing schools for the elephants, not the fleas.

Incubator units in the schools, more company-specific courses, more tutored apprenticeships and distance learning modules tied to project work, these are all possibilities that are currently being explored in Europe. The schools are finding, in short, that if the students won't come to where they are then they will have to go to where the students are. The school as an extended learning community is an exciting prospect, but it will require a lot of adaptation by all involved if it is to be more than a concept. Yet if the professional schools adapt in this way they could provide a model for the rest of education. Now that would be an act of great leadership, a goal worth striving for in a world hungry for new forms of learning.

Chapter Four

Knowledge Work and the Future of Management

Thomas H. Davenport

Does management have a future? The idea of "management"—a separate role from workers focused on the planning, oversight, and monitoring of work—was appropriate for the Industrial Age, but some would suggest that it is no longer necessary in an era of autonomous, self-motivated knowledge workers. Will teams of computer programmers, marketing analysts, researchers, and people in other knowledge-intensive jobs essentially manage themselves? Middle managers are already endangered; will senior managers follow them into the corporate dustbin?

Despite these developments, there is still an important role, albeit a different one, for management in the future. The single most important factor driving the change in what management entails is the rise and prevalence of knowledge work. Because those who are managed will be a substantially different group from workers of the past, management itself will have to change, in some cases dramatically. But what are the new tasks of management, and how will they be driven by the importance of knowledge and knowledge work?

Note: This chapter resulted from discussions with Warren Bennis about what eventually became another article. As a result, it bears his intellectual imprint, if not the actual scratchings of his pen.

A Brief Look at the Old Model of Management

The old model of management was formed to deal with a very different set of circumstances than the ones organizations face today. Industrial workers were proliferating at the turn of the last century. Many knew only craft or home-based labor and were unfamiliar with working in large organizations. Most were relatively uneducated; many were motivated to work hard only by external pressure. Employees were often in unions; managers were not. Industrial work was not yet very productive, and substantial analysis and redesign was necessary to improve it. The concept of "bureaucracy," formulated by the sociologist Max Weber, was considered a positive attribute involving professionalism, clear division of labor, and work roles that were independent of the individual.

While it's been obvious for years that this model no longer applies to the contemporary work environment, no clear alternative has come along to take its place. What attributes of the old management model still make sense, and what should be dropped? It's worth a quick review of that design for the manager's role to assess which of its aspects are still relevant:

- Management was considered a separate role from the rest of work. Managers managed, workers worked, and there was little overlap between the two sets of activities.
- Management processes assumed that workers did manual work that could be observed by managers. Work started and ended at clear times, and workers' performance was easily measured.
- Workers were assumed to be selfish and out to maximize only their own success; managers supposedly had the good of the broader organization in mind at all times.
- It was believed that a primary activity of first-line and middle managers was to convey information to and from workers, and to represent workers to senior management. Skipping links in the chain of communication was considered disloyal or rabble-rousing.
- Work processes and activities were subject to analysis and improvement, but not the activities of managers. Managerial processes were not viewed as accessible for assessment or improvement.

- Management, requiring a higher level of conceptual capabilities, was generally viewed as being superior to, and more valuable than, nonmanagerial work.
- It was assumed that managers could do workers' jobs better than any worker; indeed, it was part of the manager's responsibility to instruct workers on how to perform their jobs more effectively.
- The old model of management assumed that it is the manager's job to think, and the worker's job to do. (As Henry Ford put it, "What I want is a good pair of hands, unfortunately I must take them with a person attached!")

These assumptions about management, of course, make little sense in an economy and society in which knowledge predominates. Managing with knowledge, managing knowledge work, and managing knowledge itself all require that most of these assumptions about management must change. They have already begun to change, as managers of knowledge workers realize their inappropriateness. Again, however, what it means to manage knowledge workers has never been fully articulated. While not all organizations and work settings are knowledge-intensive, in the United States and Europe we have reached the point of critical mass at which knowledge drives the way we think about management.

Management thinkers have talked for decades about a new future for management, but the realization of it awaited the right proportion of knowledge workers and the widespread recognition that knowledge is the firm's most critical asset. The problem has been apparent, but it hasn't been solved. Peter Drucker (1969) called it a key aspect of "management's new role" to "make knowledge more productive"—an unobjectionable statement today, though it seemed strange when Drucker said it more than thirty years ago.

The Rise of the Knowledge Worker

Just as the proliferation of industrial workers created a need for a professional management class, the emergence and maturation of the knowledge worker role is the driver of what management will be in the next century. Because knowledge is an invisible asset that resides largely in the minds of human beings, management can no longer be about close observation and monitoring. Because knowledge work can and is done by managers as well as workers, strict separations between worker and manager no longer make sense. Because knowledge work has become the key to growth and differentiation in today's economy, the differential in cost and value between knowledge work and management has decreased. Management in the "knowledge economy" is a different game with different rules.

Of course, the rise of knowledge work has been foreseen for many years (Cortada, 1998). Automation in factories and farms freed most of the workforce from having to perform physical labor. At the same time, the advent of computers and the pervasive presence of information created a demand for workers who could produce the information in the first place, extract meaning from it, and take action on it. The economist Fritz Machlup (1962) did much of the early spadework on knowledge and knowledge work roles; even in 1958 he stated that knowledge workers comprised almost a third of the U.S. workforce, and that the sector of knowledge work was growing twice as fast as the rest of the economy.

By the end of the twentieth century in these advanced economies, more than 50 percent (40 percent salaried managerial and professional workers in the United States, and more than 10 percent in other knowledge work categories) of workers are "knowledge workers" whose primary tasks involve the manipulation of knowledge and information. Even before they became a majority, they had the most influence on the economy. They are paid the most, they add the most economic value, and they are the greatest determinant of the worth of their companies. Companies with a high proportion of knowledge workers—let's call them knowledge-intensive—are the fastest-growing and most successful in the U.S. economy, and have generated most of its growth in the past decade. The market value of many knowledge-intensive companies dwarfs their book value (and this ratio has doubled over the past twenty years, suggesting a great acceleration of knowledge asset value). Even in industrial companies, knowledge is increasingly used to differentiate physical goods and to fuel diversification into product-related services. As James Brian Quinn (1992) has pointed out, high proportions of workers in manufacturing firms (roughly

90 percent in semiconductors, for example) never touch the man-ufacturing process, but instead provide knowledge-based services such as marketing, distribution, or customer service.

What Are Knowledge Workers?

Of course, knowledge workers are difficult to define, and they are not all of a piece. All workers employ some knowledge to do their jobs, so we must resort to classifying them by the proportion of their time spent doing so. And there are undoubtedly several different types of knowledge workers, each requiring different work environments and leadership approaches. One obvious distinction, for example, is between knowledge creators and knowledge users. Knowledge creators are workers who create innovative new ideas and approaches for use by their organizations. This category might include scientists in research and development organizations, particularly innovative product development engineers, process designers, and creative academics.

It's much more common to *use* knowledge on the job. The garden-variety engineer, the financial auditor, and the dentist are all examples of professionals that primarily use existing knowledge, rather than creating it anew. Even a fast-food worker has to employ knowledge in the form of recipes, procedures, service approaches, and so forth. I know a CEO of a large pizza chain who argues that every worker in the organization is a knowledge worker, and unless they all use knowledge to manage costs, serve customers well, and maintain high quality standards, the organization will not succeed. However, if pizza makers are knowledge workers, who isn't? This is why definitions of knowledge workers usually include only those with a high proportion of knowledge activity.

Knowledge workers can also be distinguished by the types of ideas with which they deal. While the scope and scale of ideas undoubtedly represent a continuum, let's split it into big ideas and small ones. Big ideas are those that dramatically change people and organizations—ideas for new products, services, business models, and strategic directions. "We should develop a computer with a point-and-click operating system that's much easier to use than any other," is an example of big idea knowledge; it was someone's thinking, perhaps Steve Jobs's, at Apple Computer in the mid-1980s. By definition, an organization can pursue relatively few of these big ideas because they require a lot of time and effort to implement. Then there are the small ideas. These are minor improvements in what organizations produce or how they work. "Let's put glass shelves in our refrigerators so that customers can see through them into the back," is an example of the type of small ideas that happen every day. Small ideas are analogous to quality management and continuous process improvement; big ideas are analogous to process innovation, the start-from-scratch, think-out-of-the-box approach to change.

To which types of knowledge and knowledge work should organizations aspire, and what do their choices mean for the future of management? The most conventional view would be that only a small proportion of workers should be creators of big ideas. Workers have traditionally been viewed as users of ideas, not creators of them, and if they do create ideas they have generally been small ones. It's only researchers and senior managers to whom organizations have turned for big idea creation.

My view, however, is that the organizations that will be most successful in the future will be those in which it's everyone's job to be creating and using ideas that are both big and small. Certainly front-line workers should continue to practice continuous improvement and refinement of their own job activities, but why shouldn't they also continuously propose new products, processes, business models, strategies, and so on? Surely the most innovative and profitable firms will be those in which everyone thinks.

There are a few examples of firms in which it's everybody's job—at least almost everybody's—to think. Some are "knowledge-intensive" firms in businesses like consulting or pharmaceutical development, where professionals or researchers are all expected to create knowledge. It's much less common to find such an orientation in industrial firms, which is why Chaparral Steel is so unusual (Leonard, 1995). In this Texas-based firm, thinking is clearly everyone's job. Even the first-line "associate" is expected to work on production experiments, to identify new product offerings, and to propose new process designs. Chaparral is highly productive relative to other steel companies, although it's difficult to find steelworkers who want to be knowledge workers. Most important from my perspective, Chaparral has a very different style of management from most steel companies—its culture is nonhierarchical and workers are trusted to produce at high levels without monitoring.

Not all organizations will immediately resemble Chaparral, but because of the importance of innovation in a fast-moving, globalized economy, its useful to focus on the attributes of management that help every knowledge worker to create big, organization-transforming ideas.

What Will Management Become?

Given these important background factors, managers in the future will have to adapt their activities to the new world they'll face. In the remainder of this chapter, I'll describe some of the specific changes management may undergo, including

- From overseeing work to doing it too
- From organizing hierarchies to organizing communities
- From imposing work designs and methods to understanding them
- From hiring and firing workers to recruiting and retaining them
- From building manual skills to building knowledge skills
- From evaluating visible job performance to assessing invisible knowledge achievements
- From ignoring culture to building a knowledge-friendly culture
- From supporting the bureaucracy to fending it off

Although each of these attributes of future management may represent only an evolutionary change from how managers worked in the late twentieth century, in aggregate they comprise a managerial revolution.

Managing and Doing Knowledge Work

Perhaps the most important thing to mention about future managers is that they'll do more than just manage. In many cases, the knowledge work manager is also a knowledge worker. Managers in law, consulting, and accounting firms often have their own clients.

University administrators may still teach and do research. Managers of investment analysts in a mutual funds firm have their own industries to cover as analysts. These managers perhaps enjoy doing nonmanagerial knowledge work, and may feel it necessary to be respected by those they manage. As Rosabeth Kanter (1997) puts it, "But now, as hierarchies are deemphasized, the formal authority derived from hierarchy is less important than professional expertise in gaining the respect required for influence and leadership."

But the player-coach role creates conflicts and uncertainties. How much time should be spent doing versus managing doers? Should the manager of knowledge workers be the best knowledge worker in the bunch? Should the best worker be "wasting" time on managing? And if the manager performs too much actual knowledge work, other traditional managerial functions, such as budgeting, planning, and human resource management, may suffer. The right balance of managing and doing knowledge work varies, of course, by the particular individual and the situation. However, anyone creating or performing one of these hybrid roles should anticipate that problems will ensue on an ongoing basis.

Building Knowledge Work Communities

Knowledge workers are increasingly described as autonomous "free agents." But where will knowledge workers find community? Spending your day working with knowledge doesn't obviate the need for community—not just chat rooms, but real face-to-face contact with other human beings. Knowledge workers don't have labor unions, and they don't want them. Even the role of professional associations is fading in today's cross-functional workplace, as engineers work just as closely with marketers, manufacturers, and financiers as they do with other engineers. And as we all work longer hours, we have increasing difficulty finding community outside of the workplace.

One of the key roles of the knowledge work manager, then, is to create work communities. But on what basis? Work teams may form some degree of community, but just because team members are trying to achieve a common objective doesn't mean they want to share. And in global, virtual organizations, teams are scattered around the world. Perhaps a more viable basis for community is knowledge. Knowledge workers who produce the same types of knowledge may be the most willing to commune.

In fact, knowledge-based communities are at the heart of the recent "communities of practice" movement (Wenger, 1998). The members of a community of practice do similar work, but the purposes of their association are to share knowledge and social interaction. The members of such communities all generate knowledge, share it, and use it—generally for free. The manager's job then becomes forming these communities, nurturing and facilitating their exchanges of knowledge and social capital, and ensuring that one community overlaps with another when necessary.

Knowledge communities are already well-established in many consulting firms, where they are a primary means of connecting geographically dispersed consultants who share an interest in a particular industry, business problem, or technology. Most such groups meet face-to-face as well as electronically. But knowledge communities are also viable in industrial firms. Chrysler, for example, organized over a hundred "Tech Clubs" so that new car engineers in diverse specialty areas could share their learnings with each other. Each club has a facilitator (that is, a manager of a knowledge community) and an electronic repository for shared knowledge. The clubs are viewed as a means of nourishing shared technical knowledge in an environment where almost all work is on cross-functional platform teams. The teams have improved Chrysler's new car development, but they inhibited detailed knowledge sharing among specialists and were viewed—before the Tech Clubs—as a barrier to improved quality.

Redesigning and Improving Knowledge Work

One of the functions of management has always been to try to improve the performance of work. In the Industrial Age, this took the form of Frederick Taylor's time-and-motion studies. One might argue that many business process reengineering projects turned out to be the last gasp of Taylorism. But if today's work is knowledge work, the work improvement function must address the largely invisible steps in knowledge work production.

Knowledge work processes were largely bypassed during the reengineering movement of the 1990s; fewer than 5 percent of companies, according to one survey, attacked such knowledge work processes as new product development, marketing, or management itself. Why not, if these processes are so important to an organization's success? First, these types of activities are difficult to understand and improve, since they take place primarily in various cerebrums and cerebellums around the organization. A related problem is that the success of knowledge work process outputs can be difficult to measure. For example, we don't know if a new drug development process is working well for five to ten years, because it takes that long for new drugs to make it through the pipeline. Also, knowledge workers are characterized by their desire to work autonomously and without close direction—so they are likely to resist new work processes imposed by others. Finally, since knowledge workers are powerful within organizations, they may be better able to resist process change.

The more recent "knowledge management" movement, in which companies have attempted to capture and distribute knowledge in electronic form, hasn't helped much with regard to knowledge work processes either. Knowledge management activities have been imposed on top of existing work processes, and not altogether successfully. Few knowledge workers have any spare time today for recording their most recently learned lessons, or for taking calls from coworkers seeking their expertise. If we want knowledge workers to take on these knowledge behaviors, we will have to free up some time for them to do so. The desired behaviors—creating, sharing, and using knowledge—will have to be "baked into" the job, and unnecessary activities eliminated.

The answer to this problem is not to let each knowledge worker figure out how to free up time and attention for knowledge from scratch. Rather, a work design effort is called for, though it must be very different from the top-down reengineering of yore. In looking at over thirty attempts to improve knowledge work a few years ago, I and some collaborators discovered that this work must involve the participation of those who do the work (Davenport, Jarvenpaa, and Beers, 1996). Understanding existing work and knowledge behavior patterns is critical, so that more knowledge can be squeezed into them. And since knowledge work processes are invisible and subtle (and often not reported accurately by knowledge workers), close observation by a participant-observer (called *ethnography* in anthropology) is the best means of eliciting true knowledge behaviors.

Good knowledge work processes can also create a climate in which innovation and discipline coexist. Knowledge workers are often passionate about their ideas and won't abandon them easily. Yet it is sometimes necessary to kill some knowledge work initiatives so as to free up resources for new ones. Managers in pharmaceutical firms, for example, have noted that a key aspect of a strong drug development program is the ability to cancel projects that don't meet success criteria. But cancellation should be the result of a process, not a matter of an individual's taste.

Kao Corporation, Japan's largest consumer products firm, is an example of an organization with both a strong orientation to knowledge and learning and a strong sense of discipline when necessary. Kao's CEO talks about the company as an "educational institution," and it was one of the earliest adopters of knowledge management in Japan. But Kao also has discipline. The company had entered the floppy disk business and had become the world's second-largest producer, but by the late 1990s it became clear that the business was fully commoditized. Most large Japanese firms are slow to restructure, but Kao first closed down half and then all of the business. 1998 was the first year in seventeen that Kao had not grown profits, but it was already back on the profit growth track by 1999.

Recruiting and Retaining Knowledge Workers

Perhaps the single most important task of the knowledge-oriented manager is recruiting and retaining the best knowledge workers. In my view this is the primary factor in the success of the best knowledge-intensive firms. The Mercks, the Microsofts, and the McKinseys of the world—all highly successful knowledge-intensive firms—put extraordinary efforts into recruiting the smartest and most talented workers available in their industries, and at keeping the ones who perform well. With the lowest U.S. unemployment rates in decades and an expected shortage of workers in the next several years, the war for knowledge talent will only become fiercer.

But the importance of recruiting and retention is well-known. What is less familiar is the best approach for recruiting and retaining knowledge workers. How, for example, can firms ensure that new recruits have the basic intellectual curiosity that will motivate learning throughout their careers? My own experience as a professor suggests that having a degree from a prestigious university is not a guarantee of intellectual curiosity. One important indicator, for example, may be the degree to which an applicant has consulted knowledge about the company in question. If, in this situation involving high motivation, someone hasn't consulted a company's Web site or annual report before an interview, it's unlikely that the applicant will ardently consume knowledge after getting the job.

There are other generic knowledge worker traits in addition to intellectual curiosity. The ability to speak and write well is one. As academics have long known, the best predictor of the ability to write is having done it before. For all but the least experienced recruits, companies desiring a knowledge worker who writes should ask to see a portfolio of previous writing.

Recruiting will have to become a full-time, continual process for most managers. Instead of beginning to look for a knowledge worker when there's an opening, it will become important to look all the time. Firms should maintain a database of knowledge workers they might want to employ at some time. Cisco Systems, the fast-growing maker of Internet equipment, already has such a database—with sixty-five thousand potential employees in it. And when someone applies for a job and there's no current opening, Cisco managers keep track of the applicant's skills and backgrounds for potential future use.

Given the coming shortage of knowledge workers, the effort to retain knowledge workers will be as difficult as that to recruit them—and, of course, recruitment and retention policies are related. It will undoubtedly be expensive to retain the best workers, but cheaper than having to recruit new ones. It's also heartening that knowledge workers say that money is not the primary factor in retention. In a recent Hay Group survey of workers in over three hundred companies, workers said that the ability to learn new skills was far more important in their willingness to stay with a job than money or any other factor. Pay was the least important factor of fifty surveyed. (I must confess that I find this difficult to believe.) Workers in the survey also said they valued feedback from supervisors and information about what was going on in the company.

Companies should have well-defined procedures for dealing with the planned departure of a valued knowledge worker. At Cypress Semiconductor, for example, the structured process kicks in when a star employee declares an intention to leave. It culminates in a meeting with T. J. Rodgers, the Cypress CEO. Rodgers is a strong believer in the primacy of human assets in the knowledge economy—and has a bulldog-like personality as well. I would not want to announce my departure to him.

Unfortunately, the evidence suggests that most firms are moving in the wrong direction on recruitment and retention issues. They are telling their employees that they need to be "career self-reliant," managing their own careers and increasing their employability for a variety of jobs. But as Jeffrey Pfeffer (1998, p. 163) puts it, "the companies are then surprised when they face the very turnover that their programs have helped foster." Other research (American Management Association, 1997) suggests that the common downsizing programs in American businesses only increase turnover and lower morale for those who do remain. Perhaps the only real answer to this issue is to return, as Pfeffer advocates, to lifetime employment arrangements.

Building and Propagating Knowledge Skills

Managers have always been responsible for helping workers build their skills. At the turn of the last century, Frederick Taylor urged them to invest in workers' abilities to perform manual work. Now, of course, the skills involve knowledge acquisition, analysis, and use. As Ikujiro Nonaka, the Berkeley "Professor of Knowledge," puts it, "The learning organization must be a teaching organization." But what should the learning organization teach? Currently, very little energy is focused by either universities or employers on generic knowledge skills—how to search for knowledge, how to determine which knowledge sources are credible, how to manage personal information and knowledge environments, and so forth. Most knowledge workers underinvest in their own skills and knowledge environments. As a very simple example, if knowledge workers are receiving a hundred e-mail messages a day or more, they are spending significant time on the activity. Yet I know of not a single firm (and only a handful of universities) that offer a course or learning experience in how to manage an e-mail stream and integrate it effectively into a job.

Another component of knowledge skill-building is encouraging knowledge workers to teach as well as to learn. Managers must encourage knowledge workers to come to understand how they do their own work, and then to teach explicit and tacit knowledge to others. All knowledge workers should be held accountable not only for developing their own personal skills but also for ensuring that they are not the only ones who possess them. An organization's knowledge and learning managers should provide some guidelines as to how best to transfer different types of knowledge. Highly tacit knowledge, for example, is probably best transferred through longer-term, face-to-face mentoring relationships, while explicit knowledge can be codified (written down, for example) and transferred electronically.

Evaluating Knowledge Effectiveness

A key component of management has always been to evaluate the performance of workers. In the Industrial Age, this was a relatively easy task; an individual worker's productivity could be assessed through outputs—work actually produced—or visible inputs, including hours worked or apparent effort expended. In the world of knowledge work, however, evaluating performance is much more difficult. How can a manager determine whether enough of a knowledge worker's brain cells are being devoted to a task? What's the formula for assessing the creativity and innovation of an idea? Given the difficulty of such evaluations, managers of knowledge workers have traditionally fallen back on measuring visible inputs, such as hours worked. Hence the long hours put in by attorneys, investment bankers, and consultants. However, the increasing movement of knowledge work out of the office and into homes, airplanes, and client sites makes it difficult to use hours worked as a measure, and that criterion never had much to do with the quality of knowledge produced.

What's the alternative to hours as a measure of knowledge work? Organizations need to begin to employ a broad array of inputs and outputs, some of which are internal to the knowledge worker's mind. One input might involve the information and knowledge that a knowledge worker consulted in making a decision or taking an action (a particularly important criterion for managers). ABB, the global electrical and engineering firm, uses this factor as one of many in assessing managerial performance. Another input could be the process that a knowledge worker follows in producing knowledge work. The self-reported allocation of the knowledge worker's time and attention is a third possible input.

Outputs could include the volume of knowledge produced, the quality of the decisions or actions taken on the basis of knowledge, and the impact of the knowledge produced (as judged by others). These criteria are similar to those used for professors up for promotion, who are evaluated on the volume of books and articles they write, the impact of their research on the scholarly community, and the quality of their teaching as judged by students. In the consulting business, some consultants are already evaluated in part on the knowledge they bring to the firm and the impact it has on clients.

Creating a Knowledge-Friendly Culture

Managers have not often focused on building cultures, and when they have their approach has often been to reinforce the existing corporate culture. But knowledge work managers need to build company cultures that are in accordance with what knowledge workers want, or the workers will leave. A manager of knowledge workers quoted in the *Wall Street Journal* commented, "If you're buying intellectual equity, the culture of the company is everything."

What are the attributes of a culture that would attract knowledge workers? Drawing from Kanter and Bennis, the "Five Fs" characterize the most desirable knowledge-oriented culture (perhaps all workers would value most of these traits!): fast, flexible, focused, friendly, and fun.

The pace of business life seems to continually gain speed, and knowledge workers will want their firms' cultures to keep pace. Nothing is more frustrating than a firm that responds slowly to business trends because of bureaucratic inertia. Similarly, the knowledge-oriented firm needs to be flexible—changing business models with the environment, as many e-commerce firms do.

Knowledge workers want their firms to be focused on the business issues that matter to their firms' success. And because life is short and work is long, knowledge workers want their jobs to be friendly and fun.

The knowledge-worker culture is also a communal one. Managers must work jointly with workers to create a communal sense of purpose and vision. Knowledge workers don't want to work toward a goal because someone else has set it, but rather because they believe that it's right.

Specific knowledge-oriented behaviors must also be an integral part of the culture. It should be perfectly acceptable, for example, to sit at one's desk and read a business-relevant book—normally a knowledge behavior that's restricted to personal time. The culture should also support decision making and action based on knowledge and facts, not gut feel and intuition alone. Managers of knowledge workers must set examples with their own decisions.

Fending Off Bureaucracy

Most knowledge workers have a justifiable antipathy for bureaucracy. They would like to be able to do their work without excessive rules, policies, or formal processes. Many organizations, however, strive to control knowledge workers by implementing these very strictures. Therefore, managers of knowledge workers need to fend off the bureaucracy whenever possible, or at least provide a buffer between it and the knowledge workers. As Bennis and Biederman (1997) found out in a study of "Great Groups" of knowledge workers, including Xerox PARC, Lockheed's Skunk Works, and the Manhattan Project, most such initiatives included a manager who played the role of bureaucratic intermediary. They kept high-achieving knowledge workers happy and productive by removing barriers and giving the bureaucracy what it needed with minimal bother.

However, since managers of knowledge workers are themselves knowledge workers, many knowledge work managers will not find this an interesting way to spend time. In fact, the need to be a bureaucracy-buster may make it difficult to recruit knowledge workers to become managers. One potential solution in large groups of knowledge workers is to employ an effective intermediary between knowledge workers and the bureaucracy, someone who is not actually a knowledge creator.

The Difficulty of Finding and Keeping Knowledge Work Managers

If a good knowledge worker is hard to find, a good knowledge work manager is even harder. The role conflicts involved in doing and managing knowledge work, the need to balance creativity and autonomy with bureaucracy, and the difficulties of "herding cats"— a common metaphor for managing knowledge workers—can lead to frustrating and difficult jobs. And knowledge workers know it. For many, the power, prestige, and increased income that often accompany managerial roles are not worth the trade-offs.

In the future we may be able to look to universities for some help in solving the problem of filling such jobs. College presidents and deans often get tenured professorial appointments, so they can retreat from the pressures of knowledge work management when they burn out. Department chair positions are often rotational; each senior faculty member with any administrative talent whatsoever (unfortunately, this rarely includes all professors in the department) is expected to take a turn. Perhaps we'll see more temporary or rotational knowledge work managers over time.

Management and Non–Knowledge Workers

Not all workers are knowledge creators, and we'll still need to manage physical tasks or services that don't involve knowledge as the primary component of the job. However, even in these circumstances there are roles that knowledge can play in effective management. In well-defined service processes, for example, the equivalent to a knowledge repository is the collection of procedures that define how the work is done. For example, in ISS, the international services firm, detailed procedures specify how janitorial activities should be performed. Similarly, in the U.S. Army, formal "doctrine" specifies in great detail how military maneuvers are to be performed. Both organizations' procedures are refined continuously, making them a vehicle for organizational learning and change.

Organizations that employ non–knowledge workers can also facilitate the access to learning that will eventually equip them to become knowledge workers. United Parcel Service (UPS), for example, employs many young workers at its Louisville, Kentucky, package sorting hub who use brawn more than brains. But UPS believes that it can attract desirable workers by offering them the opportunity to complete a college degree while they work. UPS collaborates with the University of Louisville to offer special courses at times convenient for the part-time UPS workers, who generally work in the middle of the night. UPS has built a special dormitory allowing sleeping during the day.

In this sense, almost every organization needs knowledge to manage itself more effectively. Every worker relies on knowledge in some form, or would like to do so. In the future we will see more organizations that take this reliance on knowledge seriously. Knowledge will truly be viewed as the most important asset of the organization, and much of its structure, culture, processes, and management approaches will be based on what the organization knows.

Management and managers will continue to exist, but not necessarily in recognizable form. The old model of the manager who sits in an office staring down at toiling workers and occasionally makes a visit to the factory floor is now officially obsolete. The new managers look suspiciously like knowledge workers, but do more than day-to-day knowledge work. They also recruit knowledge workers, create for them a positive and communal work environment, and remove obstacles to their creative and productive activity. Rather than sitting at the top of the hierarchy, the new managers must subsume their own egos to those of the knowledge workers they manage.

Chapter Five

Boundaryless

Steven Kerr

On the topic of organizations of the future, which was our assignment, I thought I would check in with what used to be, or what is said to be, the relevant literature, and it took me back to some of the old classics, like Lawrence and Lorsch. And it turns out that the concepts of differentiation and integration have been with us in one form or another for a long time. Sometimes, they become decentralization versus centralization, other times loose coupled versus tight coupled. And the folks say that those are the right core things to do. To differentiate and integrate if organizations are to adapt to complex, changing environments.

But what didn't get said was how easy it is to do differentiation as compared to integration, for a number of reasons. One is the nature of upsets. It's the law of physics that things fall apart. Entropy. You test it by getting a jigsaw puzzle that's fully solid, you shake the box and look at it, you see what nature does to order. Or take a deck of cards that's in order, throw it on the ground, and pick it up and look at it. So nature is always helping you differentiate.

We often forget the difficulty of integration. The United States, for example, has been much better at attracting than at assimilating different groups. It's always had one of the most liberal immigration policies, but when people get here they settle down in Little Haiti, or Cuba town, or Korea town, or Japan town,

---

Note: This chapter is taken from Steven Kerr's oral presentation at the conference. It has been edited primarily for grammar and punctuation.

or China town. We haven't been really slick at learning how to integrate this thing.

Which leads me to the second factor, demographics, that also helps us to differentiate. This country does have quite a variety of people, the law protects it, and it's a difficult thing to put things back together again. In addition, you have Generation X less susceptible, it seems to me, to doing things in any common, uniform way. So you look at the integration difficulties of running an American business, for example, in places like Japan, where the diversity is less, and a common mind-set is easier to instill.

So globalization then becomes another factor. When I was at USC, we got into IBEAR—that's the international business education part—and it's the same in corporations. I'm now with GE and it's trying to go heavily into places like Japan. This creates great differentiation and these things become very hard to manage.

And then another set of factors that promotes differentiation has to do with e-business. One of the great concepts emerging seems to be the notion of being an aggregator. It used to be believed that you had to know something about the stuff you sold: Maybe you had to know how to make it, maybe you had to understand your customers. None of that seems to be in vogue any more. So places like Amazon.com decided that the ideal business model is not to get good at selling books, but to get good at selling *stuff*. And the stuff you sell can apparently be independent—it can be anything—which introduces you to a great variety of customers, and again increases by far the differentiation and consequently the need for managing well.

Another property of e-business is the low barriers to entry. Compare a guy named DeLorean to a guy named Liemandt. Both wanted to get into the car business. DeLorean spent a fortune and turned out an unsuccessful car company. In contrast, Liemandt put up a Web site called pcorder.com, took it to market, and he's selling automobiles. You can sell anything on line. You don't have to know how to make it. You don't have to make it. You just locate it and sell it. Sometimes it never even passes through your company. So you end up with a huge variety of products and services and an infinite number of customers, and the end of all this is that differentiation is easier and easier to do—it's almost an automatic consequence of doing business.

Integration, therefore, is harder and harder to do. And, again, the Lawrence and Lorsch notion was that you needed integration, you almost needed a certain level of it, but the more differentiated you were, the harder it became.

Now my shop, GE, has all of these issues, plus it has another one, which is that we're in every product, every market, every technology, and every country there is. In Charles Handy's terms, we're the biggest elephant. In fact, by some measures such as market cap, we're the biggest elephant in the world—and by other measures, we're the biggest corporate enterprise in the history of the world. Other than a church or an army, there's never been anyone that's tried to run a shop this big. Just for an example, if you broke up GE into its natural parts, you'd have twenty-two Fortune 500–sized companies. Many would be in the top fifty by themselves. And if that's not bad enough, we're acquiring organizations at the rate of five every two weeks. A hundred and thirty last year. And they're not small because when you're as big as GE, it's three-fifths of the work to bring in a small business as it is to bring in a large one, and then you don't get any bang on your income statement or balance sheet, so you have huge problems around integration.

So an answer to what's the organization of the future is that the world is giving us hugely more differentiation than we've ever had, and the organizations that solve this puzzle, that are able to stay organized, will succeed. That's the problem of organization—how do you get common output when people have so little in common? And GE gets richly rewarded for giving the impression of having solved this.

In fact what Jack Welch drills into our cortex at regular intervals is this simple statistic: The average holding company or conglomerate sells at fifteen to nineteen times earnings. In Europe they get in the low twenties. GE, it depends on the stock price of the day, is at about forty-four to forty-eight times earnings at any given moment. We're also the world's largest market cap. Over US$550 billion. The point of this is that we get about twice what we would get if the world decided we were not integrated, or what Welch calls "boundaryless." And so our biggest fear is if the world thought we were just a holding company, and yet if we're in every business and market and country there is, how can you be other than a holding company?

Which is to say, any decision you make, any action you take, any money you spend, if it makes you more integrate-able, which I'm going to call boundaryless, if it makes you more boundaryless or creates the impression that you are, don't even do the math, just spend the money. And so that's everything we do at GE. It's our belief about the organization, again more needed in a place like GE because we are more differentiated than most. But when the Amazon.coms of the world carry out their plans, they're going to have the same issues of differentiation. And the aggregators—this is going to become the way of life and doing business—are going to have those same problems.

So what we're pursuing at GE is that there are only three types of boundaries, according to Welch. One type is the floors and ceilings; that is the vertical boundaries that separate people by level. So every one of us goes home at night with information in our head that we know for certain would make our organization more effective, but we don't tell. Every one of us goes home with information in our head that would make our boss competent. There are things that you know about your boss's operating style that are just wacky. But you don't tell your boss because it's awkward. Our subordinates and students know the same things about us and they're not telling us. So imagine if all that good stuff could flow freely up and down the organization, if you could permeate the boundaries.

Inside walls separate the departments, whether it's a corporation or a university, the regions, the branches, the territories, the SBU's, the campuses. So English is resentful of Business, the West distrusts the Midwest, Sales doesn't like Production, everyone in the field hates the home office. This is how we all live.

And then the outside walls separate the organization from its suppliers, its regulators, the media, the shareholders, and in all cases, customers. So the GE answer is that those are the boundaries that you permeate. You never get there, but that is what the ideal form of organization looks like.

At GE, we say that there are only three tools to permeate boundaries. Integrated organizations move money, people, and ideas or information across boundaries. Even holding companies move money. Cash cows, growth engines, move money to other parts. That's important, everybody knows that. But what distinguishes the integrated organization or the boundaryless organization is the moving of people and ideas. In a holding company, you typically have what they call the silo or the chimney. In a boundaryless company, people move across those boundaries. And the same is true of ideas and information. At a place like GE, you make the assumption that what Plastics knows can help NBC, what Aircraft Engines knows will be fine for Capital, and so on. This is the essence of what we try to do.

I'm going to try to tell you, quickly because of time, how we try to do these things. There's an old saying that GE gets it right all the time but it doesn't. We make mistakes, just like anybody else. So, to permeate vertical boundaries, to make it easier for information to move up and down, we do things like Workout, which has been pretty well publicized in the press—the GE approach to moving down to lower levels in the organization autonomy, authority, and decision making. Again, a lot of the implications of this come from research, certainly Warren Bennis's earlier works have sought to explain it. My point is, therefore, not that it's new but that it becomes unusually important if you agree that differentiation is going up, if you agree that integration is critical, and one of the things you have to integrate is vertically across the organization. So concepts like Workout and e-business are having an effect. There is still as far as I know no rigorous research about the impact of e-mail on corporate communications. But the anecdotal evidence we get is that subordinates who are pretty intimidated to put something in writing or to say it face to face are happy to go online and send an e-mail note to tell the boss he's a horse's ass or something like that. So there happens to be greater irreverence, which is fine if you're trying to vertically integrate. Also, bosses seem more willing to ask for help and advice and to delegate and empower online than they are face to face. It doesn't seem so humiliating or something.

Inside the walls, everyone uses the same inputs. It doesn't matter what type of organization you're in, it could be a corporation or a university, and within a corporation it could be Plastics, NBC, or Lighting, it doesn't make any difference. For example, one input is people. Anybody in this room know how to get work done without people? Good, now we have something important in common. So if you have a good idea, say in a university in the

Biology Department—where the business school doesn't look for ideas—for recruiting people, or tracking them, or retaining them, or mentoring them, or disciplining them, or anything, 90 percent of that turns out to be portable. Supplies are another input. Anybody know how to get stuff done without supplies? Great. Now we have something else in common. So if you're good at bids, or specs, or algorithms or prequalifying vendors, or running e-auctions, or all the other seventy-five best practices, 90 percent of that is portable.

Then, throughput. Welch is always saying, "While some of us are bending metal, some of us are paying claims. But you map the processes, and they are amazingly similar."

And on output. There are only two kinds of outputs in this world: products and services. Whichever one you have, don't you still have to market it, don't you have to price it, whether it's tuition or a good? Don't you have to collect your cash, don't you have to quality control your product? Don't you have to have customer relations? That belief, that mind-set, we believe to be the conceptual underpinning of a boundaryless organization. But the biggest danger of these is the overhonoring and the overrespect for differences. Every specialty, every department is unique, every snowflake is unique, it's all true. But it's the enemy of having an integrated organization because you end up overhonoring and overrespecting people's differences and then you believe that no knowledge is portable. And the truth is that almost all knowledge is portable.

The last example is about the outside walls. By the way, these solutions are not unique to GE. These are just things that the organizations of the future are going to do or they're going to disappear. So at GE, for example, if you are a good customer like Wal-Mart and you ran out of stuff that you're buying from GE, you don't even tell GE about it, you just trigger your automatic signal to the GE factory and it will ship stuff to your warehouse. So you've got no inventory at your Wal-Mart and no paperwork or forms, you've got a customer now giving orders, not advice, not a plea, but orders, so the GE people can do some stuff.

Welch's one-liner about this is "If we do our jobs well, no one outside will be able to tell where GE stops and the environment begins." It's a total blurring of the inside/outside lines.

Another example is part of Six Sigma, outsiders now have the power to evaluate and reward GE employees. This example goes beyond what I used to teach when I was at the university. If you're really going to be integrated across the outside walls, it goes beyond what I just said, it actually has to do with adopting your customer's objectives as your own. In a Six Sigma quality world, you view quality through the eyes of the customers. Most of the early stuff about zero defects in total quality failed because they were built on internal measures. So businesses thought they were doing great, but their customers never felt it. The whole notion is looking at things through the eyes of your customers.

My last example is called "wing to win" because it happens to come out of the aircraft engine part of GE. GE makes engines, customers put them on the plane. Periodically the engines have to come off the plane and go back to the service shop, where they are repaired, serviced, and whatever else people do to maintain an engine. You're always setting standards to minimize the time in the shop. So you go from nine days to seven days to five days to three days. That's the old way of looking at service to customers. Here's what it looks like through the customer's eyes: An engine leaves the wing of an airplane, it may be away for nine days. If that's the number of days the plane can't fly, then that's the number of days the customer has fixed costs with no revenue from that plane. Now you say: "But only five of those days the engine was in the repair shop, the other four days it's the customer getting it to you or taking it back, or they may have a warehouse problem." When I think about things like MBO, you always talk about the accountability of goals, don't make people responsible for things beyond their control. But if you're going to be integrated across the outside walls, control has nothing to do with it. The dependent variable becomes how many days will that wing be off the engine. And all of a sudden now, GE is in there helping customers with their internal warehouse issue, it has nothing to do with anything we've committed to, but that's what the world looks like. Again, in Welch's terms, if you do a job right, you won't be able to tell where the corporation stops and the environment begins.

So in conclusion, the organization of the future still has to manage differentiation. That has not stopped being true. So integration becomes key but various forces conspire against it. Again, the more differentiated you are the harder it is to do. Boundaryless organizations can help resolve this dilemma.

Chapter Six

Trust Me On This

Organizational Support for Trust in a World Without Hierarchies

Thomas A. Stewart

April 21, 1994, was one of those mornings when Southern California lives up to its hype: the sky was clear over Santa Monica, the air pleasantly cool; a breeze that barely ruffled the blue Pacific was enough to toss the hair of the blondes who glided by on roller blades. Warren Bennis arrived to meet me for breakfast, perpetually youthful, preternaturally suntanned. *Fortune* was doing a story about how e-mail networks were beginning to change the style and content of management, and I wanted to talk about it with him as he was a professor at the University of Southern California, an expert on both the style and substance of leadership. I particularly wanted his perspective as a student (and heir to the intellectual mantle) of Douglas McGregor, the author of *The Human Side of Enterprise.*

I had eggs. He had fruit and, I think, toast. We chatted a bit about this and that; then I broached my topic. He began his reply by saying he wasn't sure he was the best person to talk on the subject— he himself wasn't all that familiar with electronic networks. He didn't quite say it, but I guessed he meant he'd never sent an e-mail message in his life. No shame in that, then: April 1994 was the month in which Mark Andreessen filed the papers incorporating Netscape, the company that made the World Wide Web navigable and popular; that month, America Online—which has more than 21 million subscribers as this is written—had just 712,000 members.

Bennis had celebrated his sixty-ninth birthday just six weeks before, and might reasonably have figured that by the time e-mail became omnipresent, he wouldn't be around.

Having warned me of his ignorance, Bennis went on to offer a set of observations and hypotheses more expert than any others I heard while reporting that story—all of them, moreover, amply and accurately borne out as electronic networks have become ubiquitous and data traffic (much of it e-mail) has grown till its volume is greater than voice traffic. Bennis himself, now seventy-five, has been known to contribute some to that torrent of bits.

Here's what he said: Networks, by definition, connect everyone to everyone. Hierarchical organizations, by definition, don't do that—they create formal channels of communication, and you're expected to follow them. He didn't use the ecological metaphors that have since become fashionable, but if he had he might have said that hierarchies are like concrete-lined irrigation ditches, where the water flows along clearly laid out, prescribed lines, whereas networks are flat, rich, mysterious Okeefenokees of every-which-way communication.

A hierarchy, Bennis went on—this was the key point—acts as a "prosthesis for trust." Organization charts—showing who reports to whom, who owes fealty to whom—define more than reporting relationships. They are the trellises on which trust's fragile vine twines and blooms. Indeed, as he reminded me, bureaucratic rules and procedures came into being in part as safeguards against untrustworthy behavior like nepotism, favoritism, and corruption. Bennis said, "That organizational armature reinforces or replaces interpersonal trust."

Reinforcement and replacement: Both are important. People in organizations act from many motives and are acted on by many pressures. Personal trustworthiness might need reinforcement by organizational strictures; if the rules are clear enough and the hierarchy strong enough, personal trustworthiness might not even be an issue. In *The Organization Man,* William H. Whyte showed how in large, hierarchical corporations, the Protestant ethic, with its notion of individual responsibility for one's actions, mutated into an organizational ethos.[1] In that regime, real interpersonal trust is unnecessary: its doppleganger will do. You can count on me because you're my boss; I can count on you for the same reason;

together we can count on others because the boss of bosses has told us what he wants. Everyone has his place, and everyone else knows what that place is. Position substitutes for persuasion. In theological terms, it's a rule of law, not grace—and it works.

When a network becomes the main means by which information is conveyed and work gets done in a corporation, those hierarchical crutches are knocked away. Networked organizations have few promotions to give out, and rank is unclear. Colleagues might be thousands of miles away. Rewards may go to teams, not individuals. Those teams are likely to be interdepartmental—so that hierarchical power, position power, isn't around to guarantee that work gets done. More and more often these teams are temporary—like floating crap games, Bennis said that morning—which disband when the project is done; today's team leader might be tomorrow's underling. Networks encourage people to operate informally, outside the rule of law. Relationships therefore depend much more on cooperation than on control. Cooperation, in turn, depends on trust.

Flattened hierarchies and networked relationships change the sources and uses of power—a subject about which there's a fair amount of scholarship. Few businesspeople I meet are mystified by power. Yes, bosses can't throw their weight around as they once did, but power is still easy to recognize, and when the boss says "Jump!" the reply is still "How high?" more often than it's "Why should I?"

Networks also change the sources and uses of trust. That's a subject far less studied. A visit to Amazon.com and a simple search on the word "power" turns up 28,003 possible titles, versus just 1,819 for "trust"; most of the books in each case fall into categories like self-help that are not pertinent to management of organizations—but the fifteen-to-one ratio of study feels about right. Yet, Bennis argues, trust is more important. His newest book *Douglas McGregor, Revisited* (written with Gary Heil and Deborah C. Stephens) says: "Gathering information, and above all developing trust, have become the key source of sustainable competitive advantage."[2]

Trust, unlike power, baffles people. How do we create a climate of trust in the company? How do I know if we can trust our suppliers? How can I make sure that people will do what they say they will do, when they don't report to me? How can we reconcile the need to protect confidential information with the desire to be open? People find these questions much harder than questions about power. When Owens-Corning moved into its airy, elegant new office building on the banks of the Maumee River in Toledo, Ohio, the CEO, confident of his authority, had no qualms about having a glass-walled office; indeed, he insisted on it. But the legal and accounting departments worried about whether their secrets would be safe behind glass, same as they did at Alcoa, when it moved to new space across the Allegheny from its old tower in downtown Pittsburgh. In these days of hacker attacks and hyper-competition, information systems managers are rightly zealous about security. Whom can we trust? Without pretending to answer that question—or indeed to do more than raise questions—I hope in these pages to suggest some of the sources and uses of trust in a postmodern corporation.

Real trust is hard even between people who have chosen to be together and have years to work on it, like spouses. It's harder still where they have little or no say in selecting their colleagues and where time is short. Impossible where an organization is large. The goal of real interpersonal trust might be misguided as well un-attainable: Certainly there are limits to the trust between colleagues or between boss and subordinate, since everyone retains the option to end the relationship. Trust at work therefore needs support—forces that create incentives for trustworthy behavior and reassur-ance for people who rely on others. In the absence of hierarchy, what organizational strictures will keep someone in line?

Trust's first truss is competence: I can trust you if I believe you're good at what you do, and cannot trust you if I doubt your skill. We trust competence all the time, with automobile mechan-ics, physicians, computer technicians, chefs.

Life at work demands that kind of entrustment more and more often. Traditionally industrial tasks were handed from one department to another—from research to development to design to manufacturing to distribution, sales, and service. At each stage, department heads vouched for the competence of their staffs. In each functional department, the boss became boss by virtue of being the best—at least, that was the idea. In an earlier life I worked for a large publishing company. One day the chairman walked by while I was typing something, poked his head into my office, and asked, "How fast can you type?"

"About fifty words per minute," I answered, looking up from the manual machine I ostentatiously preferred to use.

He said: "If you ever want to be the head of a Fortune 500 company, you have to be able to do everything better than everyone else. I type sixty." Leave his arrogance aside (not to mention the fact that few Fortune 500 CEOs could type at all in those days)— what's interesting about his quip is the assumption that the boss has to be best at everything, a notion almost as quaint as typewriters and carbon sets.

"Smarter Than My Boss" says a button I keep in my office. I won't say whether that's true in fact (power being something recognizable), but it's true in theory. The boss today isn't the most talented specialist in a functional department but is instead Peter Drucker's conductor-CEO, a coordinator of specialists. The conductor knows the score best, but the trumpeter knows how to blow the horn. When musicians have trouble with a passage, conductors say, "Take it to your teacher"—who is not the boss. The twenty-eight-year-old CEO of a dot-com company told me, "The role of 'manager' or 'boss' never existed for me. My role is to look for new and emerging markets and help us get there." The boss expects the specialists—the finance people, the techies—to work more or less unsupervised.

So the boss trusts in their competence—but what about judging it? In the functional organization, that wasn't a problem. The old-style chief engineer hired, trained, evaluated, and promoted other engineers, assigning people to jobs he could do himself, on the basis of his expert knowledge of their ability—he chose to delegate, rather than to entrust. The leader of a team consisting of a butcher, a baker, and a candlestick maker has less ability to evaluate and no choice but to entrust. "I leave it in your hands," the generalist tells the butcher, because the details of meat-cutting are a mystery.

So trust needs a second crutch: community. With or without computers, networked organizations naturally spawn informal groups of like-minded souls. When these communities emerge around a common discipline or problem—a work-related subject like graphic design or the behavior of derivative financial instruments—they become "communities of practice." The term, coined in 1987 by Etienne Wenger and Jean Lave of the Institute for Research on Learning, has come into such widespread use that a search on the Web turns up about 4,400 hits, four times as many hits as for the phrase "on becoming a leader."[3] These communities are where work and (particularly) learning occur. I elsewhere described them as "the shop floor of human capital, the place where the stuff gets made."

Communities of practice support trust because they create and validate competence, a role performed by functions in hierarchical companies. The boss may not know which butcher is best, but the other butchers do. And when butchers get together, they kibitz, teach, and form groups to work on unsolved problems. General Electric demonstrates the role of informal communities in creating trust, or at least something that substitutes for it.

General Electric's core competence is leadership; leadership development, therefore, is the company's most important business process. GE executives say they spend between a quarter and half their time on these issues. With 340,000 employees, GE might easily be an impersonal, difficult-to-navigate company; with a highly competitive culture, it might be a place where ideas are hoarded and clever politicians squash good businesspeople; with businesses ranging from medical equipment manufacturing to freight-car leasing, employees might be expected to have few skills and know few people outside their specialties. Instead, largely because the place is threaded through and through with communities of practice, the company is remarkably informal, so successful at creating topflight executives that it consistently produces more than it needs and exports its "trade surplus" in talent to companies around the world, and so networked that everybody at GE, it seems, knows people in every other GE business everywhere. In 1999 I visited GE businesses in eight European cities accompanied by an American-born, London-based media relations manager.[4] Unsurprisingly—it was her job—she knew the senior leaders of the businesses. It surprised us both, however, that in every city every time we went to a meeting with a dozen or so employees, she ran to embrace someone she'd met and worked with at one of GE's many training and networking events. Ask any GE person about the value of attending courses at Crotonville, its fabled leadership development institute. The answer is always, as it is with any great school, "The people I met were more important than the courses I took."

These communities play a key role in leadership development at GE. The company has elaborate formal leadership programs. There's training—not only at Crotonville but in many other locations—and every candidate for a leadership position in the company undergoes extensive training in Six Sigma quality methodologies as well as in traditional subjects. To evaluate talent, GE uses a forced ranking of employees into "A, B, and C players," a second ranking in which every manager rates all direct reports on a strict bell curve regardless of letter grade, and—most important— an annual staffing review, called Session C, for which all GE professional employees submit self-assessments and career-development plans and during which they are evaluated by squads of senior managers, with the top people and those singled out for high potential also reviewed at headquarters in Fairfield, Connecticut. CEO Jack Welch himself takes part in Session C evaluations of several hundred people.

The formal processes are so rigorous they would amount to hazing were it not for the role of GE's many communities of practice. The place is full of them—manufacturing councils, finance councils, technology councils—literally hundreds of interdisciplinary and interbusiness affinity groups. Through them (and through action-learning projects in training), GE's young leaders form the networks of friendships they will use during the rest of their careers with the company. They're expected to bring ideas to share at these meetings, where their friends and equals debate them, improve them, and take them home to implement in their own businesses. It is here that they get noticed, and it is from these communities that managers learn who's really good, who's really up-and-coming. Leadership, like any art, is easier to recognize than it is to define. Good "grades" in reviews and accomplishments in training, however searching the tests or superb the school, cannot create, show, or anneal leadership talent—and cannot produce trust—the way communities of practice can. Without these communities, GE's leadership development processes would be more competitive and political, and less cooperative and effective. It's essential to see the conclusions of the development processes verified by the communities in which a candidate participates.

Commitment, a third source of and support for trustworthiness, is an adjunct to both competence and community, neither of which necessarily implies loyalty to the organization. Indeed, communities of practice create a rival allegiance, where the interests of a community (for example, advanced research in cardiology) might conflict with the goals of an employer (such as a managed care company).

Trust obviously depends on the degree to which people are willing to support the organization's purposes. This is not a question of motivation. As Douglas McGregor argues, people are intrinsically motivated—but to do what? The convicted spies Kim Philby and Aldritch Ames were highly motivated men, but their goals were diametrically opposed to those of the government intelligence organizations they claimed to serve. As we ask people to be more entrepreneurial, as we flatten hierarchies so that bosses supervise fifteen or twenty people instead of six or eight, as we empower people, it's vital that there be a shared commitment to the same mission and values. Moreover, in a knowledge economy, the nature of work has changed. Repetitive, unthinking jobs—adding spreadsheets, filing sales reports, running routine tests—have been automated; in general, we are asking all workers—and especially managers and knowledge workers—to think and to make decisions. We need their inner gyroscopes aligned with the corporate compass.

That can't happen unless people know what they are committing to. Statements of vision and mission are notoriously vacuous; they breed cynicism, not trust. George Bailey, a partner in the consulting business of PriceWaterhouseCoopers, once printed up half a dozen companies' vision statements, then challenged their CEOs to identify which one was theirs. Half failed. And who wouldn't? Most companies could get better mission statements if they used Mad-Libs, or tried the Dilbert Web site, which will generate both mission statements and performance reviews by randomly combining buzzwords and bromides. It just gave me, "Our mission is to completely negotiate enterprise-wide materials while continuing to proactively leverage existing error-free solutions to exceed customer expectations." I couldn't agree more—or care less.

What's needed is a clear understanding of what makes the difference between success and failure, and how that translates into behavior and decisions. No more hiding the business model behind high-sounding nonsense. One company makes money by being the low-cost producer: We drive hard bargains, are a no-nonsense kind of place, are fussy about expense reports and impatient with slow learners, and if that makes you uncomfortable, don't work here. Another makes money by being the leader in innovation: We'd rather see half-baked ideas than fully cooked ones, and if you haven't failed around here, you haven't tried. A third makes money by coddling customers—making sure, however, to deal only with customers who will pay for pampering. It's crucial to link the mission to the business model; crucial, too, that personal success—career advancement—comes to people who commit to the behavior you ask of them. The company that asks for innovation and rewards punctiliousness should not be surprised if its creative people seem alienated.

Some companies have strong-flavored cultures. GE is an example, a culture strong enough that I can frequently recognize GE people without being told that's where they work. The Pentagon's culture is so clear that Hollywood can dress someone in mufti yet let you know he's a military officer with just a few words and facial gestures. Hewlett-Packard is another strong culture. I can't feel it, but Debra Engel, an HP alumna who went on to 3Com and now is a venture capitalist, can. People who worked at HP can almost sniff the presence of others who did, she told me once, by way of explaining how it was she had ended up in a conversation with the only other HP alumnus in a room of three hundred people. GE, the Pentagon, and HP are high-commitment organizations. You know you're there, and you know what you're supposed to do.

Beyond competence, community, and commitment, trust of course depends on communication, which can be its best friend or its worst enemy. That morning in Santa Monica, Bennis said that communication "will take a hell of a lot more time than it used to. And it will take a lot of emotional labor on the part of the leader." He understated the case.

Hierarchies can lie, and get away with it pretty well. Naked emperors go unchallenged. Incoming CEOs rewrite history with an avidity Orwell would recognize—and for reasons he would understand. Their newest trick is to take a big restructuring charge as quickly as possible after taking office, thereby reducing current earnings so that, a year later, they can boast the improved results while polishing their résumés in preparation for their next gig.

A revolutionary way to build trust: tell the truth. A few years ago the corporate communications head at AlliedSignal asked me: "What news travels faster than any other news through a factory?" He answered himself: News that a competitor won an order the company was bidding for. "And what news," he went on, "is never, never, never even mentioned in any plant newspaper?" It was a struggle, he said, to get the editors of those newspapers to understand that credibility mattered more than cheerleading.

"If you can't say something nice, don't say anything at all" might be good etiquette, but it's bad management, certainly in the age of networks. Rick Levine, Christopher Locke, Doc Searls, and David Weinberger, the authors of *The Cluetrain Manifesto,* a rabble-rousing, best-selling credo of the post-hierarchical age, exaggerate only slightly when they say: "There are no secrets. The networked market knows more than companies do about their own products. And whether the news is good or bad, they tell everyone. . . . As with networked markets, people are also talking to each other directly inside the company—and not just about rules and regulations, boardroom directives, bottom lines. . . . We are immune to advertising. Just forget it."[5] Open-book management, an outgrowth of McGregor's (and Bennis's) thinking, turns out to be inevitable as well as desirable. "Is democracy inevitable?" Bennis asked in 1964. He was talking about geopolitics, but his answer—it is—was also correct when it comes to the management of organizations.

One of trust's important, little-noticed allies—and the last I'll mention—is cupidity. (I'd have preferred another word—reward, perhaps; but after competence, community, and the rest, I needed one that begins with "C.") The point here is simple and obvious: If trust is a source of competitive advantage, it should pay. Failure always breeds mistrust—backbiting, toxic politics. "I get the willies when I see closed doors," says Nametk, the protagonist of Joseph Heller's novel *Something Happened,* and we all know why—something's not right, and "they" don't trust us to know what it is. Trust needs to be seen to be good business. Bosses should display it in stormy times as well as in balmy, palmy ones. Instead, when the going gets tough, managers dust off their old command-and-control hats, destroying the comity that's their best chance of getting out of the mess. That's got to change.

Business begins with trust. It begins with a deal: If you pay me X, I will give you Y. As companies abandon bureaucratic mechanisms, their leaders need to understand that trust is as important to management as it is to relationships with customers. Trust is hard, and it should be "hard stuff," not "soft stuff"—that is, it should be a virtue that can be documented and even measured, and not just in employee-attitude surveys. For that to happen, leaders will have to understand that trust isn't magic. It doesn't occur by itself. It can be created—and of course destroyed. Managers need to use the tools of trust as deftly as they do the tools of power.

Part Three

The Leader
of the Future

Chapter Seven

Bringing Leadership Lessons from the Past into the Future

James M. Kouzes
Barry Z. Posner

"The future has no shelf life," declares leadership guru Warren Bennis in Chapter One. He could have easily been paraphrasing the legendary New York Yankee skipper Yogi Berra, who observed: "The future ain't what it used to be!"

Predicting the future is often a fool's game. Think about Charles Duell, who as commissioner of the U.S. Office of Patents might have known better, but as early as 1899 pointed out: "Everything that can be invented has been invented." Or consider President Grover Cleveland's prophecy in 1905: "Sensible and responsible women do not want to vote." Decca Records in 1962 declared that "guitar music is on the way out"—which explains why the company turned down the Beatles. Fred Smith's student paper proposing the idea for an overnight delivery service (that is, FedEx) earned the following comment from his Yale management professor: "The concept is interesting and well-formed, but in order to earn better than a 'C,' the idea must be feasible." And it wasn't so long ago that Ken Olsen, Digital Equipment's CEO, was so bold (or rash) as to wonder aloud that he couldn't "imagine why anyone would want a computer in their home"—let alone their laps! Even Microsoft's Bill Gates insisted that "640K of memory ought to be enough for anybody."

In looking ahead, especially for the upcoming generation of leaders, our point is that the future is uncertain. However, there are lessons from the past that will continue to be an important part of the future's landscape. In fact, research strongly suggests that the ability to look first to our past before we march blindly forward actually strengthens our capacity to see the future more clearly. Here's what we think are four enduring principles to guide the millennium generation of leaders as they travel into the future.

Lesson One: Leadership Is Everyone's Business

Myth associates leadership with superior position. It assumes that leadership starts with a capital "L," and that when you're on top you're automatically a leader. But leadership isn't a place, it's a process—and this becomes all the more important to appreciate going forward in time. Leadership involves skills and abilities that are useful whether one is in the executive suite or on the front line, on Wall Street or Main Street, on college campuses, community corners, or corporations.

And the most pernicious myth of all is that leadership is reserved for only a very few of us. This myth is perpetuated daily whenever anyone asks, "Are leaders born or made?" Leadership is certainly not a gene, and it is most definitely not something mystical and ethereal that cannot be understood by ordinary people. It's a myth that only a lucky few can ever decipher the leadership code. Of all the research and folklore surrounding leadership, this one has done more harm to the development of people and more to slow the growth of countries and companies than any other.

Our research continues to offer convincing evidence that leadership is an observable, learnable set of practices. In nearly two decades of research we have been fortunate to hear or read the stories of over 7,500 ordinary people who have led others to get extraordinary things done. There are millions more. If there is one singular lesson about leadership from all the cases we have gathered it is this: leadership is everyone's business.

Just ask Melissa Poe of St. Henry's School in Nashville, Tennessee. As a fourth-grade student fearful of the continued destruction of the earth's resources, Melissa wrote a letter to the president of the United States, asking for his assistance in her campaign to save the environment for the enjoyment of future generations. After sending the letter, she worried that it would never be brought to the president's attention. After all, she was only a child. So, with the urgency of the issue pressing on her mind, she decided to get the president's attention by having her letter placed on a billboard. Through sheer diligence and hard work, the nine-year-old got her letter placed on one billboard free of charge and founded Kids for a Clean Environment (Kids F.A.C.E.), an organization whose goal is to develop programs to clean up the environment.

Almost immediately, Melissa began receiving letters from kids who were as concerned as she about the environment. They wanted to help. When she finally received the disappointing form letter from the president it didn't crush her dream. She no longer needed the help of someone famous to get her message across. Melissa had found in herself the person she needed.

Within nine months more than 250 billboards across the country were displaying her letter free of charge, and Kids F.A.C.E. membership had swelled. As the organization grew, Melissa's first Kids F.A.C.E. project, a recycling program at her school, led to a manual full of ideas on how to clean up the environment. Her impatience and zest motivated her to do something and her work has paid off. Today there are more than 200,000 members and 2,000 chapters of Kids F.A.C.E.

Melissa Poe is proof that you don't have to wait for someone else to lead. You don't have to have a title, you don't have to have a position, and you don't have to have a budget. By viewing leadership as a fixed set of character traits or as linked to an exalted position, a self-fulfilling prophecy has been created that dooms the future to having a limited set of leaders. It's far healthier and more productive to start with the assumption that it's possible for everyone to lead. If we assume that leadership is learnable, we can discover how many good leaders there really are. That leadership may be exhibited on behalf of the company, the government, the school, the religious organization, the community, the volunteer group, the union, or the family. Somewhere, sometime, the leader within each of us may get the call to step forward. Ordinary people are capable of developing themselves as leaders far more than tradition has ever assumed possible.

Lesson Two: Leadership Is a Relationship

Despite all the advances in technology, after all the irrational exuberance over the Internet has come and gone, we'll learn again what we already know—leadership is a relationship. Sometimes the relationship is one-to-many. Sometimes it's one-to-one. But regardless of whether the number is one or one thousand, leadership is a relationship between those who aspire to lead and those who choose to follow.

Evidence abounds for this point of view. For instance, in examining the critical variables for success in the top three jobs in large organizations, Jodi Taylor and her colleagues at the Center for Creative Leadership found that the number one success factor is relationships with subordinates. Even in this nanosecond world of e-everything, personal opinion is consistent with the facts. In an online survey the techno-hip readers of *FAST COMPANY* magazine were asked to indicate, among other things, "Which is more essential to business success five years from now—skills in using the Internet, or social skills?" Seventy-two percent selected social skills compared to 28 percent for Internet skills.[1] Even when Internet literati complete a poll online, they realize that it's not the Web of technology that matters the most, it's the web of people.

Similar results were found in a study by Public Allies, a nonprofit organization dedicated to creating young leaders who can strengthen their communities. Public Allies sought the opinions of eighteen- to thirty-year-olds on the subject of leadership. Among the items was a question about the qualities that were important in a good leader. Topping these young people's list is "Being able to see a situation from someone else's point of view." In second place, "Getting along well with other people."[2] Young and old alike agree that success in leadership, success in business, and success in life has been, is now, and will be a function of how well we work and play together.

We recently asked a real, live twenty-something youth leader, Tara Church, the question about leadership in the future. "What do you think, Tara? In thirty-five years how will leadership be different?" She replied: "I don't think what fundamentally drives people will change all that much. What we do has to have meaning.

Leaders have to be able to enlist people in a common cause, and I don't think you can do that without being in someone's presence."

At the heart of the relationship is trust. Without trust you cannot lead. Exemplary leaders are devoted to building relationships based on mutual respect and caring. In a recent PriceWaterhouse-Coopers study on corporate innovation in companies listed on the Financial Times 1000, the researchers reported that trust was "the number one differentiator" between the top 20 percent of companies surveyed and the bottom 20 percent. "The top performers' trust empowered individuals to communicate and implement change in order to turn strategic aims into reality," said the investigators.[3]

Similarly, customer loyalty is the secret weapon on the Web. When Web shoppers are asked to name the attributes of e-tailers that were most important in earning their business, the number one answer is "a Web site I know and trust. All other attributes, including lowest cost and broadest selection, lagged far behind. Price does not rule the Web; trust does."[4] Long before "empowerment" was written into the popular vocabulary, leaders understood that only when their constituents feel strong, capable, and efficacious, and when they feel connected with one another, could they ever hope to get extraordinary things done.

Lesson Three: Leadership Starts with Action

When Charlie Mae Knight was appointed the new superintendent for the Ravenswood School District in East Palo Alto, California, she was the twelfth superintendent in ten years. She encountered a district in which 50 percent of the schools were closed and 98 percent of the children were performing in the lowest percentile for academic achievement in California. The district had the state's lowest revenue rate. There were buckets in classrooms to catch the rain leaking through decrepit roofs, the stench from the restrooms was overwhelming, and pilfering was rampant. Gophers and rats had begun to take over the facilities. As if this weren't challenging enough, Knight had to wrestle with a ten-year-old lawsuit, whose intent was to dissolve the district for its poor educational quality and force the children to transfer to schools outside their community.

These challenges would discourage almost anyone. But not Knight. After assuming the post, she immediately enlisted support from Bay Area companies and community foundations to get the badly needed resources. The first project she undertook was refurbishing the Garden Oaks School.

Volunteer engineers from nearby Raychem Corporation repaired the electrical wiring and phone systems. A volunteer rat patrol used pellet guns to eliminate the pesky rodents from the site. The community helped paint the building inside and out, and hardware stores donated supplies. Before long, local residents began calling to find out what color paint was used for the school so they could paint their houses in a matching shade. They went out and bought trees and sod and planted them in front of their homes. New leadership came forth from parents who began to demand more of a say. In response, an "Effort Hours" program for parents was set up so that they could volunteer time at the school. Teachers began to notice that something was happening, and they wanted to be part of it too. The district was on a roll.

Within two years of Knight's arrival, the children exceeded the goal of performing in the fifty-first percentile on academic achievement scores. Today one of the district's schools has climbed above the seventieth percentile, miles above the first percentile where they had started. The district was one of the first schools in the state to use technology in every discipline, outdistancing every school in California technologically, and it was the first elementary school to join the Internet. The lawsuit has been dropped. And for the first time ever, East Palo Alto received the state's Distinguished School Award, based on its improved test scores and innovative programs.

If we are going to have a future—let alone thrive in one—we learn from Knight that leaders don't wait (in fact can't wait) for grand strategic plans to be completed, new legislation to be passed, or consensus to be built. Like other leaders, Knight knew she had to get started. "It's hard to get anybody excited just about a vision. You must show something happening," Indeed, when high school students were asked to describe a time they had acted with integrity, their cases were ultimately about leadership. Faced with a challenge, some deviation from the norm, routine, principle, or belief, they felt compelled to take action. Many of these young people said they had no choice but to take action (to lead).[5]

Leaders, Peter Drucker once observed, are "monomaniacs on a mission." We agree. They seize the initiative. Starting a new organization, turning around a losing operation, greatly improving the social condition, enhancing the quality of people's lives demands a proactive spirit. Waiting for permission to begin is not characteristic of leaders. Acting with a sense of urgency is.

In our well-intended efforts to thoroughly diagnose the situation, to craft artful change programs, and to build broad consensus, we stall progress. By all means be true to intervention theory and practice, but also get things moving. Focus on small wins—things like fresh paint and clean school yards. Set up little experiments instead of grand transformations. Transformation is a scary word. It may even discourage people. It may also fuel cynicism. Little successive victories earn a lot of credit, and they inspire confidence. As the Jedi master Yoda instructed the young Luke Skywalker: "Try not! Do, or do not. There is no try."

Lesson Four: Leadership Development Is Self-Development

Self-awareness is central to being a successful leader. And this is precisely what Dan Kaplan, president of Hertz Equipment Rental Corporation, told us: "I know who I was, who I am, and where I want to be. So, in other words, I know the level of commitment that I am prepared to make and why I am prepared to make that level of commitment, personally. I know what it takes to achieve success for me. That success for me comes from paying a big price, putting a lot of work and lot of sacrifice behind it."

Kaplan's words reflect an ancient commandment: *Know thyself.* Warren Bennis called the "management of self" (knowing your skills and deploying them effectively) a leadership commandment. "Management of self is critical," he says, because "without it, leaders and managers can do more harm than good. Like incompetent doctors, incompetent managers can make life worse, make people sicker and less vital . . . some managers give themselves heart attacks and nervous breakdowns; still worse, many are carriers, causing their employees to be ill."[6]

At Santa Clara University, we take as our mission the education of leaders with competence, conscience, and compassion. Nothing particularly unique about the competence piece, but our attempts to make people more conscientious and compassionate require an exploration both of the inner territory and of our relationship with others. Conscience informs and develops the ethical and moral dimension inherent in all human beings, regardless of their religious or cultural background. Compassion nurtures the human desire and will to fashion a more humane and just world. In the framework of leadership, it is making a difference in the world and in the lives of others. As Ignatius of Loyola, the founder of the Jesuit order, explained: "To know and not to do, is not to know."

Self-knowledge is an essential part of becoming a leader. To become a leader you must become yourself, and this prescription is one of life's most difficult. "But until you know yourself, strengths and weaknesses, know what you want to do and why you want to do it, you cannot succeed in any but the most superficial sense of the word."[7] The better you know yourself, the better you can make sense of the often incomprehensible and conflicting messages received every day: Do this, do that. Buy this, buy that. Support this, support that. Decide this, decide that. We need internal guidance to navigate the permanent white water of today's environment.

Diane Dreher, professor of English at Santa Clara and chair of our Faculty Senate, a few years ago wrote a book titled *The Tao of Personal Leadership*. In this book she describes the process of "leveling up one's self concept" and points out that new experiences test us in many ways. They draw on our internal resources, our knowledge, our skills, and an ever evolving sense of self. She tells a story about a friend of hers who was climbing mountains in Peru, pausing periodically to survey the majestic view and reflect on her life. The progressive ascent became a process of self-discovery.[8]

Leaders take us to places we've never been before, but before we can get anyone else signed up for the journey, we've got to convince ourselves to venture forth. We've got to find out what's important to us. What we care about. We've got to find our voice. As Anne Lamott, in her book *Bird by Bird,* observed: "and the truth of your experience can only come through in your own voice."[9]

In his witty book *Management of the Absurd,* psychologist and CEO Richard Farson writes: "In both parenthood and management, it's not so much what we do as what we are that counts. . . . There is no question that parents can and should do worthwhile things for their children, but it's what they are that really matters. . . . The same dynamic occurs in management and leadership. People learn—and respond to—what we are."[10]

All of the new and growing number of books these days on soul, spirit, and spirituality in the workplace are ultimately about finding one's voice. The failure to do so means we often end up with a vocabulary that belongs to someone else; we're the proverbial Theory X managers with a Theory Y vocabulary. These managers *talk* the talk, rather than *walking* the talk.

Finding a voice is most definitely not a technique. It's a matter of time and searching—soul searching. As an artist friend once explained to us: "There are really three periods in an artist's life. In the first, we paint exterior landscapes. In the second, we paint interior landscapes. And in the third period, we paint our selves. This is when you begin to have your own unique style."

The same sense of appreciation about one's work, one's expressions, and one's life applies to the *art* of leadership. Most leadership development is still at stage one. It's still mostly about painting exterior landscapes, mostly about copying other people's styles and trying to mimic the great leaders. If we're to "level-up" and move beyond stage one, we need to enter the dark inner territory so that we can emerge from it into the light where we find our own true voice.

In search of excellence—an important book title at the end of the twentieth century—in a meta sense echoes the right call. Because it is not for us to be "in search of perfection." Perfection is neither natural nor particularly human. What is natural is to keep on growing throughout life. Consider this hypothetical story about a talented baseball player. As a batter, this man was phenomenal: He always got a hit, and every hit was a home run. And as a pitcher, he struck out every batter. So what would be the consequence of such a player? Simply put: To ruin the game![11]

The moral is that like baseball, the leadership game is not for perfect people. If we somehow managed to become perfect, no one would let us play with them. What makes the game exciting is the process of discovery, the unexpected, the probabilities. And that's exactly what the future holds in store for all of us.

Keep On Learning

Learning is an essential part of the leadership process for every-one involved. What carries us through life is our ability to grow, to discover new possibilities in ourselves, in others, and in our worlds. Successful artists, inventors, scientists, executives, and lead-ers in any field never lose that spirit. When they don't know what they're doing, they embrace the experience, realizing with every fiber of their being that they're learning and that learning is what life is all about. Just like fruit on the tree, when we stop growing, we start to rot.

That's precisely why leadership has to be everyone's business. Why leadership will always be a relationship. How action brings forth the leader within. And, in the end, how leadership is about developing oneself to be an instrument for making a difference. And these principles ring true—whatever the future has in store for all of us.

Chapter Eight

Leadership as the Legitimation of Doubt

Karl E. Weick

The purpose of this chapter is to develop an allegory for leadership in the twenty-first century, an allegory built around a moment in Warren Bennis's life. As he describes in his commentary at the end of this book, Bennis gave an evening lecture at the Harvard School of Education while he was president of the University of Cincinnati. Everything came together in a superb performance. During the upbeat Q and A session after the speech, Bennis was startled when the dean, Paul Ylvisaker, asked quietly, "Warren, do you really love being president of Cincinnati?" Bennis did not have a snappy answer. In fact, he didn't have any answer. After an interminable silence, in a room that quieted dramatically, Bennis finally said, "I don't know." Shortly thereafter, he came to the realization that he loved being a college president but hated doing a college presidency, and left Cincinnati.

Why do I flag this as a moment that can carry the message of leadership for an entire century? Notice what Bennis did not say. He did not say, I can't choose between yes and no. The question of whether he loves being president is not a problem in decision making. It is deeper than that. It is an issue of meaning, direction, and sensemaking. Standing in front of that Harvard audience, Bennis was facing a job, a university, a calling, and his own leadership theories with a mixture of puzzlement, ambivalence, and honesty. Leaders who stand in front of the new millennium and resist the temptation to treat it glibly or breathlessly are in the same position.

I want to argue that, given what Bennis faced, he called this one right. When he said, "I don't know," that was a strong act of leadership, not a weak one. It was strong because it positioned him for the sensemaking that he needed to do, not for the decision making that would come later as a minor by-product of sensemaking. To lead in the future is to be less in thrall of decision making—and more in thrall of sensemaking (Weick, 1995). That is the theme I want to develop.

Think first of the world Bennis faces at the moment of Ylvisaker's question. It is a world that is partly unknowable and unpredictable. It is a world into which people have been thrown. By thrown, I mean that people can't avoid acting, can't step back and reflect on their actions, can't predict the effects of their actions, have no choice but to deal with interpretations whose correctness cannot be settled once and for all, and they can't remain silent. Anything they say shapes both events and themselves. These are the givens that shape sensemaking.

This feeling of thrown-ness, and the need to make sense of it, are just what we would expect if we took seriously the psychological implications of quantum theory and chaos theory. Both of these theories suggest that the world is less like a machine and more like shifting patterns of relationships. These patterns are unknowable because any effort to measure them changes them. These patterns are also unpredictable because very small differences in initial conditions can lead very quickly to very large differences in the future state of a system (McDaniel, 1997). In an unknowable, unpredictable world, sensemaking is all we have. Rueben McDaniel put the point this way:

> Because the nature of the world is unknowable (chaos theory and quantum theory) we are left with only sensemaking. Even if we had the capacity to do more, doing more would not help. Quantum theory helps us to understand that the present state of the world is, at best, a probability distribution. As we learn from chaos theory, the next state of the world is unknowable. And so we must pay attention to the world as it unfolds. Therefore, it is a good thing that we can't do more than sensemaking . . . because then we would only be frustrated by our inability to know. But believing enables action, which leads to more sense (sometimes), and

taking action leads to more sense (sometimes), and sensemaking connects actions to beliefs (sometimes) [private communication].

It is the combination of thrown-ness, unknowability, and unpredictability that makes having some direction, any direction, the central issue for human beings, and by implication, the central issue for leaders. Sensemaking is about navigating by means of a compass rather than a map. "Maps, by definition, can help only in known worlds—worlds that have been charted before. Compasses are helpful when you are not sure where you are and can get only a general sense of direction" (Hurst, 1995, p. 168). Maps may be the mainstay of performance, but the compass and the compass needle, which function much like human values, are the mainstays of learning and renewal. If people find themselves in a world that is only partially charted, and if leaders also admit that they too don't know, then both are more likely to mobilize resources for direction making rather than for performance.

If I had to convert this broad portrait of leadership challenges into a set of contrasts, they would include the following. As unknowability and unpredictability become more prominent hallmarks of the twenty-first century, we can expect to find conditions such as these:

- Uncertainty will be based less on insufficient facts and more on insufficient questions.
- There will be fewer experts and more novices.
- There will be more of a premium on staying in motion than on detaching and reflecting.
- There will be more migration of decisions to those with the expertise to handle them, and less convergence of decisions on people entitled by rank to make them.
- There will be fewer attempts to capture the big picture and more attempts to capture the big story, with its ongoing dynamic, plot.
- There will more focus on updating and plausibility and less on forecasting and accuracy.
- There will be more improvisation and fewer routines.
- There will be more humility and less hubris.

The Value of Uncertainty

If we compress this set of predictions into a singular speculative picture of the effective leader, we can see why that person begins with the assertion, "I don't know." The effective leader is someone who searches for the better question, accepts inexperience, stays in motion, channels decisions to those with the best knowledge of the matter at hand, crafts good stories, is obsessed with updating, encourages improvisation, and is deeply aware of personal ignorance. People who act this way help others make sense of what they are facing. Sensemaking is not about rules and options and decisions. Sensemaking does not presume that there are generic right answers about things like taking risks or following rules. Instead, sensemaking is about how to stay in touch with context.

In the face of all the recent rhetoric about "new rules," we are better off playing up the fact of "newness" and playing down the possibility that this newness will necessarily take the form of rules. What's new is the context. What's new is the need for direction. What's new is a premium on updating. And what's new is the need to fall back on the compass rather than the map. We often run into the image of maps when people reaffirm Count Korzybski's famous caution, *the map is not the territory.* Even though the map never was the territory, and even though people still get confused when they forget this, it is conceivable that the image of maps and territories itself is dated, and the lowly compass may be the better image. Even though the compass is not any closer to the territory than is the map, it is much harder to mistake the compass for the territory. A compass makes it clearer that we are looking for a direction rather than a location. And a compass is a more reliable instrument of navigation if locations on the map are changing. Regardless of whether one has a map or a compass, it is less crucial that people have a specific destination, and more crucial for purposes of sensemaking that they have the capability to act their way into an understanding of where they are, who they are, and what they are doing. While the effective leader may sometimes be able to point to a specific destination that people find compelling, it is more likely that the effectiveness lies in the ability to set in motion a process for direction making.

When bewildered people ask, "What's the story?" the crucial thing is to get them moving, observing, updating, and arguing about feasibility and plausibility. A powerful means to do this is for the leader to answer the question by saying, "I don't know what the story is, but let's find out." That reply is more subtle than it sounds. A plausible story is actually not something that one "finds." When the leader says, "let's find out," what the leader really means is, let's create the story. The good story is not simply lying out there waiting to be detected. Instead, the good story comes from experience that is reworked, enacted into the world, and rediscovered as though it were something external. Bennis and the other leaders know that the discovered story is an implanted story, a story whose origins are more internal than they appear.

Let me give an example of what I've been talking about by describing a leader and a leadership style that embodies what I have said. This example comes from my research on the antecedents of wildland firefighting disasters. One of the five best wildland firefighters in the world is Paul Gleason. Much of his fame comes from his work in over five hundred serious fires, as crew chief in charge of nineteen other firefighters from the Interagency Hotshot Crew (the Zig Zag crew). Gleason said that when fighting fires, he prefers to view his leadership efforts as sensemaking rather than decision making. In his words, "If I make a decision it is a possession, I take pride in it, I tend to defend it and not listen to those who question it. If I make sense, then this is more dynamic and I listen and I can change it. A decision is something you polish. Sensemaking is a direction for the next period."

When Gleason perceives his work as decision making, he feels that he postpones action so he can get the decision "right" and that after he makes the decision, he finds himself defending it rather than revising it to suit changing circumstances. Polishing and defending eat up valuable time and encourage blind spots. If, instead, Gleason treats an unfolding fire as a problem in sensemaking, then he gives his crew a direction for some indefinite period, a direction that by definition is dynamic, open to revision at any time, self-correcting, responsive, and with more of its rationale being transparent.

Gleason's commitment to sensemaking is striking. When crews fight fires, they post a lookout whose job is to monitor the relationship between the oncoming fire and the crew and to warn if the distance between the two gets too small. On some of Gleason's especially hazardous fires, where there is danger of rolling rocks or windblown spot fires, he has assigned as many as sixteen people to be lookouts, leaving only four people to actually fight the fire. In the Dude fire near Payson, Arizona, which was an active, dangerous fire, Gleason worked part of the time without gloves so he could get a fuller sense of the weather conditions. He clothed himself as if he didn't know for sure what his surroundings were. It paid off. The first day of fighting this fire, around 1:45 in the afternoon, he felt a few drops of rain on the back of his hands. He knew there were no thunderstorms in the area, inferred that he must be feeling *virga*—condensation from a huge column of smoke that had iced over on top and was about to collapse—and he now knew that it was time to act. He moved firefighters into a safety zone just before the column collapsed. When it did so, it pushed fire in all directions and six people who were some distance from his safety zone were killed.

Leading by the Compass

Gleason's example nudges us to think more carefully about what it means to lead when one is thrown into an unknowable, unpredictable context in which the most one can hope for is a plausible direction and plausible updating. Just such a situation is what may have confronted Bennis at Harvard and leaders at the millennium. The nature of leadership when sense is up for grabs has some distinctive properties. I want to suggest that, in the face of doubt, leaders are best served if they focus on animation, improvisation, lightness, authentication, and learning.

Animation

Successful sensemaking is more likely when people stay in motion, have a direction, look closely, update often, and converse candidly. This logic derives from the basic process that is involved. That process is embodied in the rhetorical question, How can we know what we think until we see what we say? People need to act in order to discover what they face, they need to talk in order to discover what they think, and they need to feel in order to discover what it means. The "saying" involves action and animation, the "seeing" involves directed observation, the "thinking" involves the updating of previous thinking, and the "we" that makes all of this happen takes the form of candid dialogue that mixes together trust, trustworthiness, and self-respect.

What is subtle about all of this is that it is surprisingly indifferent to content. In a way, any old prescription, any old change program, any old mantra or guru or text will do, as long as that program *animates people* and gets them moving and generating experiments that uncover opportunities; *provides a direction; encourages updating* through improved situational awareness and closer attention to what is actually happening; and *facilitates respectful interaction* in which trust, trustworthiness, and self-respect (Campbell, 1990) develop equally and allow people to build a stable rendition of what they face. Whether people become animated because of "new economic rules," or total quality, or learning organization, or transformation, or teachable points of view, or action learning, or culture change, or whatever, they are more or less likely to survive depending on whether their program engages or blocks these components of sensemaking. It is the thrust of this argument that there is nothing special about the content of change programs per se that explains their success or failure. What matters is the extent to which the program triggers sustained animation, direction, attention, and respectful interaction. It is these four activities that make it easier or harder for people to collectively make sense of what they are facing and to deal with it.

Improvisation

When people are thrown into an unknowable, unpredictable environment, there is also a premium on improvisation. Improvisation can be defined as reworking previously experienced material in relation to unanticipated ideas that are conceived, shaped, and transformed under the special conditions of a current performance (adapted from Berliner, 1994, p. 241). Improvisation involves the flexible treatment of preplanned material. It is not about "making something out of nothing." Instead, it is about making something out of previous experience, practice, and knowledge during those moments when people uncover and test intuitive understandings while their ongoing action can still make a difference (Schön, 1987, pp. 26–27). What is noteworthy in improvised action is a certain ad hoc adroitness (Ryle, 1979, p. 129). Improvisation materializes around a simple melody, formula, or theme that provides the pre-text for real-time composing and embellishment. Outside the field of music, these melodies are the *directions* that are so important for sensemaking.

The role of the leader during improvisation is suggested by Dan Isenberg's (1985) description of battlefield commanders. On battlefields, commanders often "fight empirically" in order to dis-cover what kind of enemy they are up against. "Tactical maneuvers will be undertaken with the primary purpose of learning more about the enemy's position, weaponry, and strength, as well as one's own strength, mobility, and understanding of the battlefield situation. . . . Sometimes the officer will need to implement his or her solution with little or no problem definition and problem solv-ing. Only after taking action and seeing the results will the officer be able to better define the problem that he or she may have al-ready solved!" (pp. 178–179). Commanders essentially hold a diag-nosis lightly and tie their understanding to activity. This is akin to a simple melody that is embellished until a more appropriate melody emerges from the embellishments. A hunch held lightly is a direc-tion to be followed, not a decision to be defended. It is easier to change directions than to reverse decisions, simply because less is at stake. This is what both Gleason and Bennis have taught us.

Lightness

A leader who says "I don't know" is a lot like a foreman who yells "drop your tools" to wildland firefighters who are trying to outrun an exploding fire. Firefighters who ignore this order and continue to carry heavy tools like chainsaws retreat more slowly. All too often, they are overtaken by the fire and perish. There have been at least twenty-three fatalities just since 1990 where this happened. I think analogous crises occur when a leader says "I don't know" and followers refuse to drop their heavy tools of logic and ratio-nality. Those tools presume that the world is stable, knowable, and predictable, something the leader has disavowed. The leader who says "I don't know" essentially says that the group is facing a new ballgame where the old tools of logic may be its undoing rather than its salvation. To drop these tools is not to give up on finding a workable answer. It is only to give up on one means of answering that is ill-suited to the unstable, the unknowable, the unpredictable. To drop the heavy tools of rationality is to gain access to lightness in the form of intuitions, feelings, stories, experience, active listening, shared humanity, awareness in the moment, capability for fascination, awe, novel words, and empathy. All these nonlogical activities trigger interpretations that have some plausibility and feasibility. And all these activities are made more legitimate when a leader says "I don't know." That admission forces the leader to drop pretense, drop omniscience, drop expert authority, drop a macho posture, and drop monologues. The lightness of listening and exploring is the consequence.

Dropping one's tools to regain lightness and agility is old news. Nowhere is this better stated than in the ancient epigram (Lao Tzu, cited in Muller, 1999, p. 134) that reads,

> In pursuit of knowledge, every day something is acquired;
> In pursuit of wisdom, every day something is dropped.

But old as the ties among dropping and lightness and wisdom may be, they tend to be forgotten in an era where leaders and followers alike are preoccupied with knowledge management, acquisitions, and acquisitiveness. When Bennis says to Ylvisaker, "I don't know," this comment suggests that something more than a pursuit of knowledge is involved, and something more than acquiring the title of president is at stake. When Bennis says he doesn't know, that is a polite way of saying, this isn't about knowledge and acquisitions at all. It is about something different, something more elusive, something more like a quest where the directions are less clear. When any leader suggests that the issue ahead is more about wisdom than knowledge and more about dropping than acquiring, this has an important effect on followers. It makes it legitimate for them to contribute in kind. A leader who drops heavy tools candidly and publicly is more likely to encourage similar acts in others. Having dropped their heavy tools, people are in a better position to watch closely and interact respectfully to begin to form some idea of what they do face. The likelihood that this will happen at all depends on their capability for lightness.

Authentication

One of the early pioneers in the study of organizational behavior, Harvard's Fritz Roethlisberger (1977), adds yet another twist to the Bennis prototype for leadership in the future. Roethlisberger was struck by the fact that the vast majority of problems that executives complained about had the same form. He repeatedly heard that many people in organizations were not doing what they should be doing, in spite of numerous policies and standards designed to make sure that workers would do what they should. Accounting people weren't providing the information they were supposed to, supervisors weren't supervising, marketing people weren't working with production people, and so on. In a fascinating conjecture, Roethlisberger said it was as if the organization were undoing all the things the manager did when that person planned, directed, and coordinated. He went on to speculate that the undoing seemed to exhibit the mathematical property of reciprocalness. Thus the relation between the manager and the organization was either like multiplication and division, leaving an identity number of one, or addition and subtraction leaving an identity number of zero. In either case, the executive's contribution was nil. What Roethlisberger wanted to find out was what was responsible for the apparent undoing.

At this point in his discussion, Roethlisberger describes two extended cases where people don't do what they are supposed to be doing. One is the famous Harvard case called the Dashman Company and the other is a real-life experience of one of his students, a stubborn engineer named "Hal" who was appointed superintendent of maintenance shortly after being exposed to Roethlisberger's teaching. In the Dashman case, a newly appointed VP of purchasing, Mr. Post, sends out a directive to twenty decentralized purchasing agents saying that from now on, any purchasing contracts over $10,000 should be cleared with the top office. All twenty agents say they will be pleased to cooperate. But nothing happens. Not a single contract crosses Mr. Post's desk. The case stops with the new VP asking his assistant, Mr. Larson, a veteran of the firm, what he should do. Roethlisberger's students fumble with diagnoses for most of the classroom hour. With thirty seconds left before the bell, Roethlisberger says the following:

> If you stop to think for a moment, none of us knows what the situations in the plants really are, because none of us has gone to the plants to find out. We have just been speculating about what the situations there might be. This applies to Mr. Larson in the case as well as to us in the class. Until these speculations are checked, we may be mistaken. Hence, whatever Mr. Larson can say that might help to move matters in this direction may be the first simple step needed. Perhaps Mr. Larson with one sentence can preview a simple logic for Mr. Post to take the first step. So, dear students, please reflect and ponder until we meet at the next hour about what such a simple one-sentence response to Mr. Post's query, "What should I do now?" should be [pp. 176–177].

The sentence Roethlisberger was reaching for was this one. Mr. Larson might say, in response to Mr. Post's question of what he should do now, "I don't *know;* but perhaps if you or I or both of us went to visit the plants, we might be able to find out" (p. 177; italics in original). Regrettably, even with days to think about it, few of the students came up with this answer. And those who did often deemed the visit a gimmick to get people to cooperate the way they were supposed to. One student, Hal, who thought it was a gimmick, went back to his plant, was promoted to supervisor of maintenance, and assumed his new position. No sooner had he begun the new assignment than the shop steward called and said, "What the hell is going on in your department?" Biting his tongue, and stifling his overwhelming desire to say, "Who the hell do you think you're talking to?" Hal said, "I don't know. Why don't you come to my office and tell me." The steward came, voiced the grievances, Hal listened, and they worked through their differences.

While these cases may have a quaint 1950s ring to them, set that feeling aside for the moment and look at what is happening. When leaders say "I don't know," this is a nonstereotypical response—they are supposed to know—and the response is truthful; it is factual in the sense that it states what the situation is; it establishes leader credibility in an unknowable world; it invites rather than precludes finding out more; it takes advantage of an immediate point of entry into an ongoing, here-and-now situation; and it strengthens rather than weakens relationships. In terms of the seven conditions for sensemaking (social resources, clear identity, retrospect, cue utilization, update of ongoing impressions, plausibility, and enactment = SIR COPE) the statement "I don't know" is exemplary because it activates all seven. In turn, that means that the relationship has been fully tuned for sensemaking. When a leader says, "I don't know," that seldom stops the conversation. Instead, it invites such follow-on sentences as, I don't know, "but we might know," "but you might know and we need to listen," "but knowing is not the issue here," "but I know how to find out," "but let's talk to see what we do know for sure." Any of these follow-ons authenticate doubt, unknowability, and unpredictability as the point of departure.

Learning

The final and most obvious outcome of leadership acts that begin with not knowing is that they often end with something learned. A particularly vivid example of this point is Winston Churchill's reworking of one of the darkest moments in his life. During World War II Churchill made a colossal error when he failed to realize how vulnerable Singapore was to attack by a Japanese land invasion. This error led to Singapore's downfall. After the collapse Churchill asked four questions: Why didn't I know? Why wasn't I told? Why didn't I ask? Why didn't I tell what I knew? (See Allinson, 1993, pp. 11–12.) Those four questions are questions of interdependence. They are questions of sensemaking. And they are questions that are grounded in doubt. Those four questions take seriously the idea that knowledge is not something people possess in their heads but rather something people do together.

That seems to be the wisdom that lies behind Bennis's answer at Harvard. It is a wisdom that future leaders should take seriously if they want to deal candidly with what they face. It is a wisdom stripped of hubris. The leader willing to say "I don't know" is also a leader willing to admit, in Oscar Wilde's wonderful phrase, "I'm not young enough to know everything" (Kellman, 1999, p. 113).

Chapter Nine

Leading Yourself

Philip Slater

> *Leadership is as much craft as science. Analytical methods*
> *suffice for the latter, but the main instrument or tool for*
> *the leader-as-a-craftsman is* himself, *and how creatively*
> *he can use his own personality. . . . Like the physician,*
> *it is important for the leader to follow the maxim "know*
> *thyself" so that he can control some of the pernicious effects*
> *he may create unwittingly. Unless the leader understands*
> *his actions . . . he may be a carrier rather than a solver*
> *of problems.*
> —BENNIS AND SLATER, 1999, P. 127

Does this mean that leaders should undergo some sort of therapy or psychological diagnosis in order to be effective? Not at all. The most relevant aspects of personality can be examined by applying leadership theory to that "Great Group" we call the individual organism. We could simply ask that leaders apply to themselves the same principles that they use in leading others. How, in other words, do prospective leaders lead themselves?

We like to think of ourselves as self-contained, even monolithic, units. But in real life there's no such thing, for our "individual" self actually consists of a host of disparate elements. An appreciable percentage of our own dry body weight, for example, consists of bacteria, some of which have simply taken up residence, but others of which are essential to our survival (Margulis and Sagan, 1990, p. 28).

Are We Together On This?

Our whole body is a complex factory in which millions of bacteria work as subcontractors to help us maintain life. Even within individual cells, the regions called *mitochondria* are widely regarded as the descendants of independent entities, still functioning on much the same basis as their remote ancestors, bacteria that were absorbed alive by primitive one-celled organisms to create the common rootstock of all Earth's plant and animal life. They provide the energy our bodies need to keep going, and the wherewithal to repair them. "Without our mitochondria we could not lift a finger. In fact, it is these swarms of ancestral bacteria, working night and day in all our cells, that keep us alive" (Sahtouris, 2000).

To make matters more confusing, we're also full of contradictory impulses, as well as mental creations such as dreams over which we have no control, body parts that rebel and produce symptoms we don't understand, and so on.

Sociologists used to work themselves into a tizzy whenever anyone compared society to an organism, because they thought it implied some kind of monolithic unity. But today we know how little unity there is in the human organism: how much internal conflict, how much "class warfare" between the mind on one hand and the lowly body on the other; how little "freedom of speech" for some feelings and impulses; how many rebellions and uprisings there are; how poor the communication between body and mind at times; how despotic the governing forces can be; and how much the poor proletarian body often suffers as a result.

Contradiction and inconsistency are the rule, not the exception, in human behavior.

A Miracle of Coordination

Yet any moderately healthy human organism is an astonishing enterprise. When we consider the millions of living entities that operate it, the amount of information it processes, the rich mix of conflicting impulses and beliefs it serves, it's a miracle of coordination. And if it manages to achieve anything at all in the world it's even more deserving of the appellation "Great Group" than the examples in *Organizing Genius* (Bennis and Biederman, 1997). Consider what even the most ordinary organism can accomplish in a single day: successfully making billions of subtle adaptations to its physical environment, receiving and organizing billions of bits of data, acquiring, ingesting, and processing several different types of fuel for itself—oxygen, water, food— healing itself when injured or attacked, generating new ideas, and so on.

But who "runs" this group? We like to think we run it with our minds, but this is like the authoritarian scientist who missed out on a great scientific breakthrough in biology because he was looking for a "boss cell" (Tannen, 1998, pp. 13–15). Most of an organism's functions are performed quite well before it can even be said to have much of a mind. With regard to 99.99 percent of what goes on in the human organism the mind doesn't have a clue.

I may notice I have an open sore on my tongue, for example. I have no idea how I got it. It looks, when I examine it, as if someone took a chunk out of it. It's hard to ignore, but I try, and finally, in sleep, succeed. Sometime during the next day I remember it and take a look. It's gone. How was this done? I don't remember giving the order.

While playing tennis an opponent dribbles a dink shot over the net. I rush desperately for the ball, thinking only of getting a racket on it. But when I do, it whistles crosscourt for my best shot of the day. I don't recall giving that order either.

Micromanaging the Organism

On the other hand the orders I do give playing tennis seem often to be ignored, and I'm not alone in this. My group of elderly tennis players is not known for powerful serving, and our second serves are viewed by the receivers much as a cat views a bird with a broken wing. Yet I've noticed that we win quite a few points off those second serves, and I know why. There's just too much time to think about all the things you can do to that weak serve—opportunity knocks so loudly it throws your timing off, and your return all too often ends up in the net. This is what comes of letting the boss get too involved in day-to-day operations.

Yet we all try to micromanage our bodies. When we get the message from our body that we're tired we ignore it and drink coffee. When we get too jittery we have a drink. We push and prod, ignore messages we don't want to deal with, try to control our internal functioning with drugs, and so on. Until our "staff" has a sick-out in protest.

Who's the Boss Around Here?

Who really heads up the human organism? And how does this CEO operate? Does it lead or does it manage? And how well? Clearly there's an integrative and adaptive element of leadership that exists below the level of human consciousness or we would die every time we took a nap. It may well be that this nameless—largely unconscious—coordinating function is our true leader. But when we think or speak about *self* we're usually referring to a conscious entity—to the mind, or to what is generally called the ego.

From a DNA viewpoint the individual's only function is to reproduce itself ("a hen is just the egg's way of making another egg").

As individuals, of course, we take a different view of the matter—seeing our own survival as an end in itself. When people don't we think there's something very wrong with them.

To address this universal concern each human organism has a department assigned to deal with threats to personal survival. This bit of ourselves we call the ego, and most of us identify totally with it. But the human organism is very complex, and we're on automatic much of the time. While my ego is making plans, the rest of my organism can perform complicated tasks, process food, and balance itself internally in a thousand ways. A healthy organism may get out of bed, turn off the alarm, go to the bathroom, go jogging, wash, get dressed, prepare and eat breakfast, drive to work through crowded city streets, listen to the car radio—constantly making the most complex adaptations without any help at all from the ego, which may be entirely absorbed in security issues—that is, thinking about getting rich, powerful, famous, or loved.

Now the ego is a very simple mechanism compared to the organism as a whole. All its intricate thinking and planning is just an elaboration on one binary distinction—threat versus no-threat. Digital computers, which are also binary, are modeled on the ego.

Ruled by an Idiot

This may sound odd. What could be more complicated than the productions of logical thought? But the fact that the ego *makes* things complicated doesn't mean the ego *itself* is complicated, but quite the reverse. This is what we mean when we say a picture's worth a thousand words (an understatement if you've ever seen a picture digitized on a computer). The words make things complicated for us because they're too simple for the task of conveying what the picture shows. The picture *is* complicated, and therefore makes things easy for us to grasp.

Yet most of us are ruled, with varying degrees of tyranny, by our egos. How did this come about? How could such a simpleton gain so much control over something so subtle and complex?

The Despot

The reason is that in times of danger, binary simplicity is just what the doctor ordered. When a big rig is bearing down on us we want simple binary answers—run–don't run, left–right, forward–back. And the ego is superbly gifted at processing this kind of information quickly. In times of stress we give the ego dictatorial powers.

But who defines "times of stress"?

What the ego is not good at is deciding how severe a threat is, or when it's no longer serious enough to worry about. This, after all, isn't a binary question. And to make matters worse, the ego has a vested interest in not answering it.

In this respect the ego is no different from other despots. The Roman dictator Cincinnatus was famous because when the crisis he was called in to deal with had passed he gave up power and went back to his farm. In this he was unique. When the time comes for most emergency leaders to go back to the farm they start to hem and haw and find excuses. The state of emergency becomes a way of life.

There's always something to be nervous about if you're inclined that way, and how could you *not* be inclined that way if it was your job? How could you justify your existence otherwise? If the threat is gone you'd better find another one.

When the USSR—the prime excuse for forty-five years of bloated military budgets—collapsed with a pitiful groan, as Warren

Bennis and I had predicted twenty-five years before, the Pentagon didn't say, "Oh, I guess we were wrong about that big threat, we won't be needing all this stuff now!" They invented new dangers.

The ego is no different. It says things like: "I know we have a hundred million dollars, but what if we lost it all? Better make some more!" Or, "I know the bully who beat us up in the third grade is a bank teller in Akron now, but what if he comes back? Better add to our gun collection!" Or, "I know I've slept with three different women this week, but what if tomorrow I'm all alone and unloved, or I become impotent or it turns out I'm gay? Better find someone new!" None of this is conscious, of course, for the ego, like all despots, keeps its operating maneuvers in the dark.

In a Chronic State of Siege

The ego keeps excellent records of life-threatening situations. Unfortunately, its filing system makes no distinction between situations that are truly life-threatening today and those that may have felt life-threatening in infancy but are life-threatening no longer. Alienating a parent, for example, feels life-threatening to a toddler, and whatever strategy the child stumbled on to avoid losing a parent's love may continue to get the nod from the ego long after the child reaches adulthood. The strategy may be overachieving, underachieving, being meek, being aggressive, being tidy, being a slob—whatever made the child feel safe.

We learn through mistakes. We learn to avoid major errors by making small ones and incorporating that experience. Such learning is deeper and more permanent than any warning, advice, or instruction. Pediatricians say that a toddler with no bruises is overprotected. Bruises are the way we learn to sense our way in the world. An organism that takes risks doesn't need to send every little piece of information through Central Processing before acting.

But the ego doesn't like this. Its job—the justification for its existence—is to anticipate threats. It's not interested in learning, creating, exploring, adventure—only in avoiding mistakes.

When egos become despotic they censor information—a process psychologists call *denial,* or *repression.* Only "relevant" data gets past the censors—information that justifies the ego's control. Like other despots, the ego hates negative feedback, because it always includes the message that it's arrogating too much power to itself.

Internal Memos Ignored

The ego doesn't like to hear, for example, that it's driving the body too hard, or subjecting it to too much stress, or harming it with addictions. It doesn't want to hear messages from the unconscious, in the form of dreams or unbidden thoughts, that it's propelling the organism on a life course that will cause untold misery.

It doesn't even want to hear intuitive messages that the organism is entering life-threatening situations. People who have been beaten, shot, or raped often report that just before entering a dangerous situation they had a feeling of foreboding that they ignored or dismissed. In other words, the scouts did their job and the message was delivered to the despot but the despot ignored it.

How can it be that the ego, whose sole function is to protect the organism from danger, sometimes—in its obsession with control—fails to do even that?

First, the ego is often forced to choose between two dangers—an old chronic one and a new acute one. The old chronic one is the danger of losing parental love. It's the one that says things like "Don't be a wuss, guy" or "Be a nice, sweet girl and do what the nice man tells you." And this old chronic danger often gets the nod, because it's familiar and the ego knows how to deal with it. Furthermore, the ego, like all despots, makes no distinction between threats to the organism and threats to itself. Responding to intuition feels like a challenge to the ego's position, so intuitive reports are routinely ignored.

Despots maintain their power by incessantly warning of potential dangers: "The enemies of our nation are everywhere! We must be eternally vigilant!" The ego uses the same strategy. It manufactures threats, and claims that if it were weakened the organism would be plunged into chaos.

What's Good for Me Is Good for the Country

The ego's fear of losing its grip on the organism is what we call anxiety. It feels the same as fear of an external danger but no real danger is present. We feel we ought to be doing something to protect ourselves, but we don't know what it is we should be guarding against. This is the function of anxiety: to encourage us to give more power to the ego, just as all dictators drum up war scares to shore up their position.

At this point the ego can scarcely be called a capable leader for the organism—acting against many of the organism's best interests and probably hastening its demise. It has become blind and rigid, to the point where not only is the organism in constant stress and misery, it is also in increasing danger. The ego's rigidity makes it unable to adapt to changing conditions and its narrowness makes it unable to absorb necessary information. As is so often the case in life, the protector becomes the most serious threat.

In some cases the ego becomes so dictatorial that it's unwilling to allow the organism to sleep. Normally an organism will pull the plug on the ego for a third of each day, so that the populace can get its work done without constant government interference. But many egos are so tyrannical they're willing to sacrifice the health of the organism to their own obsession with control.

Many people find themselves in this condition today. At some point early in life they called in the Marines and now can't get rid of them. They're kept in a state of chronic mobilization by being continually reminded of obsolete dangers. The ego may claim that safety lies in being uptight, punctual, and reliable, or that it lies in being slovenly, disorganized, and helpless. *What reveals the despot is the consistency—the use of the same strategy in all situations,* protecting us from dangers that have long since vanished.

Evaluating Your Internal Leader

While all egos show tendencies toward micromanagement and excessive control, they vary widely from person to person. This raises an important issue for leaders in tomorrow's world. It will be hard for them to function as flexible, democratic leaders in tomorrow's fluid organizations if their egos are behaving like yesterday's rigid despots.

Since the world is moving too fast for the cumbersome rigidities of authoritarian control, and since a leader's most important tool is the leader's own personality, all potential leaders need to ask leadership questions of their egos.

Consider the following examples:

• "Effective leaders are willing to make decisions, but they typically allow members of the group to work as they see fit" (Bennis and Biederman, 1997, p. 20).

Does your ego allow your body, your impulses, and your intuition to function as they were designed to do? Or does it attempt to limit and constrain them? Is it only comfortable when it feels that everything the organism does is a result of its own conscious control?

• "Leadership is not so much the exercise of power itself as the empowerment of others," and the idea that "the leader controls, directs, prods, manipulates . . . is perhaps the most damaging myth of all" (Bennis and Nanus, 1985, pp. 224–225).

Does your ego empower the rest of you? Does it allow the organism to pursue its own optimal functioning or does it push, prod, and manipulate it? Does it give free rein to your unconscious to divulge its creative imagery? Or does it dismiss such imagery as irrelevant and pointless? Does it allow your musculature to express itself in nonutilitarian activities? Or does it restrict it to boring, monotonous tasks? Does it express gratitude for the wonders that the body accomplishes in maintaining, healing, and balancing this complex organism, rewarding it with release, rest, and whole-body gratifications? Or does it simply demand more and more of it, noticing it only when it fails in some way or breaks down?

• "The leader must be willing and able to set up reliable mechanisms of feedback so that he can not only conceptualize the social territory of which he is an important part, but realize how he influences it" (Bennis and Slater, 1999, p. 127).

Does your ego respond to feedback? Does it listen to your intuition—that is, to right-brain, holistic insights? Or does it shoot the messenger? Does it respond to pain, fatigue, and other physical symptoms with attention, care, and concern for the afflicted area, or does it shout down these messages with painkillers, stimulants, and other forms of symptomatic relief? Does it listen to messages from the unconscious or dismiss them as the ravings of cranks? Is it ever quiet when information is flooding in from all parts of the organism, or is it continually talking or looking at its watch?

Does your ego have an adequate understanding of the enormously complex system of which it is a part, and on which it depends entirely for its continued existence? And does your ego have an adequate awareness of the impact its demands and preoccupations have on the organism as a whole?

Why It's Important

Democratizing your ego is important today because of the way the world is changing. For thousands of years we've lived in a global culture that was authoritarian and hierarchical—a culture obsessed with exercising control over nature, other people, and our own emotions. Today we're moving at an accelerating pace toward a democratic and synergistic global culture—one more comfortable with spontaneous process, more accepting of what looks like chaos; a culture in which control is something that emerges, not something imposed. This is what Mary Parker Follett called "self-creating coherence" (Metcalf and Urwick, 1942, p. 200).

Modern writers such as Kevin Kelly (1998), Stan Davis and Christopher Meyer (1998), William Knoke (1996), Virginia Postrel (1998), and Thomas Friedman (1999) often use organic metaphors in talking about the new economy. It behaves like a biological community, they say—evolving and developing without centralized control. People are beginning to visualize organizations in the same way.

But how do people who have grown up with a more mechanistic concept of the world deal with this changing environment? Will those who've been schooled in the belief that their world—or their organization—will unravel without the exercise of their conscious control be able to adapt? Who will find this new world congenial? Who will find it oppressive, frustrating, terrifying?

Fresh Eyes

When change occurs, those who are uncommitted to the status quo—the outsiders—are in the best position to take advantage of it. Outsiders have fresh eyes—they haven't been indoctrinated with obsolete assumptions. It was the untaught child—uncommitted to the etiquette of authoritarianism—who saw that the emperor had no clothes.

This is perhaps why women today are making their greatest gains in cutting-edge industries. "If the male was the prototypical industrial worker, the information worker is typically a woman. . . . Of the people whose job title falls under the category of 'professional' . . . the majority are women (Naisbitt and Aburdene, 1990, pp. 220–226).

The "glass ceiling" that often keeps women from reaching the top of the corporate ladder may prove to be a blessing in disguise, as more and more women abandon these corporate dinosaurs to start new businesses of their own in cutting-edge fields. Women are starting their own businesses at twice the rate of men, their sales and workforces booming, and they're more likely than male business owners to have Internet access and Web sites (Jackson, 1999).

Pretrained

Another reason women adapt well to the new economy is that it demands just those skills women specialized in during the centuries they were locked into their traditional gender role—mediating, anticipating, negotiating, compromising, recognizing the needs of others. As a group women are better attuned to the demands of a democratic society. Men talk constantly about "being firm" and "standing tall" and "standing up to" people, as if working collectively on a problem were a matter of maintaining an erection. But rigidity is not a virtue in a democracy, and solving social problems is not a form of hand-to-hand combat.

Deborah Tannen finds that women often make better managers than men because they're more likely to involve employees in decision making, leading to more enthusiastic implementation (Tannen, 1998, p. 181). Men have traditionally tried to dominate the environment and make it predictable, but women have always had to live with confusion and chaos. Women are more compelled by their biology to recognize the limits of control. Menstruation, pregnancy, childbirth, and menopause are boundary-dissolving experiences that tie them to nature, and in traditional households they had to adapt daily to the unexpected, between active small children and the whims of demanding husbands. Women are used to being involved in several activities at the same time, of being a moving center in the midst of revolving chaos.

And being comfortable with chaos is just what Kevin Kelly says is necessary to function effectively in the new network economy (Kelly, 1998, pp. 113–114). But a despotic ego—male or female— is never comfortable in a turbulent environment. An ego obsessed with maintaining rigid control over its own organism will have trouble permitting the flexibility modern organizations demand.

In the past it was assumed that if a person acted in accord with certain leadership principles, good results could be obtained. But an effective leader in the future will need actually to *be* that way. The world is becoming too fluid and shifting for compartmentalized performances. In the old days you could be a flexible leader at work and a control freak at home. But splitting yourself in this way means viewing yourself, your organization, and the world around you as mechanisms—things that your ego can control, direct, manipulate—a way of thinking hopelessly out of touch with today's world.

Vision

Warren says one of the most important qualities in a leader is vision—a clear sense of where to go. A vision creates order without demanding it, just as a boat creates the order of a patterned wake by moving through formless water.

I've observed this quite strikingly in a very different setting— theater. Inexperienced playwrights often want to direct their own plays so they can make sure everything conforms to their vision. The result is usually sterile and often disastrous. If the vision comes through the writing, the director will see creative ways of enhancing that vision—ways the playwright never dreamed of. And so will the actors, designers, composers, and so on. I tell playwriting students never to write stage directions that tell an actor how to do or say something, since it limits the actor's options and encourages phony gestures. A good actor, I tell them, will have a dozen ways of creating the effect you want—ways you haven't thought of—and will choose the one most natural and the one that most powerfully expresses that vision.

The head of an organization is in the same position as the playwright. If the leader's vision is clearly articulated it will be most effectively realized by others who share it, and bring their own creativity to it. Any attempt to control and direct their input will reduce its quality.

But a despotic ego doesn't like sharing things. It feels very uncomfortable giving up control in this way. It's always willing to sacrifice the vision to the feeling of being "on top of things."

A cliché of the Industrial Age was that it was lonely at the top. But it was only the need to control people that made it lonely. There's nothing in the world that makes you feel more connected and more understood than having other people creatively enhance your own ideas with theirs.

People don't need to be controlled and manipulated to commit themselves to a heartfelt vision, and being controlled and manipulated tends to destroy that commitment. Those trained to a mechanistic worldview often find it difficult to learn this. But it becomes almost impossible if you've never learned it in relation to your own organism.

Chapter Ten

The Context of Creativity

Mihaly Csikszentmihalyi

I have been teaching two courses on innovation and creativity, and one of the texts for both courses is Warren Bennis's *Organizing Genius.* I would like to expand on a single passage in that book, to develop some of its implications.

> Jack Welch once said of his role at General Electric: "Look, I only have three things to do. I have to choose the right people, allocate the right number of dollars, and transmit ideas from one division to another with the speed of light." Those three tasks are familiar to almost everyone involved in creative collaboration [Bennis and Biederman, 1997, p. 26].

• These three tasks are indeed essential to the healthy functioning of any organization, and to creative accomplishment in general. Let me expand on the concise observation contained in this quote, and unfold some of its implications.

In my own work, I have argued that Creativity with a capital "C"—the kind that changes the way we see or understand the world—never happens in the mind of a person exclusively (Csikszentmihalyi, 1996, 1999a, 1999b, 2000). It can be observed only in the interrelations of a system made up of three main elements. The first of these is the *domain,* which consists of information—a set of rules, procedures, and instructions for action.

What we call a culture is a collection of thousands of such domains. They include, for instance, the domains of religion, mathematics, poetry, recipes for making BBQ sauce, the rules of basketball—you name it—our thoughts and actions are ordered and directed by the information contained in domains we absorb from the culture we belong to. Creativity does not happen in a vacuum; it always involves a domain of some sort. One is never creative in the abstract; instead a person may be a creative musician, or a creative scientist, or a creative basketball player. To do anything creative, one must operate within a domain. In fact, creativity can best be understood as *an idea, product, or action that changes a domain.*

A corporation such as GE could be thought of as a culture in a microcosm. It too contains information organized within domains—the concerns and procedures specific to the various divisions of the organization. If the firm wants to be creative, the first step is to make the information contained in these domains accessible to everyone in the company, since most creative ideas arise when previously unrelated material becomes connected. This is why Welch is right to say that ideas must circulate in an organization with the speed of light.

• The second component of a system is the *field,* which includes all the individuals who act as gatekeepers to the domain. It is their job to decide whether a new idea or product should be added to the domain. New ideas and products are constantly being thought up, but few are worth remembering or implementing because they are no improvement on the status quo. According to Peter Drucker (1985) only one out of five hundred new patents ends up making any money, and the same proportion holds for works of art or music. It is therefore important for any organization that aspires to creativity to have gatekeepers who can choose well among the many innovations the ones that are worth supporting. At General Electric, Jack Welch is the highest representative of the field who must "allocate the right number of dollars" to transform ideas into reality. If the field is too permissive and accepts novelty indiscriminately, or if at the other extreme it is too conservative and does not stimulate and reward worthwhile novelty, the organization will suffer as a consequence.

• The third component of the system is the *person.* Creativity occurs when a person makes a change in the information contained in a domain, a change that will be selected by the field for inclusion in the domain. This is where Jack Welch's "right people" come in. How does one recognize the right person, that is, the person who wants to innovate and who is likely to come up with something creative?

There are many characteristics that mark someone as a candidate for creativity. I will only mention a few that I feel to be the most important ones. In the first place, a person should enjoy pushing the envelope of a particular domain. Someone who loves to make music and delights in coming up with new tunes has a reasonable chance of coming up with something new that others will also appreciate. The same is true for an engineer or a marketing executive: nothing is more important than wanting to do one's job for its own sake. Too much concern for making money or for acquiring power and fame are warning signs that the person's priorities are not really promising as far as creativity is concerned. On the other hand, promising signs are interest, curiosity, and an almost childlike naïveté that questions everything, that is dissatisfied with the answer: "But this is how things have always been done."

• But creative individuals alone do not make creativity happen. They need access to the right information, and they need access to resources. If any of these three elements of the system are not functioning properly, the system—whether it is an organization or a larger institution such as a nation—will not adapt creatively to its environment. For instance, if the field (for example, management) in a company is bent on compartmentalizing knowledge so that workers in production do not know what people in sales or marketing are doing or what suppliers and customers want, and no one has a clear idea as to what the leaders of the organization are thinking about, chances are that even the potentially most creative employees will not come up with ideas for any useful new process or product.

• To see how this systems model explains creativity on a large scale, we may turn to a historical example. In a critical span of barely a generation, between 1400 and 1425, a startling number of masterpieces were produced in the city of Florence. The Western world's notion of beauty has ever since then been compared against the benchmark set by a band of young men that included the architect Brunelleschi, who designed the stupendous dome of the cathedral; the sculptor Donatello, who carved the proud images of the Orsanmichele chapel; the goldsmith Ghiberti; the painters Masaccio and Gentile da Fabriano, to name only a few. How could such a small city produce so many great artists all at the same time? Did the waters of the Arno river suddenly get filled with some chemical that changed the brains of average Florentines into creative geniuses?

Without trying to take away any of the credit that rightly belongs to these superb craftsmen, it should be pointed out that they alone did not make the Renaissance happen. The sudden creative spurt that later began to be seen as the "rebirth" of Western civilization was the result of the confluence of many favorable forces that created a unique window of opportunity for the flowering of the arts. Of special importance was the development of an able field of supportive patrons and the rediscovery of knowledge that had been forgotten for almost a thousand years.

• According to the sociologist Arnold Hauser, "In the art of the early Renaissance . . . the starting point of production is to be found mostly not in the creative urge . . . of the artist, but in the task set by the customer" (Hauser, 1951, p. 41). He is echoed by many others; for instance: "the patron begins to assume a very important role: In practice, artistic production arises in large measure from his collaboration" (Heydenreich, 1974, p. 13). To understand why the customers and patrons became so involved in artistic production at that time, one must look at the broader context in which the city operated.

Florence had become one of the richest cities in Europe first through trading, then through the manufacture of wool and other textiles, and finally through the wide-ranging investments of its rich merchants. By the end of the fourteenth century there were a dozen major bankers in the city—the Medici being only one of the minor ones—who were getting substantial interest every year from the various foreign kings and potentates to whom they had lent money.

But while the coffers of the bankers were getting fuller, the city itself was troubled. The population was divided into the "fat people" and the "skinny people" who owned only their labor. Men without property were ruthlessly exploited, and political tensions fueled by economic inequality threatened at any moment to explode into open conflict. In addition, the struggle between pope and emperor, which divided the entire continent, was reproduced inside the city in the struggle between the Guelf and Ghibbeline factions. To make matters worse, Florence was surrounded by Siena, Pisa, and Arezzo, cities jealous of its wealth and always ready to snatch away whatever they could of Florentine trade and territory.

It was in this atmosphere of wealth and uncertainty that the urban leaders decided to invest in making Florence the most beautiful city in Christendom—in their words, "a new Athens." By building awesome churches, impressive bridges, and splendid palaces, and by commissioning great frescoes and majestic statues, they must have felt that they were weaving a protective spell around their homes and businesses. And in a way, they were not wrong: When more than five hundred years later Hitler ordered the retreating German troops to blow up the bridges on the Arno and level the city around them, the field commander refused to obey on the grounds that too much beauty would be erased from the world—and most of the city was saved.

The important thing to realize is that when the Florentine bankers, churchmen, and heads of great guilds decided to make their city intimidatingly beautiful, they did not just throw money at artists and wait to see what happened. They became intensely involved in the process of encouraging, evaluating, and selecting the works they wanted to see completed. As a result they developed a refined taste that made them expert at recognizing good work, and thus enabled them to be true collaborators in the creative process. It was because the leading citizens, as well as the common people, were so seriously concerned with the outcome of their work that the artists were pushed to perform beyond their previous limits.

• But having money—and the willingness to spend it—still does not a Renaissance make. It also took know-how, skill, knowledge—the information contained in the domain. The contribution of the domain was the rediscovery of ancient Roman methods of building and sculpting that had been lost for centuries during the so-called Dark Ages. In Rome and elsewhere, by the end of the thirteen hundreds, eager scholars were excavating classical ruins, copying down and analyzing the styles and techniques of the ancients. This slow preparatory work bore fruit at the turn of the fifteenth century, opening up long-forgotten knowledge to the artisans and craftsmen of the time.

The dynamics of this increase in knowledge are well illustrated by the building of the cathedral's dome. The cathedral of Florence, Santa Maria del Fiore, had been left open to the skies for eighty years because no one could find a way to build a dome over its huge apse. There was no known method for preventing the walls from collapsing inward once the curvature of the dome had advanced beyond a certain height. Every year eager young artists and established builders submitted plans to the Opera del Duomo, the board that supervised the building of the cathedral, but their plans were found unpersuasive. The Opera was made up of the political and business leaders of the city, and their personal reputations were at stake in this choice. For eighty years they did not feel that any proposed solution for the completion of the dome was worthy of the city, and of themselves.

But eventually humanist scholars became interested in the Pantheon of Rome, measured its enormous dome, and analyzed how it had been constructed. The Pantheon had been rebuilt by the emperor Hadrian in the second century. The diameter of its 71-foot-high dome was 142 feet. Nothing on that scale had been built for well over a thousand years, and the methods that allowed the Romans to build such a structure that would stand up and not collapse had been long forgotten in the dark centuries of barbarian invasions. But now that peace and commerce were reviving the Italian cities, the knowledge was slowly being pieced back together.

Brunelleschi, who in 1401 appears to have visited Rome to study its antiquities, understood the importance of the studies of the Pantheon. His idea for how to complete the dome in Florence was based on the framework of internal stone arches that would help contain the thrust, and the herringbone brickwork between them. But his design was not just a restatement of the Roman model—it was influenced also by all the architecture of the intervening centuries, especially the Gothic models. When he presented his plan to the Opera, they recognized it as a feasible and beautiful solution. And after the dome was built, it became a liberating new form that inspired hundreds of builders who came after him, including Michelangelo, who based on it his design for the cupola of St. Peter's in Rome.

Another illustration of how the field and the domain of art came into a particularly fruitful alignment in Florence at this time concerns the building of the north and especially the east doors of the baptistery, one of the uncontested masterpieces of the period, which Michelangelo declared was worthy of being the "Gate of Paradise" when he saw its heart-wrenching beauty. In this case also a special commission had been formed to supervise the building of the doors for this public edifice. The board was composed of eminent individuals, mostly the leaders of the guild of wool weavers that was financing the project. The board decided that each door should be of bronze and have ten panels illustrating Old Testament themes. Then they wrote to some of the most eminent philosophers, writers, and churchmen in Europe to request their opinion of which scenes from the Bible should be included in the panels, and how they should be represented. After the answers came in, they drew up a list of specifications for the doors and in 1401 announced a competition for their design.

From the dozens of drawings submitted the board chose five finalists—Brunelleschi and Ghiberti among them. The finalists on the short list were given a year to finish a bronze mock-up of one of the door panels. The subject was to be "The Sacrifice of Isaac" and had to include at least one angel and one sheep in addition to Abraham and his son. During that year all five finalists were paid handsomely by the board for time and materials. In 1402 the jury reconvened to consider the new entries and selected Ghiberti's panel, which showed technical excellence as well as a wonderfully natural yet classical composition.

Lorenzo Ghiberti was twenty-one years old at the time. Just as Brunelleschi had been influenced by the rediscovery of Roman ruins, Ghiberti studied and tried to emulate the Roman bronze sculptures that were beginning to be excavated at the time. And he also learned to combine the rediscovered classic style with the more recent Gothic sculpture produced in Siena and elsewhere. He spent the next twenty years finishing the north door and then another twenty-seven finishing the famed east door. He was involved with perfecting the baptistery doors from 1402 to 1452, a span of half a century. Of course, in the meantime he finished many more commissions and sculpted statues for the Medicis, the Pazzis, the guild of merchant bankers, and other notables, but his reputation rests on the Gates of Paradise, which changed the Western world's conception of decorative art.

It was this synergy between newfound knowledge, a wealthy community with good taste, and able artisans that made the Renaissance possible. Nowadays we believe that all it takes to produce creativity is to get people to "think outside the box," to be more imaginative and original. But without the other ingredients—the right kind of information and a supportive community—creative thinking alone has no chance of producing anything worthwhile. This is as true of contemporary corporations as it was true of fifteenth-century Florence. And thus we return full circle to Jack Welch's observation that Bennis highlighted: For a firm to survive in a competitive environment that requires constant creative adjustments to changing conditions, it is necessary to choose the best people, to have the best information, and to recognize and support the best ideas.

What does this way of looking at creativity suggest for those who aspire to become leaders of business and polity? In many ways, the recipe is simple. Leaders who want to support creativity do not themselves have to be creative. But they have to become connoisseurs who can recognize good new ideas and good people. It is better if such leaders are not merely specialists but have a wide horizon of interests and competencies. Most often creative new ideas arise at the interface of domains, markets, technologies. Too narrow a horizon will blind the leader to many opportunities.

As to recognizing the right people who may contribute creatively to one's organization, the best tip-off is interest bordering on obsession. It takes a person genuinely in love with a branch of work to push beyond what is known, beyond where it is safe. Of course you want to make sure that the person is competent, and honest, and so forth; but what differentiates the potentially creative worker is intrinsic motivation—the willingness to do the work for its own sake. Naturally, if one wants the organization to remain creative, such people should be listened to, given credit, and rewarded; whenever possible, their ideas should be taken seriously and implemented.

The important thing to realize is that without necessarily being creative, a leader plays an indispensable role in the process of creation. As a crucial member of the field, a gatekeeper to the domain, the individual in a leadership position holds the keys for turning wild ideas into practical reality. To call such individuals *patrons* is to misunderstand their role; they are an essential part of the creative process. Just as without the Medici and their compatriots Florence would not have known the Renaissance, without enlightened leaders our creativity will stagnate.

Chapter Eleven

Why Do We Tolerate Bad Leaders?

Magnificent Uncertitude, Anxiety, and Meaning

Jean Lipman-Blumen

To peruse Warren Bennis's remarkable oeuvre is to explore an encyclopedia of leadership. Themes are introduced and developed, then recur later more richly embellished with nuance and depth. Here, I shall select just a few of Bennis's recurring motifs—uncertainty, democratic institutions, and the limitations of leaders—to explore a frequently ignored question that bears directly on the quality of future organizations: Why do we so frequently tolerate poor, even evil, leaders? I shall use another concept—anxiety—as the needle to stitch together these seemingly unrelated themes.

Many authors examine leadership in terms of the rapidly changing external world in which it functions. In contrast, I find it useful to look inward, that is, to look at the impact of the uncertainty and change generated by that external environment on some enduring aspects of the human condition—our existential anxiety and the human search for meaning. I am concerned with these issues because the ability of leaders and their constituents to deal with dynamic uncertainty, anxiety, and meaning will largely determine the kinds of organizations we shall have in the future.

_____

Note: I am deeply indebted to my colleagues Harold J. Leavitt and Neil Elgee for their insightful comments on earlier versions of this chapter.

An Age of Magnificent Uncertitude

First, and perhaps most important, we live in an age of *magnificent uncertitude*—an uncertitude that is only bound to increase. Its magnificence, like that of Janus, the god of doorways, derives from the fact that it faces simultaneously in opposite directions: one oriented toward potential dangers, including chaos and catastrophe, the other toward enormous challenges, involving expansive, ennobling possibilities.

Potential Dangers

While all historical ages have faced uncertainty and change, our own times are characterized by unprecedented increases in the rate of change.[1] Changes and uncertitude drive our world toward greater and greater ambiguity, turbulence, chaos, and other dangers.[2] They fuel and intensify our innate existential anxiety born of the awareness that the course of our lives—including our death—is not within our control.

This deepened sense of uncertainty, heavily seasoned with complexity and lack of control, demands a response. Yet the rapidity with which things now change makes it difficult to know what response is appropriate. The press for quick decisions amid uncertainty provokes still more anxiety, a growing dread of succumbing to powerful forces beyond our control, even beyond our comprehension.

This era is also marked by spectacular experiments, scientific, sociological, and political. These efforts contain the potential for vast and intractable destruction. In recent decades, we have witnessed the *Challenger* explosion, Bhopal, Chernobyl, Kosovo, Chechnya, and many more calamities. We don't seem able to put these disasters back in the bottle. The interdependence that now laces together the globe only exacerbates the possibilities for additional chaos.[3] Thus the magnificent uncertitude of our era heightens our underlying existential anxiety, the anxiety we must repress in order to live our daily lives.

Potential Challenges

Our growing uncertitude is nevertheless magnificent, for it holds much more than danger and devastation. First, it offers the promise of growth, change, and challenge. The challenges we confront stimulate new ideas and technologies that have the potential to reweave the very fabric of our lives. The Internet, cloning, and gene therapy are just a few of the amazing technologies that can transform, for better or for worse, the landscape of this age.

Second, this Janus-like uncertitude also offers us chances for making ennobling choices. Within our unfolding world, there are myriad occasions for us to dedicate ourselves, not to our own power and glory, but to great causes that hold the promise of a positive and lasting difference for society. Opportunities for transforming the settings in which many of us live, work, and think create ennobling chances for those who seize them. Occasions for ennobling action, large and small, arise everywhere—in neighborhoods, schools, churches, industry, and government.

This age of great perturbations also prepares the way for new leaders. It is a time not simply for the charismatic leaders Max Weber associated with turbulence, but for connective leaders who can integrate the goals of diverse constituencies living in today's interdependent environment and for other new types of leaders besides.[4] Who those leaders will be, how they will act, and—perhaps most crucially—how we shall choose to respond to them will affect the very nature of future organizations and the world around them.

The organizations yet to come will inevitably operate in a vast, diverse, and interdependent environment, where uncertainty and change keep company, and where danger and opportunity are locked in a permanent embrace. Still, like the Chinese ideogram for crisis, the top character—the *wei,* danger—is the first element that we see; the *chi,* the opportunity or life force, beneath the danger, is often below our angle of vision. This essay looks to the chi, the opportunity or life force.

Uncertitude, Anxiety, and Leaders

Existential anxiety, *angst,* is fundamental to the human condition, as Søren Kierkegaard, Otto Rank, and Ernest Becker have eloquently explained. This angst stems from our peculiarly human self-consciousness, a self-awareness that painfully alerts us not only to our limitations but also ultimately to our mortality. It is a powerful force that works in tandem with our openness to life to shape our responses.

Nor does it end there. When our angst drives us to seek certainty and security, we turn to gods—divine and human—to transference objects such as parental figures, and eventually to leaders. We hold fast to leaders who take control, who can provide us with a sense of certainty—real or imagined—that we don't feel within ourselves. Such leaders can manipulate and exacerbate our uncertainty by identifying scapegoats and enemies on whom we can blame our angst. They assure us that when we destroy those evil forces, peace and security will reign supreme.

Gurus, priests, rhetoricians, con artists, bullies, political, corporate, and military leaders, as well as media stars persuade us that they have the certainty that we crave. Their rhetoric and sometimes their deeds convince us that they are anointed with powers beyond those granted to ordinary mortals, that is, that they hold the key to immortality.

We cling to leaders to repress our awareness of our mortality, our consciousness that death and destruction may strike from any quarter and at any moment. To live with this mortal knowledge, we must repress it. Constantly staring at the one real certainty, that is, our own eventual extinction, can only lead to paralysis and paranoia. Thus, we must keep it at bay with the illusion that life is somehow under control—if not under our own control, at least under someone else's. And this control is what leaders promise, implicitly or explicitly.

Accepting the illusion that life is controllable is important if much of social life is to proceed; however, examining and understanding that the apparent controllability is, indeed, an illusion is necessary for a confident society to flourish. For many, the unpalatable truth of a world roiling with uncertitude is too much to bear.

Freud noted the tendency of groups to seek illusions, arguing that they "constantly give what is unreal precedence over what is real."[5] There is a powerful reason for this, as Becker suggests: "The real world is simply too terrible to admit; it tells man that he is a small, trembling animal who will decay and die. Illusion changes all this, makes man seem important, vital to the universe, immortal in some way. The masses look to the leaders to give them just the untruth that they need; the leader continues the illusions and magnifies them into a truly heroic victory."[6]

In a chaotic, uncertain world, where we sense our smallness and the danger of being overwhelmed, these illusions provide a lifeline. Leaders who appear larger than life, who can create larger-than-life illusions, seem to connect us to the deepest aspects of life. Moreover, leaders who seem to burst beyond the very parameters of ordinary mortals create the illusion of their own immortality. Identifying with such figures enhances our own sense of self—at least sometimes. Small wonder that we weep disconsolately for fallen leaders whom we have never met face to face. Such tragedies force us to discover that they were mortal, after all. Worse yet, their death also rends our illusion of security to tatters. Albert Camus poignantly comments on this issue: "Ah, mon cher, for anyone who is alone, without God and without a master, the weight of days is dreadful. Hence one must choose a master, God being out of style."[7]

The Propensity to Tolerate Bad Leaders

We idolize the good masters and often refuse, consciously or other-wise, to see the clay feet of poor ones, even when those leaders are patently incompetent, cynical, toxic, or evil. To acknowledge their ineptitude, even their malevolence, will only stir up our dreaded insecurities. John Byrne, in *Chainsaw,* describes this phenomenon in the case of Al Dunlap, who cut a drastic swath through organi-zations and people's lives.[8] The age of uncertitude rubs raw our vulnerability to bad leaders.[9]

The illusion that leaders can both protect us and transform us into vicarious heroes lulls our anxiety. Of course, the price we pay for this enhancing illusion is high: *un*freedom and submission to the leader's dictates.[10] So, in our eagerness to quell our anxiety, we are often less willing to surrender ourselves to good leaders, who "tell it to us straight," than to put up with dishonest, incompetent, perchance evil leaders. For what does the good leader do but dis-pel our illusions, or at least make us aware of them, thereby open-ing our eyes and heightening our tension? Denying their own omnipotence, such leaders are more likely to ask for help and expect others to participate in the leadership process. This strategy also more often promotes democratic organizations.

Even the very worst of leaders, the demagogues and tyrants, offer us the illusion of security that insulates us from the pain of our anxiety. Indeed, we should note that authoritarian leaders commonly create a stronger sense that things are under their control than do democratic leaders.

Moreover, authoritarian leaders with their self-confident illusions make us feel that they alone have the knowledge and skill to keep things that way. We therefore tend to stifle our concerns about their excesses, particularly as long as we are not the focus of their negative attention.

Turning Rationalizations into Control Myths

We become quite adept at giving ourselves a multitude of rationales for not toppling bad leaders:

- It is too difficult, and it takes too much effort to unseat them.
- We don't have enough support from others, and we can't do it alone.
- To try to overthrow them is too risky.
- More important crises need to be addressed.
- Besides, they're not so bad, after all, and, at least, we know what their faults are.

Eventually, we elaborate these rationales and transform them into complex reasons why we should accept these inadequate and often destructive leaders. These transformed rationales ultimately reemerge as "control myths," deep-seated beliefs that we use to control not only our own behavior but also that of others:[11]

- We believe leaders are stronger than we are and know more than we do.
- We believe that the gods favor them, thus making it morally wrong to challenge them.
- We remain blameless for any negative fallout because they take on the tough decisions.
- We believe they have our best interests at heart. (They certainly tell us so often enough.)

- We see that leaders control valuable and otherwise unattainable resources, and we may be permitted to share in them—but only if we remain loyal.
- We take for granted this power relationship, embedded in the social structure. That's just the way things are and always have been.
- We buy into pervasive stereotypes of "leaders" and "followers" that keep both the leaders and the followers in their places.
- We perceive that the odds, based on institutional resources, overwhelmingly favor leaders.
- We come to believe the smoke and mirrors campaigns that the leaders' entourages are at pains to keep producing.[12]
- We don't join forces with other less powerful parties to overthrow bad leaders because we often buy into the stigmatizing social stereotypes that separate us from other sufferers.
- Our desire to find meaning in the world and in our lives makes us yearn to be where such meaning might emerge: where the action is, at the center of things, at the nexus of key ideas and institutions, where leaders and those who oppose them operate.[13] Any unsuccessful attempt to unseat our leaders is a direct invitation to exile from the arena of action.
- And finally, as Becker wrote, "What we are reluctant to admit is that the admiration of the hero is a vicarious catharsis of our own fears, fears that are deeply hidden; and this is what plunges us into uncritical hero worship: what the hero does seems so superlative to us."[14]

These are powerful control myths that compel us to tolerate poor leaders. The criticality and complexities of these control myths warrant far greater elaboration than is possible within the scope of this discussion. Not surprisingly, breaking free of their grasp is no simple matter.

A Different Option: Matriculating in the School of Anxiety

Tolerating poor leaders is a fearsome price to pay to avoid dealing with our anxiety. But there is another option: We can enroll in what Kierkegaard called the "school of anxiety."[15] Confronting our anxiety helps us to learn from it so that we can assume leadership roles ourselves. Of course, "learning something new, itself, produces still further anxiety," as Edgar Schein reminds us.[16] For example, taking leadership responsibility for a totally unfamiliar task commonly provokes anxiety. It is often easier to turn such an assignment over to someone who "knows how" or at least appears to have the background and skill to complete the assignment. Conversely, accepting the assignment and using the accompanying anxiety to fashion a creative solution helps an individual discover previously unrecognized personal resources and talents. This unexpected success subsequently leads to an increased level of confidence for the next unfamiliar assignment.

While confronting bad leaders—from the incompetent to the immoral—triggers profound dangers, it also offers great rewards. Taking them on allows us to act on our own integrity and authenticity, to restore our own and others' freedom, and to give meaning to our actions. Moreover, by failing to stand up to bad leaders, we remain in darkness and lose the opportunity to become our own heroes.

Anxiety is a remarkably complex force. It bears a curious relationship to both personal and social change.[17] While it may be prompted by *external* social change,[18] anxiety also stimulates *internal* psychological and cognitive change, driving us to think in new ways and expand our identity accordingly.[19] Anxiety occurs when we realize that increasing external change, innovation, and disruption all demand a response.[20] Anxiety, after all, is an invariable accompaniment to serious change. Its appearance, however, need not signal that we are in trouble, but rather that the process of change is under way.[21]

Facing up to anxiety and the accompanying pain enables us to take the next step—even in the face of fear and uncertainty. Acting despite fear and trembling is one definition of *courage,* the very stuff of heroism. Under such conditions, we are most likely to take risks, to act as our own leaders, even to reach for the stars. The process is painful, but it can strengthen us enough to stop relying on false gods and to overturn toxic leaders.

When we arrive at that point, it becomes possible to give up the "control myths" that have kept us entrapped. Then we can acknowledge and confront leaders' inadequacies and urge them in new directions. As good leaders know, developing their people's insight, critical thinking, and courage to criticize their leaders has clear benefits: It enlarges the leader's vision and strengthens the whole organization. It is the very curriculum of leadership. As Bennis notes, "Perhaps the ultimate irony is that the follower who is willing to speak out shows precisely the kind of initiative that leadership is made of."[22] Accepting the responsibility to speak out is perhaps the first step in participating in a democratic organization that calls for multiple leaders at every level.

Democracy, Personal Responsibility, and Organizational Leadership

Confronting our anxiety helps us to discover the leader within us. We begin to tap our own human potential. When many members of an organization have made that discovery, the organization becomes both stronger and more democratic. It becomes an organization in which the many, not the few, share the burdens, the responsibilities, and the rewards of leadership. So students who graduate from the school of anxiety are likely to foster more democratic organizations.

Nonetheless, a curious and sometimes frustrating circularity arises: Because democratic institutions require that we look to ourselves, they also generate anxiety. We rarely dare to practice organizational democracy in its undiluted form. Participative management in organizations, a noble movement toward democracy, often generates so much anxiety—in leaders and followers alike—that it dwindles into thinly disguised authoritarianism.[23] What does it mean when the leaders of an organization say that Joe isn't a "team player"? Most often it signifies that Joe is not sufficiently obedient, that he doesn't always follow his leaders.

Democracy takes patience and strength. It requires far more ego-strength than ego. It also demands the ability to criticize and the even more painful capacity to be criticized. In addition, democracy is messy, both in and out of organizations. It's slow, and it's not very efficient, even though it is effective.[24] In the short run, it is often easier to turn the organization over to someone who will make the trains run on time. In the longer run, however, those trains may carry people to the death camps of demoralization, downsizing, and dead ends before grinding to a rusted, depleted stop.

Democracy, at least Jeffersonian democracy, requires each of us to do our part as leaders. It is a responsibility, not a privilege, to assume some of the leadership burdens of our society, both within and beyond organizations. And surely, as Bennis has pointed out, there is more than enough leadership work to go around.

Whatever the other strengths and weaknesses of organizational democracy, for my purposes here it has one incontrovertible forte: Democracy provides a well-oiled mechanism for removing bad leaders. Although most Western organizations are far from democratic, they live in a democratic environment, amid a broad general ethos that supports democracy and abhors tyrants. That democratic ethos also values merit. To the extent that their participants matriculate in the school of anxiety, organizations can become less vulnerable to incompetent and malevolent leaders.

Facing our anxiety, albeit a painful process, is the first step toward acknowledging our responsibility for leadership and participating in a democratic society. But that is not all within the human condition that prompts us to cling to leaders.

Leadership and the Search for Life's Meaning

Another aspect of the human condition that makes us vulnerable to bad leaders, beyond existential anxiety, is the human search for meaning.[25] Our search for meaning also has two faces. On one hand, it attracts us to leaders who have the ability not simply to manage meaning but to create it. Our search for meaning is another need that evokes our dependence on leaders, bad as well as good. Sometimes the meanings are real, sometimes not, sometimes uplifting, at other times cynical and manipulative.

Some leaders offer us explanations of life, purporting to tell us why things are the way they are.[26] For as long as those explanations seem to fit the reality we experience, we are likely to accept both the exegesis and the leader who formulated it. When that explanation is shown to be illusory or inadequate, as in crisis, we are forced to look elsewhere for meaning.

On the other hand, the Janus-like quest for meaning also offers us release from the thrall of flawed leaders. Heroic striving, a part of this search, is one human strategy for dealing with the need to transcend our inevitable mortality. It frames our effort to leave behind some memorable fragment for the ages, some immortal crumb of our symbolic self that will remain when our cloak of creatureliness dissolves, when we succumb to our finitude, our mortality.

In our quest for meaning, we seek to discover that we have a significant role in a meaningful universe.[27] We need to believe, despite the magnificent uncertitude, first that the world is not a meaningless, random place, and second that the grand struggle we call our "life" has significance. The death of that meaning, in fact, can be ultimately more awesome than one's physical death.[28]

Death need not end either the significance of that life nor our symbolic self. We are aware that it is possible, at least symbolically, to transcend physical death by various means: through our biological heirs; through religious and mystical beliefs; through creative achievements in various human fields of endeavor; and through the imprint of our actions, personalities, and thoughts on others.[29] In all these ways, and more, we can leave a residue that lasts beyond our own finite lifetime.

Still, striving to determine how to satisfy this longing creates another source of uncertainty and anxiety. The meaning behind this ultimate mystery of our singular lives in a wondrous world is one that we unceasingly try to penetrate. The very best of leaders are engaged in their own personal odysseys for meaning, and they invite their constituents to join the search.[30]

Our insatiable pursuit of meaning is one of the great turbines of progress. It is manifest everywhere around us. All the great discoveries that propel contemporary life were driven by a desire to grasp the meaning of things—things spiritual, social, artistic, scientific, and technological. It is in this search for meaning that we play out our days and make our fateful choices.

If we passively surrender to anxiety, we cannot find meaning—only a false, temporary security through external leaders and other bulwarks outside ourselves. And, in this age of uncertitude, leaders themselves are becoming increasingly fragile and vulnerable, no longer able to guarantee safety to followers, even if they so desired.

Actively exploiting and transforming our anxiety into constructive tension, however, helps us discover not only internal leadership strengths but also the essential meaning of life. What are we doing here? What is worth doing? What do we want to leave as our legacy?

Using anxiety in this positive way, we can explore the "thick description" of our lives, much as anthropologist Clifford Geertz uses "thick description" as a strategy for interpreting cultures.[31] Examining our actions and our choices, our strengths and weaknesses, as well as our roles in families, organizations, and communities provides an inkling of what all this does or could mean. Self-scrutiny that pierces the mists of anxiety enables us to catch glimpses of ourselves as the leaders we might be. It is one way for us to try to apprehend and interpret our lives, the actions we take, and what they signify.

Finding and nourishing the leader within is only one aspect of our central life task. We might think of this as part of our "immortality project," that lifelong enterprise we all engage in to satisfy our symbolic selves.[32]

The more we mature, the more complex the meaning we seek. We search for meaning that plumbs the depths of our own individuality and that of others far beyond ourselves. Creating such a complex meaning system requires a balancing act between understanding and differentiating ourselves from others and integrating ourselves with the larger world.[33] Attaining this balance allows us to seek ennobling opportunities by committing ourselves to significant social enterprises.

Ennoblement and "Victories for Humanity"

Eventually, we want more than an explanation of who we are and what that means; we want opportunities to be more than our narrow selves have allowed us to be heretofore. We also want to fathom what our contribution should be to the larger world. We sense that it is time to overcome the tyranny of our ego and our dependence on external leaders. Heroically breaking free of the bondage of protective leadership allows us to wrestle with life's major challenges as we dedicate our efforts to something greater than ourselves.

In short, we seek ennoblement by committing ourselves to heroic causes that benefit others beyond ourselves, even beyond those we hold dearest. In the words of Horace Mann, whom Bennis fondly quotes, "Be ashamed to die until you have won some victory for humanity."[34]

Leaders who engage in their own quest for meaning and ennoblement will fashion organizations where they and others can find what they seek, can win such victories. It is here that immortality projects become relevant, be they the creation of a groundbreaking technology, a global industrial organization, or a soup kitchen for the hungry.

For each of us, our immortality project offers the possibility of an ennobling undertaking, a heroic act.[35] Becoming a hero often entails facing, surviving, and symbolically transcending fear and death, but there is more to heroic behavior than that.[36] Courage, by one definition, is the ability not simply to look death in the eye in the traditional heroic fashion but to see death continuously out of the corner of the eye and still function at the fullness of one's potential.[37] Instead of hiding obediently within the thicket of cultural expectations, those individuals who courageously confront life's daily dilemmas and events are enacting their own brand of heroism.

The greatness of the cause that lies at the heart of our ennobling enterprise is in the eye of the beholder. Each and every one of us works hard at our immortality project, whether consciously or not. Here, too, our existential anxiety—thickened by uncertitude and learning—is at work. So, too, is our natural striving toward life.[38] These forces catapult us beyond our ordinary limits, perhaps to cosmic heroism, demonstrating that we deserve to be up there among the stars.[39]

Where and how do our immortality projects fit into the larger scheme, even beyond the organizations in which we spend most of our days? Graduating from the school of anxiety and forgoing our dependence on leaders are clearly only the initial steps. Breaking the chains of our control myths and freeing ourselves from the bondage of bad leaders both move us along an important path. Building democratic institutions where freedom exists and everyone has a voice is another key step. Searching for a complex understanding of our self and our world vaults still another barrier. Finding the leader within and winning those victories for humanity take us beyond our creaturely selves to the expression of our noblest instincts.

Finding the leader within, our heroic self, does more than unshackle us from the external leaders to whom we so desperately have held fast. It also frees up much more leadership talent for the entire society, in every organization, at every level. This new breed of leaders will be more self-reliant and thoughtful. These will be leaders who can handle the magnificent uncertitude of our times, the anxiety it augments, and the opportunities for learning and change that both uncertainty and anxiety generate.

There are no easy answers. Still, taken together, these strategies may offer a nutritional cocktail for future organizations. They present one road map for overcoming our vulnerability to bad leaders. Then, magnificent uncertitude and anxiety will have been put to good use, and democratic organizations surely will flourish.

Chapter Twelve

The Evolving Role of Executive Leadership

Cathy L. Greenberg-Walt, Alastair G. Robertson

This set of extracts from *The Evolving Role of Executive Leadership* is dedicated to Warren Bennis, the father of modern leadership as we know it. The book is a compendium of research results, key findings, and recommendations and is designed to help leaders understand current issues and envision future challenges, making them better prepared to lead their organizations. Bennis was a primary motivating force in the development of this work, which was produced by the Accenture Institute for Strategic Change, a pragmatic "think-and-act tank" that has conducted extensive research on the key issues of executive leadership and their evolution since its inception in January 1997. We are grateful to Bennis for his leadership, dedication, and insight, which have culminated in this and over fifty articles worldwide on the subject of the future global leader based on this research. Here we address three key topics for the future of leadership:

- Shared leadership and the devolving CEO
- Leading across generations
- Global leadership—the next generation

Shared Leadership and the Devolving CEO

Shared leadership is currently the subject of some debate. How practical and effective is the collaborative leadership model? Few answers have emerged, and the global markets have provided vivid examples of both success and failure, with a few whose fate has yet to be determined.

Research findings, however, suggest that this will be the leadership model of the future. The model appears to respond best to the needs of organizations that have undergone mergers, acquisitions, or joint ventures that have simply grown to great size and complexity.

What Is Shared Leadership?

Shared leadership, at the highest level, means splitting the responsibilities of the CEO between two or more individuals. In the broader sense, it means empowering individuals at all levels and giving them the opportunity to take the lead. It is becoming more common as the old top-down management structure gives way to flatter, more decentralized forms, and is seen by some experts as a way of promoting agility, proactivity, and autonomy: "Shared leadership fosters an environment that responds in agile ways to newness. It promotes a greater degree of creative and rational thought at the levels where it is needed. It enables all individuals in the organization to test their own assumptions and those of others rather than waiting for the ideas and decisions to be handed down through the hierarchy. True shared leadership can happen anywhere in an organization" (Deiss and Soete, 1997).

In consequence, leadership expectations for any employee in a company that has adopted shared leadership have increased significantly. At a minimum, staff are expected to be their own leaders, but at some point, most are also expected to lead formal or informal teams.

Drivers of Shared Leadership

Numerous factors contribute to the adoption of shared leadership models. The most common in recent years has been the increasing, if not overwhelming, number of mergers and acquisitions. Naturally, as two or more companies unite, their executive managers must integrate (or leave), and the new board of directors determines who will lead the new company. In some recent cases, the leadership is shared between two (or more) people.

A second factor is the growing number of partnerships and alliances where executives work jointly on specific projects or assignments. Basic to their success is the ability of all to work effectively together, the leaders in particular. Often, new leadership teams are created, with representation from each of the partners in the alliance, requiring several leaders to work together effectively in a broad coalition.

Rapidly flattening, often team-based structures are a third reason for shared leadership. Flatter organizations mean sharing responsibility and accountability at all levels of the company, so that power, authority, and decision making are more dispersed, both laterally and vertically.

A fourth factor is market convergence. As markets become more complex and interrelated, the demands on leadership increase until the job is simply too large for one individual, and global alignment of strategy and performance are likely to suffer. The many competencies required for such global leadership are unlikely all to be found in one individual.

Warren Bennis finds that many CEOs see their central task as developing other leaders and actively helping followers reach their own leadership potential (Bennis and Goldsmith, 1997). Thus future leaders may move away from singular roles to shared leadership networks that may themselves alter the foundations of the organization.

Examples of Shared Leadership

Long-Term Dual Philosophy

Unilever, an Anglo-Dutch consumer goods corporation that derives some $50 billion global sales from more than a thousand separate brands, is evidence that dual leaders are feasible, providing they have the same corporate philosophy. The group has worked with a shared leadership management structure ever since 1929, when the Dutch Margarine Union merged with the British Lever Bros. Both the Dutch and British shareholdings were retained and two co-chairmen were appointed to head the group. Along with the next chairman-elect, they formed a triumvirate that operated through a complex matrix of product coordinators and national heads.

In a move to improve the quality and clarity of strategy formu-
lation, the triumvirate was replaced as part of a major restructuring in 1996. The financial structure, divided into Unilever plc and
Unilever NV, was retained, and with it the two chairmen, who pre-
side over the business of the Unilever group as the principal executive officers. But overall strategy was put in the hands of a
seven-strong executive committee, and presidents were appointed
to head the fourteen (now twelve) geographically based business
groups, with full responsibility for operations and profits. Chairmen, executive committee, and presidents form the Unilever Executive Council.

There is now a much clearer distinction between group strategy and business operations, but Unilever has also designed the
new structure to balance both global and local imperatives. It aims
to make the most of its extensive knowledge of consumers in the
158 countries in which it operates, as well as optimizing the manufacturing facilities in 88 countries.

The executive committee, the top decision-making body, is
therefore responsible for the following:

- Agreeing on priorities and allocating resources within
  the company
- Setting overall corporate targets
- Agreeing to and monitoring business group strategies
  and plans
- Identifying and exploiting opportunities created by
  Unilever's scale and scope
- Managing relations with the external world
- Developing future leaders

Business group presidents are responsible for operating their
business in the most effective way. These are the key elements of
their role:

- Taking full profit responsibility for their group
- Feeding their understanding of local market needs into
  group deliberations about future corporate strategy and the
  allocation of resources
- Executing corporate strategy

The new Unilever structure thus exhibits both forms of dual leadership: split chairmanship supported by an executive committee. The group's size and breadth of focus require a broad base of senior management expertise and experience. For companies that are merging with or acquiring others, it is essential to develop a strategy for a leadership team or teams that can be incorporated into the wider M&A plan.

Co-Chief Executive Officers

Shared leadership in its wider sense is a relatively new phenomenon, although splitting the powers and responsibilities of the chief executive between two exceptional leaders has a long history. A current example in which the role of chairman and chief executive is divided is provided by Citigroup, formed out of an equal merger between the U.S. bank Citicorp and the Travelers financial services group. Sharing the top roles are John S. Reed of Citicorp and Sanford I. Weill of Travelers. They have highly respected records in their own areas, which are seen as critical to the ultimate benefit to customers and shareholders. Observers question whether two such disparate cultures can be merged, and there have already been casualties, but the two leaders say their union is a marriage in which divorce is not an option.

Shared leadership may also be used as a change vehicle with no intention of maintaining it as a permanent structure. The U.S. long-distance telecommunications group GTE Corporation recently merged with the regional operator Bell Atlantic to create a wireless communications company. Charles R. Lee (CEO of GTE) and Ivan G. Seidenberg (CEO of Bell Atlantic) hold the co-CEO title and share leadership of the newly merged company. Lee is chairman, with Seidenberg as president. Lee brings chief operating officer, finance, and planning skills to the team, while Seidenberg's record features outstanding earnings performance and a turnaround in service delivery. He also has good experience in mergers, regulatory reform, and union negotiation. Useful as Lee's skills are in the short run, it should be noted that a natural succession back to single leadership has been planned. In 2002, Seidenberg will become the sole CEO, with Lee continuing as chairman until 2004, when Seidenberg will succeed him.

Whether shared leadership is a permanent phenomenon remains to be seen. It does not suit every situation. Monsanto and American Home Products intended to become a smoothly integrated model of co-leadership. The combined companies' board of directors was planned to have equal representation, and Robert B. Shapiro and John R. Stafford were to be co-chairmen and co-CEOs. In the end, however, the deal fell before what a statement described as "clashes of corporate cultures and CEOs' egos." As one analyst noted in the *Boston Globe* ("The Region," 1998), "It's OK if you want to have co-managers, but you can have only one philosophy and you can have only one leader."

Executive Teams

Another form of shared leadership is the executive team. The increased size and breadth of focus of merged companies demand a broader base of senior management expertise and experience. Such companies therefore need a strategy for a leadership team or teams that can be incorporated into the wider merger and acquisition plan.

In the United States, NationsBank and Bank of America opted to apply this form of shared leadership when they merged in 1998. The top team was a combination of Hugh L. McColl Jr., CEO of NationsBank, who was made chairman and CEO of Bank of America; David Coulter, former chairman and CEO of Bank of America, who was appointed the new president of Bank of America; and James H. Hance, who became the new vice chairman and chief financial officer. Thus three leaders would fill different roles and provide different experience and expertise within the new executive team, sharing a job that was regarded as too big for one individual.

Once again, however, events interfered with an intriguing experiment. Coulter resigned barely a month after the two firms joined, raising the question of how shared leadership withstands adverse market conditions—in this case, a 78 percent drop in Bank of America's net income for the previous quarter. Perhaps the new team did not have enough time to develop shared responsibility.

Strong executive teams that share leadership are not always the product of a merger. In other cases, they are put in place to maximize the best talent and capability for the firm. Global perception management firm Burson-Marsteller provides an example. The team includes Graham Phillips, chairman; Chris Komisarjevsky, CEO; Don Cogman, president and COO; and Kurt Krauss, CFO. Extremely well-managed companies such as this have figured out how to share leadership, and they have done it for a long time. The executive team is well aligned, and generally the totality of leadership is shared with specific roles performed very effectively by the various team members.

Another example is SuperStock, a U.S. company that represents hundreds of photographers, artists, archives, museums, and special collections. In addition to co-presidents, this organization has an extensive leadership team.

Partnership

In strategic partnerships and alliances, some form of shared leadership is unavoidable. Either the separate leadership teams must come together to find a cohesive structure for their business practices, or a new leadership team, perhaps with equal representation, has to be created. Where there are several participants in a partnership or alliance, demands for shared leadership can increase sharply. Many alliances now include twenty or more partners, and the leadership demands become very complex.

Bechtel, the San Francisco–based engineering, construction, and management firm, shares leadership with its partner Intergraph Corporation, which supplies software, hardware, and technical assistance for its global engineering and construction projects. Similarly, Accenture relies on its partner Kenan Communications for state-of-the-art billing and customer care solutions used by communications providers worldwide. Accenture personnel are trained in the Kenan suite of solutions, and both partners assign staff to work together on client projects. As the number of alliances and partnerships between suppliers and customers grows, this form of shared leadership can be expected to expand.

Yet other examples can be found in proliferating alliances that include the outsourcing of major corporate functions to multiple partners.

Pru-Tech, an information technology subsidiary of Prudential Assurance, has an alliance with Accenture, to which each contributes leadership and core competencies. A team of Prudential and Accenture executives was formed to design and implement information technology and related change initiatives that directly support Prudential Assurance's strategic business objectives. Their goal is to provide more responsive, personalized products and services to customers through the customers' preferred access routes.

Research Support

Demands for shared leadership will continue to increase in the future. Accenture's Global Leader of the Future Profile indicates that dimensions such as *develops and empowers people, builds teamwork and partnerships,* and *shares leadership* increase significantly in importance for future leadership. The knowledge-based organization demands leaders who are ready for the participation of their workers in decision making. Qualitative data from research participants indicate that most are already involved in some form of shared leadership; they expect to see more shared executive leadership situations ahead.

Peter Drucker has noted that knowledge workers are people who know more about what they are doing than their managers do. In dealing with knowledge workers, old models of leadership will not work. Telling people what to do and how to do it becomes outmoded. The leader will instead be a guide, asking for input and sharing information. Knowledge workers of the future may well be difficult to keep. They will probably have little organizational loyalty and view themselves as professional free agents who will work for the leader who provides the most challenge and opportunity. Skill in hiring and retaining key talent will be a valuable commodity for the leader of the future. Sharing leadership may be one way to help demonstrate this skill.

Leading Across Generations

A growing problem facing some companies is the divisions in the workforce between different generations. In the modern high-tech, knowledge-based organization, where innovation and flexibility are vital, there is often a youth culture that leaves older staff out in the cold. But any organization that is not tolerant of the different generations making up its workforce is likely to suffer through high staff turnover and suboptimal performance.

In the United States, two generations in particular seem prone to conflict. These are known as the "baby boomers," who were born between the end of the Second World War and the mid-1960s, and a younger generation, the "Generation Xers," born after that time. All workforces are (or probably should be) multigenerational, but there is some evidence of a significant difference in assumptions, attitudes, and expectations of the younger Generation Xers. In the complex modern business organization, the older generation may have increasing difficulties leading the younger with its differing values and workstyle. But more obviously, the younger generation, thrust by technology into an increasing number of lead positions, may find difficulty winning the confidence of older subordinates.

Generational Values and Corporate Culture

Traditionally, organizations have developed a strong culture based on the values of loyalty, fortitude, and corporate paternalism—generally embodied and practiced by baby boomers. But this classic culture does not appear to resonate as well with the Generation Xers. Problems arise when corporations expect their younger employees to live, work, and lead like their boomer predecessors. A senior executive at the San Francisco Forum, commenting on the need to transform the organization, explained, "Corporate cultures must become adaptive or people will leave. Young professionals today have many more options than ever before. They no longer have to bow down to the 'corporate god.'"

Companies realize that they must adapt their culture to attract and retain the best of both generations, but do not know how to initiate this change. Developing an effective multigenerational corporation requires understanding and respecting the different values and motivation of the workforce.

The Generation Xer: Educated, Driven, and Self-Aware

Because they grew up in a different social and economic environment than the older generation did, Generation Xers have developed a different value set and workstyle. Thomas Malone, professor at MIT's Sloan School of Management, has found that this group grew up with more affluence and more education than earlier generations; they are searching for responsibility and excitement based on challenge. A 1997 study by OfficeTeam, a staffing service organization based in Menlo Park, California, suggested that Generation Xers were not seeking the corporate paternalism of their parents' era, but looked for a working environment that recognized quality-of-life needs and encouraged and rewarded creativity.

A Generation Xer in one of the study's focus groups, typifying the ideals of the twenty-something workforce, asked, "Why should I have to learn a specific [corporate] language to get to the executive level? If organizational change doesn't happen, I sure as hell won't work for corporate America." The tentative conclusion is that the corporate culture and values previously revered will not satisfy the needs of the younger generation.

Searching for a potentially more rewarding and challenging career than can be offered by large companies, many Generation Xers have expressed their entrepreneurial spirit by starting their own businesses. Having witnessed their parents endure layoffs, mergers, buyouts, and general uncertainty, Generation Xers are driven to develop the self rather than to proclaim loyalty to the corporation. Emphasizing the shift, a participant in San Francisco said, "Now people will only do things for themselves or for other people they value, not for the organization." In the Czech Republic, the younger participants echoed this point, expressing their desire for more individual expression, accountability, reward, and opportunity.

Younger generations always strive to develop their own identities and to make their mark. American Generation Xers seem to be more ready than their parents were to move from firm to firm to develop their specific skills, and in Silicon Valley or Wall Street, for example, many will take new jobs literally across the street to achieve greater responsibility, recognition, and reward. Whether they are forming their own businesses, working for start-ups, or contributing to Fortune 500 companies, these people seem to be searching for experiences that stimulate their interest and recognize their contributions. They put a high value on training, challenging roles, and constant feedback.

The Baby Boomer: Experienced, Loyal, and Directed

The values of loyalty, patience, stability, and judgment are strongly held by the baby boom generation. It formed these ideals while being promoted in older corporate cultures. Fitting the organization's image was highly regarded and rewarded in most organizations. Being a company player was an ideal for many in this generation. Some boomers in the focus groups stated that they placed more emphasis on the success of the corporation than on their own personal development. Self-awareness and personal mastery have not always been highly valued by this generation, but it is now indicating a need and desire to develop these competencies.

Baby boomers have thrived in a business environment that provides direction and fosters broad skill building. Whereas Generation Xers tend to move from employer to employer to develop a specific set of skills, many boomers have been at one firm long enough to develop a wide range of skills and organizational knowledge. It is not uncommon for a boomer to have shifted from research and development to sales, then to finance, before eventually moving into a leadership position. Experience in different areas within the organization provides insight and skills beneficial in analyzing results and strategic planning. Boomers have learned how to monitor the company's progress to predict outcomes and manage the workforce.

In addition to developing deep business knowledge, boomers' years of experience have taught them to place a high value on building relationships on which they rely for guidance and ideas. These relationships are generally formed with other boomers and are founded on honesty and trust. However, as some organizations have discovered through often-ineffective mentoring programs, boomers rarely develop strong relationships with younger generations.

Misperception of Values Leads to Conflict

Generation Xers have succeeded in casting off the label of slackers. However, they are now viewed by boomers as a workforce of educated, driven self-starters who also exhibit impatient, disloyal, and self-centered behavior. Rather than being lauded for their strong understanding of personal and career needs, Generation Xers are criticized for moving from employer to employer as they develop their skills and résumés. But they are not inherently disloyal and impatient: they are searching for an environment that provides development and recognition, while promoting a balance of personal and career needs.

The difficulty in leading a multigenerational workforce is not purely an older generation's misunderstanding of a younger one's values. The skills and ideals of the baby boom generation are not being recognized by younger employees. Boomers have a wealth of knowledge gained through both work and life experience. Unlike some of their younger counterparts, boomers have lived through recessions and have worked in a struggling economy. Many have stayed with one firm long enough to witness the consequences of their business decisions. While the baby boom generation values the skills and relationships gained through experience, Generation Xers tend to undervalue them. They often misperceive boomers as being stifling, unenergetic, and resistant to creativity.

The expanding markets in Central and Eastern Europe provide an extreme example of the differing values and attitudes of the younger and older generations. Following the collapse of Communism, a large number of younger leaders come to the fore—leaders who, educated under a totalitarian regime, are now developing their own individualism, particularly in the areas of accountability, responsibility, and reward. Participants in the Prague focus group indicated that Czech employers hesitate to hire anyone over thirty.

One message came through clearly across all geographic regions: it will be important for both older and younger generations to understand one another's distinct values and harness these differences for success. The challenge facing the organization of the future will be to capitalize on the entrepreneurial spirit of its younger leaders and the insight of its experienced executives.

Generation Xers as Leaders

Although multigenerational conflict affects many organizations, the high-tech, electronics, and software industries have felt the impact most strongly. This tension results from having a large number of skilled Generation Xers in leadership roles, coupled with the lack of understanding and trust between the generations. Due to the need for rapid product innovation and development in high-tech industries, many leaders are appointed for their technical knowledge and creativity, rather than their experience and business acumen. Often the employees with the greatest technical expertise, the knowledge workers, are the skilled Generation Xers rapidly moving up the organization.

Bruce Tulgan, founder of RainmakerThinking Inc. (a New Haven, Connecticut–based research and consulting firm that explores the role of Generation Xers in the corporation), stated, "more and more twentysomethings are being put into management and leadership roles. As a result of these young leaders, many of the old-fashioned work rules are being pushed aside" (Lewis, 1998). This shift may result in increased support for innovation and creativity, but it often leads to organizational problems. Leadership is difficult regardless of age and experience, and Generation Xers face an uphill battle.

While highly competent technically, they often lack the presence and strategic decision-making skills needed to be effective in the executive suite. Many of these young leaders have not accumulated the experience, knowledge, and professional relationships that contribute to making sound decisions. Bob Hunter, an Accenture managing partner, stated, "Today, because of the extra weight of technology, [young workers] jump into the role [of leader] without the full set of competencies" (Joyce, 1998). It is important that Generation Xers have a chance to develop that full set before they try to lead others.

Some Generation Xers do posses the competencies and vision to be effective in leading a multigenerational workforce, but their age and lack of experience leads others to assume they are also unskilled and ineffective. Many boomers feel threatened by the rise of the younger technical specialists, believing that their experience and business knowledge have been devalued. In their resentment, these boomers may fail to support the young executives. Such a mutual lack of support and understanding can lead to distrust and increased tensions between the boomer workforce and the Generation X executives.

Guidelines for Leading a Multigenerational Corporation

Although the strengths and potential limitations of each generation can be identified easily enough, the challenge is in successfully integrating the positive characteristics of each group. Clearly there is no single model for success. As a young participant in Prague said, "There should not be any models. Organizations need to focus on people's individuality and strength, which cater to new ideas and innovative thinking." Successfully leading a multigenerational corporation will come from the understanding of difference, tolerance of ideas, and the sharing of knowledge.

Although conflict between the values of the baby boomer generation and those of Generation X may seem natural, it is the synergy of these two work groups that will provide the most successful leadership in the future. To develop this synergy, corporations need to develop an understanding and open culture that supports individuality and provides guidance to employees. The resulting strong corporate culture will develop from the bottom up, not from the top down.

The support of a group of diverse people is best achieved by providing them with representation in the decision-making process. A multigenerational leadership team provides a voice for the concerns of both the boomers and Generation Xers, who can then be more effective in developing a vision for the company that is shared by all. By bringing together both cohorts in the leadership roles, companies can expand the competency set of the executive suite. Differing values and experiences can often lead to conflict, of course, but the "constructive abrasion" of the diverse styles also is likely to lead to new forms of value creation.

Leaders are becoming younger. While most twenty-something professionals have the technical skills and creativity to drive the organization into the future, many do not have the business skills and experience necessary to provide direction and guidance to others. Mentors not only transfer basic business skills and knowledge but guide young employees in developing their individual leadership characteristics. Leadership is not a competency that can be effectively taught in the classroom; it is best developed through experience and observation.

It is obvious how mentoring benefits Generation Xers, but baby boomers also gain from this experience. Younger employees can transfer technical knowledge and act as a sounding board for new ideas. The greatest benefit of interaction between the two groups is the development of cross-generational relationships built on trust and respect.

Companies gain when they develop an environment in which employees feel that their contributions are rewarded and their concerns are noticed. This can be accomplished by promoting the formation of smaller communities within the organization. Communities can be formed around project teams, common interests, and skills. Smaller groups can provide their members with performance feedback and direction much more accurately than the larger corporation is able to do. The smaller groups' setting makes it easier for employees to maintain their individuality. Rewarding communities for their results allows the employees' entrepreneurial spirits to thrive. Employees are more readily going to take ownership in a work group where they can see the results of their actions. A community structure helps employees develop personal pride in their work and loyalty to the organization.

Global Leadership: The Next Generation

In partnership with the Accenture Institute for Strategic Change, Keilty, Goldsmith and Company (KGC) investigated the attitudes and opinions of the next generation of U.S. leaders. A student at the University of Pennsylvania, Lauren Wagner, was commissioned by KGC to interview a hundred student leaders on the top undergraduate business programs across the United States (as determined by *US News & World Report,* September 18, 1997).

This research was designed to obtain the views of the under-twenty generation on the characteristics they think will be important for the leader of a more global organization in the next millennium. These young leaders provided their opinions on the changing business environment and how successful leaders in the future will adapt. By tapping into the beliefs and values of the next wave of young professionals, present leaders will, presumably, be better prepared to meet the leadership challenges of the next few decades.

Although the beliefs and values of this group of students are similar to the young executive profile, their responses lacked the cynicism and determined individualism expressed by the Generation Xers currently facing the challenges of the corporate world. The under-twenty group perceives organizational change as inevitable, and is less concerned or possibly less aware of the conflict that will accompany such change. In contrast, the corporate image portrayed by the working Generation Xers was one of change, but also one of conflict and uncertainty. The findings from the undergraduate interviews underline the need for organizations to develop and promote a common set of corporate values.

Analysis of the responses revealed certain key themes that send a strong message about the future of the business environment and its leaders. The undergraduates identified behavior that successful leaders must develop in the expanding global workplace:

- Communicate a global vision.
- Be technologically savvy.
- Embrace an open-minded leadership style.
- Champion diversity (style, culture, and leadership).
- Display flexibility and respect toward employees.
- Foster a corporate culture of teamwork.

Global Vision and Communication

The next generation recognizes that the increasing convergence of business across industries, regions, and competencies will continue to push organizations' vision and scope beyond national borders. They understand and expect a global leader of the future to pursue opportunities throughout the world; virtually all reaches of the globe are fair prospects to compete in the fierce business environment of the future. The students understood that it was not enough to have a global vision. A leader must also have the ability to communicate the company's position in the global marketplace, and to communicate the vision to all levels of the organization to gain the support of all employees.

Technology

The power of technology to transform the work environment they will join is not lost on the interviewees. Advances in information technology and the introduction of the virtual marketplace are radically altering the way business is done. It is up to the leader of the future to be technologically savvy and use the technological resources necessary to make the company more efficient and competitive. To pass on the global vision that is so important, leaders must use technology to improve the quality and expedite the flow of communication.

Open-Mindedness

Due to the rapid pace of organizational change, the number one characteristic identified by students for "the global leader of the future" is open-mindedness. Participants believe that a leader who embraces the status quo will be easily defeated by a competitor who is willing to try new ideas, seek out new opportunities, and change as needed—both within the corporation and the industry. Innovation is key to the continued success of an organization, and using this key depends on having a leader with an open mind.

Diversity

Open-mindedness is not only beneficial in embracing innovative ideas or new technology, it is also essential when recruiting, managing, and leading a global, multigenerational workforce. It is the responsibility of a leader to be open to all kinds of people and recognize the opportunities and different perspectives that diversity brings to an organization without regard to gender, race, or religion. This person should be intolerant of sexual and racial discrimination and harassment and should also promote people fairly. Participants noted that cultural diversity training and international experience will be an integral part of the leadership development process. Students believed that all leaders should have some sort of international experience, whether that means traveling abroad or working overseas.

Flexibility and Respect

Recruiting and retaining good people will in part depend on leaders' respecting employees and being sensitive to their needs. Participants considered that leaders now more than ever need to respect the people that work with them. Talent is becoming a scarce resource, and in competitive labor markets, firms need to find ways to keep the talent they already have.

Today's student leaders predict a need for extraordinarily flexible leaders to transform today's organizations. The key to this new work environment is freedom and trust. Employers will expect more from their workers, but in return will be more responsible to their employees. Interestingly, student leaders expect a form of flexi-time to be offered, where the hours will be set depending on when individuals work their best, and to be able to work in any environment they feel comfortable, including telecommuting. This flexible culture is perceived to be possible in an organization where the leader respects different work styles and values. Relaxed dress codes, day-care services, and a family-friendly environment are just a few of the many changes that this generation expects to see in the organization of the future. This generation of workers will value mutual respect between employer and employee and greater individual freedom within a productive, flexible work environment led by personable, respectful, and tolerant leaders—real or virtual.

Corporate Culture of Teamwork

Along with the flexible work environment, future workers look forward to a changing corporate culture that values teamwork highly, in an environment that is more relaxed and places less emphasis on formal titles. The leader of the organization can create an atmosphere that encourages teamwork, where employees benefit from the success of the group and not from personal maneuvers at each other's expense. However, teamwork will prove to be more difficult to achieve as flexi-time and a virtual organization become the norm. Although members of this generation value a more relaxed, collective, and collaborative culture, they are aware of some of the inherent challenges that it will pose for leaders.

Charisma

Charisma is one characteristic that, the younger generation believes, will always be vital to successful leadership. Executives may have all the necessary technical and industry knowledge, but they will not be effective if they cannot motivate and empower those who are subordinate to them. A leader must be charismatic so that others will follow without feeling that they are being "bossed around." Charisma is a key component of gaining the respect of employees and leading the workforce through influence, rather than through formal authority. As the command-and-control model of power loses the respect and loyalty of the younger workforce, the need for charismatic leaders is increasing.

Ethics

Young leaders place great value on ethics. Ethical behavior was identified as a key characteristic of the leader of the future and was thought to be sorely lacking in current leaders. Some felt that ethics would become the most important characteristic of future leaders. Executives must lead through example and establish the ethical standards for the company. An optimistic group, 50 percent of those interviewed, thought that ethical standards of companies would rise in the future, 22 percent thought they would fall, and 28 percent thought they would stay the same or were undecided.

Summary

With the aid of Warren's personal leadership and dedication to elevating future insights on the topic of leadership, we have been successful in developing this perspective. We hope you agree that the next generation of leaders faces unprecedented global change. However, we hope you also agree that armed with this knowledge they can face those challenges with practical and effective models based on broad leadership experience coupled with a global picture of future leadership needs.

Chapter Thirteen

When Leadership Is an Organizational Trait

James O'Toole

Increasingly, the identities of corporations are mere reflections of the personalities of their leaders. Today, a business magazine won't run a cover story about Ford Motor Company; instead, it will feature the company's CEO, Jacques Nasser, in a full-color spread. Even in the high-tech world—where one would expect the full focus of attention to be on the latest cyber gizmo—the public eye is riveted more on the persona of CEO Scott McNealy than on his company's red-hot Java product—and hardly any heed is paid to Sun Microsystems as a corporation. Indeed, recent research shows that the perceived image of a high-profile chief executive brings a premium to a company's stock. Investors thus join journalists in the personification of corporations, focusing on the characters, biographies, and alleged charisma of CEOs. As a result, American business organizations are more often than not portrayed as shadows of the "Great Men" who sit in the chief executive's chair. In the

Note: This chapter is a summary of the findings of a study undertaken by Booz•Allen & Hamilton and the University of Southern California's Center for Effective Organizations for the World Economic Forum. It is based on surveys and interviews conducted for that study. The author gratefully acknowledges the contributions of his Booz•Allen colleagues, Paul Anderson, Bruce Pasternack, Karen Van Nuys, and Tom Williams, and his colleagues at the center, Cristina Gibson and Alice Yee Mark. A related version of this chapter appears in the January 2001 issue of *Strategy+Business.*

most extreme case, for all intents and purposes Warren Buffet *is* the Berkshire Hathaway corporation.

And academic theory follows practice. Over the last decade, the parsing of leadership styles has become de rigeur in American business schools, the subject of practical (and arcane) professorial research, as well as stacks of graduate dissertations. In continuing education seminars, in MBA classes, even at the undergraduate level, professors now teach students each to adopt the "right leadership style" for themselves—using "360 degree feedback" to make them aware of how they are perceived by others and, especially, to learn how to manage those perceptions. And for those who are severely leadership-impaired, there is always that growth industry called executive coaching.

This focus on personality is peculiarly American, perhaps an outward manifestation of our collective unconscious—on which the image of George Washington astride his powerful white steed is indelibly depicted. In recent times, Europeans have tried to resist such personification of leadership. Indeed, thanks to the likes of Hitler, Lenin, Stalin, Franco, and Mussolini, Europeans were more than happy to concede the whole sorry field of leadership studies to Americans after 1945. If you don't count the scads of books written in French about Charles De Gaulle, Americans owned the subject of leadership for most of the second half of the last century. And, during that time, we applied our theories not only to political leaders but, unique in the world, to leaders of business corporations.

And, of course, we got it wrong. "We" meaning those of us in American business, academia, consulting, and journalism who habitually discussed, studied, and wrote about leadership solely as an *individual* trait. While this obsession on a single personality is occasionally appropriate—particularly when the founding entrepreneur is still running a company—evidence offered here indicates that this perspective often skews analysis away from organizational factors, which are the more important drivers of performance. My colleagues and I came to this conclusion quite by accident. In early 1999, we began a research project on Strategic Leadership in conjunction with the World Economic Forum. For the last decade, leadership sessions had been a good draw at the Forum's annual Davos conclave, but Forum members had started to grow tired of the usual bill of fare: a thin gruel of CEO war stories, anecdotes, and homilies. So we were charged with putting a little beef on the Davos leadership menu. We formed a research team and set out to create something that didn't exist: a data base of hard information about the soft subject of leadership.

Working with Forum member corporations, we began our efforts with traditional premises about leaders—but soon were surprised to discover that the relative performance of large corporations cannot be explained adequately by measures of the individuals who head them. Note that operative word, *adequately*. As predicted, we discovered that most of the large global companies we studied operate, to one degree or another, under a traditional model of strong individual leadership at the top. Moreover, the quality of that leadership bears on the overall performance of those companies. But we also noticed that a few of the companies we studied—and some business units within others—are characterized by a different pattern of leadership. Instead of leadership being a solo act, an aria sung by the CEO, in these organizations it is a shared responsibility, more like a chorus of diverse voices singing in unison.

Significantly, this characteristic is more than the frequently observed phenomenon of "cascading" leadership (in which a strong leader at the top empowers other leaders down the line). Although cascading is often a part of what we observed, more to the point *in these organizations many of the key tasks and responsibilities of leadership are institutionalized in the systems, practices, and cultures of the organization.* Typically, cascading leadership depends on the continuing support of whoever is the leader of an organization at any given time; what we observed is behavior that is not personality-dependent. Eventually, we realized we were observing a form of leadership that is rooted in systems, processes, and culture. Without the presence of a high-profile leader (or "superior" goading or exhorting them on) we observed that people at all levels in these organizations . . .

- Act more like owners and entrepreneurs than employees or hired hands (that is, they assume ownerlike responsibility for financial performance and managing risk).
- Take the initiative to solve problems and to act, in general, with a sense of urgency.

- Willingly accept accountability for meeting commitments, and for living the values of the organization.
- Share a common philosophy and language of leadership that paradoxically includes tolerance for contrary views and a willingness to experiment.
- Create, maintain, and adhere to systems and procedures designed to measure and reward these distributed leadership behaviors.

Obviously, we did not invent this model of leadership, nor do we believe that it is necessarily new. Doubtless, it has been around a long time and we, like others, missed it because we were blinded by the powerful light that emanates from high-profile leaders. We were also prisoners of the current wisdom about the necessity for personalized, take-charge leadership—particularly in times of rapid change. Moreover, it is important to stress that the organization-based model we identified was not the only one we observed in our study, nor was it necessarily always the most effective. In fact, the two most successful companies in our sample operate on two different models, Oracle being headed by a single strong leader, and Enron with widely diffused and systematized leadership responsibilities. Thus we are not advocating a newly discovered "best way to lead"; instead, we are calling attention to a previously unnoticed—but equally viable—alternative to the traditional leadership model. Among other things, this discovery helps to explain some persistent contradictions to the dominant model of leadership. *If leadership were solely an individual trait . . .*

- Why is it that some companies continually demonstrate the capacity to innovate, renew strategies and products, and outperform competition in their industries *over the tenures of several different chief executives?* Intel, for instance, has been a rip-roaring success under the leadership of, in sequence, Gordon Moore, Andrew Grove, and now, Craig Barrett.
- Why is it that some CEOs who have succeeded in one organization often turn in so-so performances in the next? Consider George Fisher, who was a star at Motorola, but far less effective at Kodak. (Conversely, why is it that some companies headed by singularly unimpressive CEOs nonetheless rack up good performance records?)

- Why is that academics are unable to quantify the relationship between CEO style on one hand and organizational performance on the other? (In fact, they have found no objective correlation between those two factors—concluding, unhelpfully, that "it all depends.")

Moreover, as history shows, businesses that become dependent on a single leader run a considerable risk. If that individual retires or leaves (or dies in office), the organization may well lose its continuing capacity to succeed—witness the performance of General Motors after Alfred Sloan, ITT after Harold Geneen, Polaroid after Edwin Land, and Coca-Cola after Roberto Goizueta. More frequently, organizations learn the hard way that no one individual can save a company from mediocre performance—and no one individual, no matter how gifted a leader, can be "right" all the time. As one CEO said, "None of us is as smart as all of us." Since leadership is, by definition, doing things through the efforts of others, it is obvious that there is little that a business leader—acting alone—can do to affect company performance (other than try to "look good" to investors).

In light of these observations, it should not have been so surprising that our research revealed that, in many successful companies, *leadership is treated as an institutional capacity and not solely as an individual trait.* It turns out that many corporations whose familiar names perennially appear on "most respected" lists are ones with the highest institutionalized leadership capacities. Like individual IQs, companies have collective LQs—leadership quotients—that can be measured and compared. (Moreover, unlike individual IQ an organization's leadership capacity can be bolstered through appropriately directed effort.) Hence, we now are better able to explain why companies like Intel, ABB, GE, Enron, BP, Ford, Nestlé, and Motorola continue to renew themselves year after year, and over the tenures of many different leaders: Such companies are not only chock-full of leaders from the executive suite to the shop floor, they make conscious efforts to build their LQs, that is, their overall organizational leadership capacities.

That last point requires an important clarification. To our surprise, we discovered that some companies with continuing records of success do not pay much, or any, attention to traditional—that is, *individual*—leadership development. Instead of asking "What qualities do we need to develop in our leader?" these companies continually ask "What qualities do we need to develop in our organization?" And, though this may seem to defy the current wisdom about the importance of leadership, on reflection it squares with experience. At Motorola, for example, there has been a decades-long pattern of self-renewal that has continually belied the predictions of Wall Street analysts who, on at least four occasions, have written the company off for dead. When it has suffered one of its periodic setbacks, how could Motorola reasonably be expected to turn itself around without a take-charge leader like Jack Welch at its helm? But it has done so repeatedly, and under the collective leadership of several different individuals. In light of what we have learned from our study, we posit that the secret sauce at Motorola is the company's strong, institutionalized leadership capacity—systems consciously created by former-CEO Bob Galvin's leadership teams over a period of thirty years.

And the effectiveness of the organizational leadership model should not come as a surprise to those who have tried to change the behavior of a CEO—or of any executive whose career has been validated by rising to the top. Powerful executives tend to see leadership as positional. To them, by definition, the CEO is *the leader* of the corporation. For example, a couple of years ago we suggested to the CEO of a Fortune 500 company that he (and his executive team) might benefit from a leadership development program. He looked at us as if we were space aliens and testily replied, "If the board thought there was someone who was more qualified to lead this company, they would have named him and not me." Given that such ego-driven denial is fairly common in executive suites, it makes practical sense that the high-LQ companies in our study focus on identifying business-related activities as the source of leadership development—that is, they stress improving the ability of their leaders collectively to do their central tasks, rather than on trying to fix them as individuals.

The lesson we take from this is *not* that individual leadership behaviors are unimportant, but that in some cases, at least, it may be more effective to treat them as secondary to organizational issues. Moreover, it is far easier for leaders to learn to do things differently in terms of business processes than it is for them to change who they are. (Nearly a century of experience with psychoanalysis proves that it is almost impossible to change basic individual traits, and that the rare successes come only after considerable time and effort.) And, hopefully, certain leadership behaviors—as opposed to the ingrained factors we call personality—can be changed more effectively in the context of organizational and business imperatives. In our experience, individual leaders often see more clearly, and less threateningly, how they have to change personally as leaders— and why they must do so—when the reason is business-related, as opposed to fixing them personally.

Using Leadership Data as an Objective Focus for Change

In effect, our research uncovered an alternative model not only of leadership but of organizational change as well. By surveying the behavior of over three thousand leaders at all hierarchical levels— and buttressing these observations with hundreds of interviews— we are in the process of creating an objective data bank about alternative ways leaders bring about strategic and organizational change. This body of data has allowed our research team to pin-point specific business systems and processes that leaders use as levers to bring about significant shifts in organizational behavior and, ultimately, improvements in business performance. For example, at one large global high-tech company we surveyed leaders at five different levels to collect data on sixty items related to the effectiveness of twelve categories of systems that leaders use to affect behavior (see Exhibit 13.1).

Exhibit 13.1. Measuring Twelve Organizational Systems

Our growing leadership data bank now includes information gathered from surveys completed by over three thousand managers at all hier-archical levels in ten large organizations based in Asia, Europe, and North America. We also interviewed twenty to forty individuals in each of these companies to gain a qualitative perspective on each organization's per-ceived strengths and challenges and, in particular, how their leaders used systems and processes to affect behavior.

Our survey instrument asks respondents to score their organizations on sixty-five measures of behavior, for each measure giving two scores, the first for "managers directly above me," and the second for "people at my level." Instead of measuring attitudes, the survey asks respondents to use a seven-point scale to score the degree to which individual leaders did specific things (for example, "hold people accountable for their performance").

Responses are grouped into scales designed to produce quantitative scores for each company in terms of the effectiveness of the twelve organizational systems, or leadership capabilities, in the following list, as well as four composite measures (behavioral coherence, organizational coherence, behavioral agility, and organizational agility). This information is then analyzed and fed back to leaders of each company, allowing them to see how they score in comparison with other companies, how their various business units differ, and how leadership performance measures up at various levels within the organization. They can then use this information as the basis for corrective action.

At each company we studied, we measured the extent to which each of the following twelve organizational systems enabled leadership:

- *Vision and Strategy:* Extent to which corporate strategy is reflected in goals and behaviors at all levels
- *Goal-Setting and Planning:* Extent to which challenging goals are used to drive performance
- *Capital Allocation:* Extent to which capital allocation decisions are objective and systematic
- *Group Measurement:* Extent to which actual performance is measured against established goals
- *Risk Management:* Extent to which the company measures and mitigates risk
- *Recruiting:* Extent to which the company taps the best talent available
- *Professional Development:* Extent to which employees are challenged and developed
- *Performance Appraisal:* Extent to which individual appraisals are used to improve performance
- *Compensation:* Extent to which financial incentives are used to drive desired behaviors
- *Organizational Structure:* Extent to which decision-making authority is delegated to lower levels
- *Communications:* Extent to which management communicates the big picture
- *Knowledge Transfer:* Extent to which necessary information is gathered, organized, and disseminated

In parallel interviews, we discovered that there were competing theories about the reasons why this company was not as profitable as its competitors. When we then analyzed the survey data and fed the results data back to the top management team, they were able to compare the relative effectiveness of their systems to those of other companies in our study. They discovered that they did well on about eight of the key systems we measured, average on two, but that their scores for performance appraisal and decision making were near the low end of the scale. The data was unequivocal: top management wasn't holding operating heads to their commitments, and decision making was based more on relationships than on objective facts. The team members, who had been in denial about some of this—and divided about what was causing the rest—were then able to come to grips with their organizational leadership problems, and to create an agenda for repairing the broken systems. They were also able to identify a "concrete layer" in their hierarchy where transmission of messages from the top was getting stuck on the way down the line.

The executives then began a change process by feeding the data back to the next two levels of the organization, building consensus about the roles and responsibilities of each level, clearly identifying what needed to be done and by whom. In the process, they asked us to prepare cases of how other companies dealt with similar problems, and they discussed these in a series of four workshops over a two-month period, building a common language about, and approach to, leadership. In sum, they were able to consciously build their organizational LQ by addressing the systems that had the greatest impact on performance. The bottom line is that, by using those systemic levers, the executives became more effective change agents and leaders than had been the case in the past when they had worked with organizational development experts to alter their individual leadership styles. They came away from the data-based exercise with the belief that, although one has to be born with charisma, almost all of them could learn how to better manipulate a small set of enabling management systems. Moreover, they now had an objective way to measure the extent and degree to which the changes they had initiated had been adopted by leaders down and throughout the company.

Building Organizational Coherence and Agility

In the highest-LQ organizations we studied, leaders at all levels use such ordinary systems as goal setting, communications, capital allocations, and recruiting in a conscious way to create two prime attributes of long-term organizational success: coherence and agility. *Coherence* means that common behaviors are found throughout an organization that are directed toward the achievement of shared goals. And *agility* is the institutionalized ability to detect and cope successfully with changes in the external environment, especially when such changes are difficult to anticipate. Until recently, scholars had posited that companies with high levels of coherence were "built to last," and that the task of leadership was to get the right fit, or alignment, among key institutional characteristics. But we discovered that not all institutional coherence is good. For instance, bureaucratic alignment anchored in the habits of the past is deadly, as we documented in a couple of the companies we surveyed. Similarly, although agility has often been identified with corporate success, we found that too much of that good thing leads to chaos and wasting resources on duplicate efforts.

What we found is that organizations need to be coherent and agile at the same time. In fact we discovered that not only were the operating systems of high-LQ companies directed to those two ends, *the leaders viewed their prime task as creating those attributes*. (These quantitative findings from our survey are consistent with recently espoused qualitative theories about the centrality of organizational "alignment and adaptability" offered by such scholars as Harvard's Ronald Heifetz, Stanford's Charles O'Reilly, and Columbia's Michael Tushman.) Significantly, one of the highest-performing companies in our study, Enron, actually aligns around agility: that is, its leaders rigorously measure and reward the seemingly loose entrepreneurial behaviors of market-responsiveness and risk taking. In essence, Enron creates organizational coherence around shared business objectives while simultaneously encouraging the agility to meet discontinuous threats and opportunities. More specifics about Enron in later sections, but first we should address some points of natural skepticism likely to arise concerning our approach and findings.

A Distinction with Consequences

Does it make any real difference whether leadership is treated as an institutional capacity or as an individual trait? Because fundamental premises drive behavior, when leadership is thought of as an organizational trait there are profound consequences for almost everything that follows. For example, because ABB views leadership organizationally, its highly respected former CEO, Percy Barnevik, could retire at age fifty-four in full confidence that the company had the capacity to carry on successfully without him (thus freeing Barnevik to take on even greater responsibilities for the Swedish Wallenberg family, ABB's largest shareholders, and allowing the company to make several needed changes in structure that had been closely identified with Barnevik's tenure). Because Intel sees leadership as an organizational trait, the company did not miss a beat when Andy Grove retired as CEO—in fact, it was well positioned to move on to a higher level, with the capacity to take on new strategic challenges. How often is it that a company not only doesn't go into the tank when a CEO as respected as Grove steps down, it actually renews itself with a fresh line of products and promising new areas of business? And the reason for the successful hand-offs at ABB and Intel is not simply good succession planning. The key factor is that neither company is dependent on any one, two, or half-dozen key individuals for its ongoing success. As observers note, neither company talks much about individual leadership at all. Instead, they focus on building the human capacity to manage the systems that, in fact, are at the heart of their respective successes. And that is what we found at our high-LQ companies.

The Role of Enabling Systems

In essence, we found that there is something palpably different about a company that emphasizes building enabling systems versus one that depends on a single personality at the top. Since the contributions of every leader are seen as important, there is concerted effort to define and measure leadership behavior down the line—and parallel emphasis on accountability at all levels for how the enabling systems are used—and to make certain that they *are* used. But what do we mean by enabling systems? Here are four examples of such systems (from the list in Exhibit 13.1), and how the high-LQ companies we studied use them in order to institutionalize leadership:

Goal Setting and Planning. Some of the companies we studied religiously institutionalize the process of setting challenging goals to drive performance. Although it often has been remarked that great individual leaders constantly challenge and stretch their followers, we discovered that institutions can also do this through the use of disciplined organizational processes. In several of the companies we studied, there were formal mechanisms that ensured that leaders at all levels and at all times have a clear sense of how the organization is doing relative to its goals. Moreover, individual leaders are rewarded (and, yes, punished) based on rigorous measurement of performance against goals. While most organizations pay lip service to setting stretch goals—and to measuring the things that are most important to success of their business—we found that a few rare companies actually do it, and stick with it, no ifs, ands, or buts. This was an especially welcome finding because, in the personality-based organizations we studied, the punishment of poor performers either didn't happen or, when it did, was seen as a sign of "the boss" playing favorites. But in the most structured and disciplined of the processes we observed, there is a high degree of involvement in goal setting, and highly participative processes of establishing performance metrics—thus ensuring a climate of organizational fairness previously associated only with the actions of an unusually trustworthy leader.

Risk Management. Perhaps the most surprising finding in our study was the importance of risk management systems in creating a sense of leadership down the line. In some companies, we found formal processes designed to make certain that everyone understands the size and likelihood of the key risks facing the business. In light of this knowledge, leaders at all levels become willing and able to take prudent risks, and they are enculturated to (and rewarded for) avoiding negative financial surprises. Because processes (not personalities) are paramount, capital allocation is seen as an objective process of pursuing business objectives (rather than personal agendas). Thus people are confident not only that objectively defensible projects will be funded but that the system behaves fairly when making all capital allocation decisions.

Communications. There is a striking consensus among scholars and practitioners about the centrality of communication to the role of the leader. Significantly, we found some companies where this important task was viewed to be the responsibility of *every* leader at every level—and that they were evaluated on how well they performed this task. In companies where leadership is institutionalized, we found that leaders at all levels spend a significant amount of time communicating the big picture—the vision, strategy, mission, and purpose of the organization. At the operating level, leaders provide ready access to information that others need to do their work. In particular, we found that those who have the most relevant information have the greatest impact on decisions.

Recruiting. All companies recruit. But in high-LQ companies, recruiting is a prime task not of the HR department but of operating managers at all levels (including the CEO). These companies make a conscious effort to define selection criteria for new recruits that are closely related to overall corporate goals. Some, like sports teams, even recruit "the best talent available regardless of position," instead of looking to fill specific niches. Moreover, they consciously include leadership criteria in their recruitment profiles. For example, they look for people who are interested in developing subordinates, and who see leaders as teachers rather than bosses.

Different in Countless Ways

While this discussion may sound familiar, what is striking is that none of the companies we studied stresses all twelve of the systems we identified. Instead, they each focus on managing a few systems tightly, while leaving the others loose. For example, one high-performing corporation keeps tight control of vision and communications, but leaves it to the business units to make decisions relative to structure, recruitment, planning, and the rest. Significantly, we found no pattern in the choice of systems that are stressed, and no correlation between performance and the systems emphasized. What seems important is that there be a clear focus on any two or three key systems—the particular choices being driven by the strategy, industry, or challenge faced by the company. As noted earlier, the two highest-performing companies in our sample are exact opposites of each other (Oracle has a traditional leadership model, and Enron is a high-LQ company), and they each emphasize quite different systems. Yet these two dissimilar organizations are mirror images of each other in making clear and conscious choices to stress certain systems—and then disciplining themselves to follow through with the application of those systems.

When all of the sixty-plus variables in our study are analyzed—the regressions run, the variations standardized, and the chis squared—what the highest-performing companies seem to have in common is that they *consciously choose* what systems to emphasize. Leadership is thus a rational and analytical process, and not a natural trait with which some fortunate few are born. Related, when the highest-performing companies we studied create a system, announce a major managerial policy, or introduce a change in process, *they stick to it in a disciplined way and hold leaders at all levels accountable for behaving consistently with the chosen course*. In contrast, the lower-performing companies we studied are often characterized by arbitrary policies, inconsistent enforcement of systems, and the lack of follow-through in both implementation of policy and change initiatives. We found this distinction to be as true for companies like Oracle that operate with a traditional model as it is for those like Enron where leadership is institutionalized.

The Moral Equivalent of Individual Leadership

With specific reference to the high-LQ companies we studied, we think they may have developed the moral equivalent of great individual leadership. While having a Larry Ellison, Jack Welch, or Percy Barnevik at the helm is obviously desirable, and companies who have such talented leaders are indeed fortunate, such good fortune is rare. But companies with a high LQ get many of the benefits of such leadership, even if the individual in the executive suite is not a star performer. And when the individual in charge is sadly less-than-stellar, strong systems can help to make up for the morale-sapping effects of arbitrary, erratic, indecisive, weak, or egotistic leadership. It is here that students of organizational theory will recognize shades of what Max Weber was struggling with over a hundred years ago when he advocated bureaucracy over the only alternative available at the time: personality-driven leadership. While Weber may have solved the problem of capricious and politicized management, his solution—bureaucracy—merely substituted the problems of immobility and rigidity that came to characterize not only his beloved Prussian civil service but, in time, the likes of General Motors, IBM, and AT&T. But now, after a century of struggling between the Charybdis of arbitrary leadership and the Scylla of bureaucracy, high-LQ companies may have resolved the Weberian dilemma. These companies are not only both coherent and agile, they are also not burdened with the vicissitudes of arbitrary leadership.

Case in Point: Enron

Enron is a particularly instructive case of how a high institutional leadership capacity can contribute to business performance. As recently as a decade ago the company was an unlikely candidate to be chosen as *Fortune* magazine's "most innovative company" in 1999 (and again in 2000). In the late 1980s, Enron was a slow-growing Texas-based gas pipeline company. Today it is one of the fastest-growing, most entrepreneurial corporations in the world, moving into countless new lines of business (such as power marketing and bandwidth trading). Enron management transformed the company by consciously creating the opportunity for many leaders at all levels of the organization to take risks, create new businesses, and share in the fruits of their success. They started the process of change through an expensive recruiting initiative. Competing against the attractive enticements offered by high-tech companies and high-paying financial institutions, Enron successfully recruited two hundred MBAs from top schools to come to back-water Houston with an unambiguous charge to shake things up.

Enron's CEO, Kenneth Lay, may not have had a detailed blue-print of what all those energetic young people would do when they got on the job, but he established an environment in which they could think creatively, speak up, try new things—and motivate the existing corps of managers—all in the belief that "exposure to new talent stimulates people to do better work." And he kept it up: Enron has pursued a vigorous recruiting effort in each subsequent year. And, to build organizational coherence, the company introduced a free internal labor market (allowing people to move around easily), and it provides training that enables them to "own their own employability." It inaugurated a policy in which there is freedom to fail without penalty if people take the right kinds of risks, and Lay gives the hundreds of new leaders Enron has recruited a free hand in running the businesses they create—and a healthy financial stake in their success. As the many leaders of Enron now say, "We are given the freedom and financial wherewithal to succeed." Not coincidentally, Enron also was chosen last year as one of *Fortune*'s "ten best corporations to work for."

Lessons for the Next Generation of Leaders

A message that emerges loud and clear from our study is that CEOs like Ken Lay don't need to know all the answers, and they don't have to do all the work of leadership by themselves. In fact, Lay defined his task as creating the systems under which others would be encouraged to do all the things that typically end up on the desk of the do-it-all leader. We believe that in many, if not most, corporations it is easier to motivate and reward leaders down the line to take up the mantle of leadership themselves than it is for a single CEO to provide detailed direction to hundreds, even thousands, of managers. To this end, it is instructive to review in passing how some of the companies in our study have used the survey data we have reported back to them. At the annual World Economic Forum meeting at Davos, Lay was joined on a panel by leaders from Oracle, Renault, and one of India's largest companies, Godrej & Boyce. They addressed common themes: The value of assessing the level of coherence and agility in their organizations; the usefulness of locating the "concrete layer" in their hierarchies where the transmission of messages to the front line get blocked; the importance of identifying and communicating the right leadership model for the organization given its particular challenges and aspirations; and the absolute requirement of pinpointing what systems should be given the highest priority in order to build the organization's leadership capacity. And all of these steps are facilitated by having objective and comparable data.

Collecting and feeding back hard data about institutionalized leadership is still a new concept, and much remains to be done to make the information gathered both reliable and useful. What gives us hope that the effort is worth the candle is a comment made by a top executive in one company we studied—an organization where not all the information fed back about leadership capacity was positive: "At least now we can discuss leadership without defensiveness. Instead of threatening egos, which is never effective, we can talk about needed changes in terms of organizational tasks. And almost everybody can buy into that process." We have found that there is nothing like a little objective data to overcome denial and to get leaders focused on the collective work that needs to be done.

Our message to young leaders is not that the personality-driven model of leadership is headed for extinction, nor do we believe that it should be. Clearly it will continue in small and start-up companies, and in places where appeals to the human heart must be made in order to bring about drastic change that requires considerable sacrifice (paradoxically, the impetus to move toward the organizational model probably requires the personal leadership of a Bob Galvin or a Ken Lay, individuals willing to forgo personal glory for the collective good of their enterprise). Nonetheless, we believe that more CEOs of large companies may be drawn to the organizational model of leadership for the simple reason that it is potentially more productive—and satisfying—to become a leader of leaders than it is to risk trying to look like George Washington on a white horse. The bad news—at least for those who like a *People Magazine* approach to business journalism—is that there may be fewer "cover boy" CEO leaders in coming decades. The good news is that there may also be much more effective corporate *leadership*. As we now have learned, leadership need not be just a solo act.

Part Four

How Leaders Stay On Top of Their Game

Chapter Fourteen

Just Say Yes!

Tom Peters

My wife, Susan, and I, on short notice, invited her mom, age seventy-four, to come down from New Canaan and join us for a Midtown dinner in late February. She said, "No." Period. I've known Joan Sargent for a long time. If she's anything, she's self-certain.

When we arrived in town from Vermont, we were therefore nonplussed to find a message from Joan saying, "I'll be arriving at seven."

We were pleased. (Yes, I have a great relationship with my mother-in-law.) And surprised. We obviously asked her why she'd changed her mind.

Short answer: *"I decided to say 'Yes.'"*

Longer answer. She recalled a friend who'd had a vigorous life into her nineties. "She said she had three 'secrets,'" Joan recalled. "First, surround yourself with good books on any and every topic. Second, spend time with people of all ages. And third, push yourself to say 'Yes.'"

She went on to say that she had not intended to drive down from Connecticut. (For those among readers who haven't had a chance to age a bit, peripheral vision goes for all of us who have pretty damn early, and night driving is a pain, especially in rain or snow. And the weather was foul.) But she remembered her friend and determinedly decided to say Yes.

Hurrah!

We had a lovely dinner. But for me the peak experience was the friend's advice. It made eminent sense, especially because I had this article to write on "How Leaders Stay on Top of Their Game."

My only problem at that point: How do I extend the article to the allotted standard academic fifteen pages. It pretty much seemed to me that Joan's friend had said about all that needed to be said. Namely:

- Surround yourself with books of all sorts.*
- Pal around with folks of all stripes and ages.
- Just say yes.

Bigger message: Work assiduously at staying fresh!

Warren Bennis has been saying *Yes* to anything and everything . . . and professionally peering around corners and through concrete walls for seven decades. He and Peter Drucker and Alvin Toffler and Charles Handy have few or no peers at perspicacious peering. (Is it coincidence that they are good pals?)

Bennis & Co. gave me marching orders for this paper. I am now judged ancient enough—swell, fellas!—to have been accorded the mantle of "staying power." "How'd you do it?" I was asked to answer in this piece. And, then, somehow, my personal observations were to be tied to the leadership milieu at large in these bizarre days . . . where staying on top of one's game is at once more important than ever and more difficult than ever.

Hence . . . to the Staying Power Annals of Tom Peters, "on the scene" since 21 July 1980, when *Business Week* featured my commentary in a piece summarizing the early research into "excellent companies." God knows what will follow. I have avoided personal ruminations like this as if they were the plague.

Thirty-One Ways Leaders Stay on Top of Their Game

I haven't a clue. Me and "staying power": I never think about "sticking around." A reporter once asked, "What do you hope to be

---

* Candid admission. Susan asserts that #1 on the list is "surround yourself with dogs." She and her Mom (and I) are over-the-top dog lovers. I refuse to "fact check" this with Joan, because I prefer my recollection. So for any of you who'd prefer dogs to books, or would feel moved to add a fourth to my list, feel free to do so. It works either way, as far as I'm concerned, though I admit such factual flexibility does doubtless fly in the face of academic canon. Not the first time.

doing at eighty?" I snapped, "I hope I won't still be writing for the *Harvard Business Review.*" I meant it! And now it's ten or so years later . . . and my pen/keyboard is not yet stilled. (Ye gads . . . maybe I will be doing this—whatever it is—twenty years from now.) I don't have a plan. Never had a plan. *Hope I never do have a plan.* Years ago I had a power boat on Lake Champlain. Named it *The Cromwell,* after Oliver. My rationale was a Cromwellian quote: "No one rises so high as he who knows not where he is going." (Or words to that effect.) I like that.

(Let's try a touch of honesty: Perhaps my "staying power" comes from the absence of true hobbies . . . not so rare among "my type." Thence, I scramble to "stay up" simply because I'm terrified and don't have an inkling as to what I'd do if I didn't! Damn!)

I have no staying power. I get bored easily. *Hence, no staying power is the real secret to my staying power.* I have lots of stamina, but no staying power. I flit from idea to idea. Or, better said, from passion to passion. Though I used the word *flit,* it's not really appropriate. I fall in love easily. And my passion knows no bounds. (For a while.)

I think boredom is my "secret." Unless I'm totally turned on by the idea I'm chasing, I'm miserable. ("Thomas *E.* Peters," my wife calls me. The "E": Excess. What else?)

Where does the low boredom threshold come from? No idea. I suppose that I wear an idea out. Become exhausted. And then scurry on. (Which is not quite candid. I flit from idea to idea. True. But there are very important constants: for example, the "Bias for Action" that was Bedrock Principle No. 1 in *In Search of Excellence.* Also bedrock: Passion rules!)

I am a finisher! Though a flitter . . . albeit a passionate flitter . . . I am not a flake. Warren Bennis and Patricia Ward Biederman, in *Organizing Genius,* call their Great Group members "dreamers with deadlines." Me, too. It . . . whatever "it" may be . . . is not real until I've written it up. Gotten it published. I have a finisher's compulsion. Always have. In the most trivial ways. Recently got hooked on computer solitaire. You'd be amazed—appalled?—at the detailed scoring records I keep.

I am fearless . . . with pen in hand. I am a wimp in face-to-face dealings. (Fear of rejection, on which, more anon.) But within the confines of my writing studio (often as not a United Airlines cigar tube) I am a slayer of dragons. The fierier the better. I don't quite get this. But, then, I don't get most of this stuff. I'm like a bomber pilot, perhaps, only able to kill at long distance?

I only see a little around corners. Much as I hate it, I'll come clean. I have been remarkably successful. I think it's because of my limitations. I see around corners, all right, but only "short corners." I see—by sheer accident—exactly far enough ahead to be provocative . . . but plausible. In my grad school reading, I was exposed to a social psych researcher, Somebody McGuire. He demonstrated a "Zone of Acceptance," relative to the change process. If the case for change is too bland, then *ho hum* is the response. Too far out, and *doesn't apply to me* is the reaction. But in the middle ground, one is "interesting enough" to be interesting without being beyond the pale. I have made a career of that Zone of Acceptance sweet spot—by accident.

If I were smarter, I'd be less useful. It's a fact . . . I think.

There is nothing that doesn't interest me. I love section "D" of *USA Today!* It provides better clues to tomorrow than the *Wall Street Journal.* I groove on magazines in dentists' offices. I find the whole wide world a hoot!

Why? No idea!

What I love to do most—for the sheer anti-snobbery of it—is to cite *USA Today* and other "lowbrow" journals, and to tie their stuff to big trends. I love to connect far-fetched dots! Again: For the sheer hell of it! (Rule No.1 for fending off boredom: *Amuse yourself.*)

I am terrified of falling behind. Fear has its (big) place in my life. I got "here." *God alone knows why.* I l-i-k-e it "here." (Wherever here may be.) The Web is, in fact, changing everything. Perhaps no one over the age of twenty-seven has the right to pronounce about anything. (There is a big part of me that believes that. Snicker if you will.)

I am investing millions—literally!—in my Web site. Why? It's fun. (Keeps that boredom at bay.) *And I'm afraid not to.*

Maybe this is all a sham. Maybe I do not have staying power . . . at this amazing point in time. At this moment—when it matters most. When the world is wobbling at an unprecedented rate. I'm far from sure—and farther every day—that I am, in fact, fresh. Stuart Crainer penned a lovely piece (per me) in *The Times* (of London) stating that I was the only one of the "established gurus" to have embraced the Web. Fine . . . good on me . . . but is it enough? (Yes, I do think about these things. Obsess on them, truth be known.)

I am a "garbage man." Big secret: I read everything. Flying off to [wherever]. Grab fifteen *(no baloney)* mags at the airport kiosk. Spend the next four hours poring over them. Emerge with forty torn out pages. Convert same into ten new presentation slides. Use four of the new slides . . . tomorrow morning. One from *Cosmopolitan.* One from *Vanity Fair.* One from *Sports Afield.* One from *Scientific American.* Not to mention a Bill Parcels quote snared from the *New York Post.*

MCI guru–madman–Cool Irish Dude Bill McGowan was a self-professed "garbage man." He spotted trends by sucking up stuff from any damn source you can mention. I loved Bill. And I've shamelessly stolen his garbagic secret!

I love ambiguity! No . . . I *adore* ambiguity. I love messes. I love great fiction. (I love Warren most . . . he doesn't know this . . . because his favorite playwright is Samuel Beckett.) I especially love it when I am "accused" of inconsistency. My mentors-in-chief (more later), such as Karl Weick and Gene Webb and Charles Handy and Warren, groove on mess and ambiguity. (Especially Karl Weick, in my book.)

Bottom line: I love life . . . *because it is so absurd!* Why is this my bent? Beats me. (Talk to one of my many shrinks—or don't. I never got anywhere with shrinks because I looked at our "exchanges" as mortal combat. I never really participated. My loss, I suspect. Though I'm not sure.) Fact: My first shrink wanted me to smell the roses, be more "balanced." I thought that was stupid. Still do. Never got over it. I'm proud to say I don't have a single good "balanced" friend. God knows, not Warren.)

I hate labels. OK, for a while I was "the excellence guy." (Pleasantly vague.) But—I'd like to think—I am not categorizable. Peter Drucker has a unique place in the Management Heavens. So I would not (dare not) compare myself to His Eminence. But . . . my conceit . . . we are the only management "gurus" who are label-*less.* I've done my "excellence thing." And my "customer thing." And my "women's thing." And my "design thing." And so on. Pin me down if you will. I bet you can't. (Redux: Boredom rules!)

My mom made me an obsessive reader. Bless you, Evelyn Charlotte Snow Peters. You have given me no greater gift.

I picked my mentors well. Warren's book—*An Invented Life*—at its most personal is a mentor's book. I once tried my hand at autobiography. The result stunk, except, my friend and publisher Sonny Mehta said, the mentors chapter.

I got lucky. (Like Warren Bennis.) I had a Vietnam mentor, Captain Dick Anderson, who was my Captain Bessinger. Then I got doubly lucky. At the big, impersonal Stanford Business School, I latched on to my most important mentor in life . . . Gene Webb. The intellectual mentoring was, of course, invaluable. (Understatement.) But the "life mentoring" was worth a million times more. (The S.O.B. died early, in 1994. What a rotten thing to do to a mentee.) Karl Weick and I have only been together in person a couple of times; but Karl remains my litmus test; how would Karl look at this, I ask myself, at least a few times every month. Karl may be appalled, but . . . everything I write must pass the "Karl test."

Truth is, Warren and I also have little facetime on our record. Nonetheless, Warren has inspired me by the very fact of Being Warren . . . and not acting as if I was totally full of it. (He hasn't a clue as to how important his little notes are to me.) Hal Leavitt and Charles Handy have also been more important than most of my blood relatives. They have taken me seriously, and, given my limitless respect for them as absurdly thoughtful humans (as much as "influentials" in my field), they have made a big impact on my life. Their work per se has been a guiding influence. As has their willingness to take me seriously. (Has anybody ever succeeded big-time with *high* self-esteem? Low esteem is so valuable!)

Bigger message: *None of us in this field, I dare say, have paid enough attention to the "luck" of mentoring in the shaping of leaders.* (On second thought, perhaps some of the political scientists have.)

I am pissed off at prior miscues. Self-hatred. Strong term—the basis of many a suicide. *And most success?* In any event, I am most motivated by my irritation at the stuff I got wrong last week or last month or last year. (I get so much wrong.) (*In Search of Excellence* was a radical book. Right? Then why are "globalization" and "information technology" missing from the index?)

Message: Usefully directed self-loathing makes the world go round. Maybe.

I am not a "people person." But people fascinate me. Bob Waterman and I argued—the true "revolutionary aspect" of our book—that "soft is hard." That is, the people stuff and the passion are what matters in the end. ("Take that, Harvard B. School," we sputtered in 1982. Hint: We were right!) And yet, I'm *not* a "people guy." God's truth. I am an observer. The "people stuff" turns me on. As an analyst. Maybe that's good: If "soft is hard," then "hard is soft." You've gotta be able to look at the "soft stuff" dispassionately.

I love cabbies. I really don't get this one. Damn. I hate self-reflection. Point is: I love talking to cabbies. Hate (mostly) talking to CEOs. Low self-esteem? Not clear. Mostly, I think, I identify more with cabbies than with CEOs. And find them more human and more interested in humanity. Or maybe it's something else entirely. My wife glommed on to this. Yes, I have had some success. Enough so that "everybody" wants something from me. An endorsement. (God, it's their life's work. How can I not . . . Or: "ten minutes of your time . . . five minutes . . . to review this business plan." Whatever.) Cabbies don't want a bloody damn thing except a decent tip and the very temporary loan of an ear. Bless them.

Speaking of love: *I love business.* Per se. I read *Business Week* and *Fortune* and *Forbes* because the Theater of Business turns me on. I think this is, in fact, no small thing. My sixth sense tells me—clearly!—that a lot of people in "my field" are not moved by business. Per se. For one (big) thing, this love affair is helpful because "keeping up" is a pleasure, not a pain. (It also—obviously—increases my credibility enormously.)

Bob Schwartz, another Warren pal,* developed a similar taste for business; he figured that most interesting social experimentation, driven by the relentless storms of the marketplace, occurred in business. True—times ten or ten thousand—in the Internet World.

I am a hopeless suck-up. Bill Clinton needs everyone to love him. *Me too!* I cherish integrity. Get high on my "prickliness." But you must love me. Note to Warren: Not enough on this in the leadership literature. That is, the tension between a pointed view and the desperate need to please.

---

*Are there any interesting people who aren't F.O.W.?

I want to be provocative as hell. (It's my trademark brand.) And I want to "reach out and touch" every member of an audience of twelve thousand I'm addressing at the Moscone Center. (It's my "secret," which, in fact, makes the provocative part work.)

I had a breakthrough moment re "this stuff." It's a variation on the suck-up theme. I was giving a speech to 4,500 ACE Hardware store owners. It went incredibly well. And . . . I figured out why. (Perhaps.) For that hour I was "with" them . . . *I was a hardware store owner.* Please feel free to laugh. But I think I'm right. It's a version of a top actor's Trick No. 1. Trust me: For that hour, I owned a hardware store in Burlington or Palo Alto. Every remark I made— substance and exact choice of language—was consistent with my role-du-jour. When I started thinking on this, I realized I'd been a doctor . . . while addressing the American Medical Association's top thousand leaders in Miami ten days before. Perhaps this obser- vation is of no use to you, but it has been to me. Success in big-time public speaking = assuming the shape of one's audience.

I am nauseatingly competitive. This is embarrassing. It's a P.C. World—and one is not to own up to raw, naked aggression. But . . . I am bloody competitive. (I even chuckle—secretly, till now—at: "It's not good enough for me to win. You gotta lose." Sick.) But, we are, after all, on the topic of staying power. And I believe that Pete Rose and I do share this trait: No. 1 is fun! *And I wanna stay near the head of the league tables, in an absurdly more competitive "guru market" than fifteen, or five, years ago.* To fail to admit to it ruins this piece.

Energy rules me. Biographer Strat Sherman says Jack Welch's ace is "2,000 percent" more energy than the rest of us. Well, my secret is 995 percent more energy than most. Fact: People—audiences— respond to energy per se. Trust me. (This is a big deal.) (Susan says I'd be just as successful on "the circuit" if I read from the phone book. My horrid secret: I fear she has a point.)

Message: Again, pick the right genes?

Retirement sucks. If you don't buy this, then you don't have a chance of understanding the idea of "staying on top of your game." 'Nuf said.

You must put yourself at risk. Regularly. If you're not scared you're not growing. That's my reluctant but clear conclusion. There is a type of Generic Speech that I can give—to twenty-two or twenty-two thousand—with 1.83 hands tied behind my back. But what about speaking to the Legal Department (as I did in late '99) of Philip Morris? I love such speeches. They scare the hell out of me. I am paid a huge sum to address a group I have no business addressing. Whoops—better figure out something interesting to say.

Message from me to me: Put thyself in Harm's Way a dozen times a year. Or go hopelessly stale.

I groove on young people. Message 2000: If you don't groove on young people . . . hang up your spikes. You/I/we must honor youth!

I love Vermont. (God's great and personal gift to me: Grey Meadow Farm, West Tinmouth.) And I'm glad my (albeit minuscule) corporate HQ is in the center of the new universe: *Palo Alto.* I n-e-e-d the energy of the absurdly youthful Internet Revolution to seep into my pores—regularly.

Diversity is my God. If you grew up in the South (or, in my case, the Near South . . . Annapolis) in the 1940s and 1950s . . . you are forever shamed at the misbehavior of white folks. (Message to South Carolina and Georgia: For God's sake take the Confederate flag down!) But I haven't got a P.C. cell in my body. It's simple (to me): *America's strength is her entrepreneurial and creative energy . . . read, diversity.* (Mess rules!) A friend of mine weeps at the national anthem; I don't (too many memories of Goebbels and mindless—mindful?—symbol worship). I do weep when I see a business gathering that features Jesse's Full Rainbow. (Sadly, I rarely feast upon such a sight.)

Unless you are pissing people off . . . you are not alive. OK, those are not the precise words MLKjr. or Gandhi would have chosen. But it is a fact. I am (as noted) a pleaser. But I also know that if everybody loves you, you are pushing no hot buttons. Hence, I have learned—reluctantly—to take pleasure in the Nasty Notes as well as in the syrup-flavored variety. Nasty = Getting through.

I'm wildly ambivalent about this. Post *In Search of Excellence,* I had a 1984–1986 resurgence as The King of Customer Service. Worthy topic? Absolutely. Yet . . . "it" was a clear by-product of childish, self-indulgent behavior that resulted from a schedule (two hundred+ speeches per year) that would have killed a horse. I was overstressed. Understatement. I would get very pissed at some little slight—and make (almost literally) a congressional case of it.

And the world lapped it up. What I did was, in fact, of value—self-indulgent or not. But I'm also deeply ashamed of the immature self-indulgence.

Bigger point: *Some things piss me off!* For example, "Board" pictures from big companies—in 1999 or 2000—that consist . . . in 1999 or 2000 . . . of *old white males.* (Bob Waterman told some interviewer, "Tom is not happy unless he's angry about something." 'Fraid there's more than a grain of truth to that.)

Dunno why, but I've gotten the nerve to publish my personal piques. Anger keeps me fresh? (Bigger leadership point: Does anger at "stupid stuff" motivate most successful change agents?) My case: As I said, I'm really not a "people guy," but I do get infuriated when institutions are stunningly dumb, as when a Board of Directors bears no resemblance whatsoever to the market the company serves.

It—whatever—is a hoot. (And if you don't get that . . . forget "staying power." No baloney.) A big deal headhunter tells me that that "sense of humor" is No. 1 on her list of Must Have traits for any big-time job candidate. Former governor Ann Richards says the same thing. (Ann Richards = Best governor Texas has had or has.)

Message: Be serious. ("I regret that I have but one life to give . . . ") Message: Never take yourself seriously. And a hundred hundred hackneyed-but-true aphorisms. . . . If you can't take the heat, stay out of the kitchen. (Lordy, Bill Clinton gets that one! To his eternal credit.)

When you love what you do, you're alive. My shtick: P-a-s-s-i-o-n. Passion, energy, commitment, and care make the world go round. Or: *Just say no to Ritalin . . . for 99.99999 percent of kids.* I love the obstreperous ones! (And you?) Life = Technicolor.

Quotes (OK, I don't like doing this either, but these *are* WWRU—Words Worth Remarking Upon):

"Well-behaved women rarely make history."—Anita Borg, Institute for Women and Technology

"When was the last time you asked, 'What do I want to be?'"—Sara Ann Friedman, *Work Matters*

"I want to be thoroughly used up when I die."—George Bernard Shaw

"I am an American, Chicago born, and go about things as I have taught myself, free style, and will make the record in my own way."—Saul Bellow, *The Adventures of Augie March*

"Everything can be taken from man but one thing: the last of human freedoms—to choose one's own attitude in any set of circumstances, to choose one's own way."—Victor Frankl, psychologist and Auschwitz survivor

"You are the storyteller of your own life, and you can create your own legend or not."—Isabel Allende

"Blame nobody. Expect nothing. Do something."—Coach Bill Parcels

Weird Rules

Psychologists and psychiatrists piss me off, mostly. They want me (and others) to be normal. And cheerful. But I hate "normal." And "cheerful." I like the screwed-up folks. Adjustment? What an awful idea. I love maladjusted folks who have monster egos—who think they can change the world, and occasionally do. And occasionally for the better. *Maladjustment interests me far more than adjustment.* And I think that "competent" is the worst thing you can accuse a fellow human of being!

There is a role for "our types" (management "experts") who study the creation of terrific systems that "get the most" out of "ordinary people." It's just that there is no role for me—or Warren, I believe—in such pursuits. The Silicon Valley Miracle is my coming-out party: *Weird rules!* The "gales of creative destruction" (J. Schumpeter) have engulfed us all. And what a merry wind storm howls around us! Reinventing the world!

I waited table for nine years to earn tuition bucks in high school and college. I am, thence, waiter-sensitive. And: I hate "normal" waiters and waitresses. Every meal and every table is a leadership and theatrical opportunity of the first order—if your head is screwed on right. I am far too old to be a Pollyanna. Threw away my rose-colored glasses years ago. (Truth is, I veer toward cynicism. Hence, my clinical depression.) Yet I do think we can mostly all make a good thing out of whatever thing we're engaged in. And I am sure that systems aimed at "optimizing" mass behavior suppress human engagement and thence thwart peak performance—in the restaurant and on the flight deck. (As I write, the *Wall Street Journal* features a piece attributing Southwest Airlines' incredible safety record to management's allowing SWA pilots lots more discretion than other airlines. Upshot: SWA pilots are engaged! Upshot: A spotless, nearly three-decade safety record.)

Passion—engagement—rules! (Believe it.)

I surprised myself. (Stunned myself, is more like it.) I was on a BBC TV religion show a coupla years ago. The likes of Bishop Tutu had been on previous segments. I was tired. (Tired = Primitive response = Truth?) "What gives you your obvious fire?" the interviewer asked. I blurted out, "Robert Strange McNamara.

"My [professional] life stands as counterpoint to the bloodless, dispassionate analytic approach to private and public enterprise that McNamara epitomized." No baloney: I felt a great weight had been lifted from my shoulders when I said it.

We needed a modicum (or more) of organization at Ford (and in the Army Air Corps) when McNamara arrived. Just as we needed—desperately—Frederick Taylor sixty years earlier. But— no surprise to followers of human affairs—we overdid it. Grotesquely. We proudly drained the passion from enterprise. (Thank you Fred Taylor, Peter Drucker, and J. K. Galbraith—the Man Who Never Got Anything Right.) I love Warren. And Karl. And Charles. But my pick as Management Book of the Last Twenty-Five Years is Henry Mintzberg's magisterial *The Rise and Fall of Strategic Planning.* So thorough. So damning. So final.

Yes, in the end, I'm motivated to stay around. To still be writing when McNamara dies. To quash dis-passion!

I wanna be a player!

The thought of having been around during this incredible-wonderful-awful time and not having participated in it is too much to contemplate. Period. In my so-called trademark presentations, I conclude with this from Emile Zola:

> If you ask me what I have come to do in
> this world, I who am an artist, I will
> reply, I am here to live my life out loud.

Chapter Fifteen

Heroic Leadership's Greatest Battle

The Defeat of Disappointment Versus the Disappointment of Defeat

Jeffrey Sonnenfeld

Various bromides greet us amid losses regarding how we must squeeze the lemons of life into lemonade. For leaders, however, life's adversity can turn hard-earned assets into monumental barriers to recovery. Leaders can enjoy such resources as great popular recognition, vast networks of supporters, and gushing pools of finances. Yet celebrity, popularity, and wealth do not insulate them from fate.

There is no cruise control for leaders to coast on the momentum of recent triumphs. Today's evidence of good fortune could evaporate with tomorrow's events.

This point is dramatized well for us in the headlines. Professors Warren Bennis and James O'Toole properly celebrated the proven leadership strengths of AT&T CEO C. Michael Armstrong for his two and a half years of turnaround efforts to build the biggest cable television operation and a powerful wireless division while demonstrating his passion for his work and his employees. They wrote in the May-June 2000 *Harvard Business Review,* "His direct reports will tell you of his warmth. How natural it is to follow him. And they will tell you how he transformed AT&T from a moribund giant into a nimble competitor" (p. 172).

Unfortunately, the very day that issue hit the newsstands, the *New York Times* tore into Armstrong following a day of shockingly bad financial performance, "It was the worst day for AT&T's investors in more than a dozen years and Mr. Armstrong probably had not had such an unpleasant professional experience since he took over the company. . . . AT&T simply has not been able to escape its deteriorating legacy . . . and is running out of chances with impatient investors who are hoping that AT&T's future is now" (Schiesel, 2000, p. C-1).

This review does not mean that Bennis and O'Toole were necessarily hasty in their celebration of Armstrong. Quite the contrary, the skills they identified may be just the tools needed for recovery. Clearly the reported loss of faith in Armstrong was a professional and personal disappointment for him. How he embraces such a setback will help determine his genuine heroic qualities.

Former president Jimmy Carter challenged a group of CEOs at one of my conferences to consider how they would recover if the American public had fired them. Despite failing to be re-elected, Carter continued tirelessly in his humanitarian, public health, and diplomacy missions, heavily promoting democratic reform around the world, and has become revered by virtually all as the greatest *former* U.S. president. Leaders should not be measured by how they bask in the gratification of their accomplishments. Rather, they should be measured by how they respond when fate deflates the joys of hard-earned triumphs. How well do they pick themselves up and get back in the race?

Creating Triumph from Tragedy

This quality of resilience is critical in the lives of creative figures such as leaders and artists. The rise, the fall, and the recovery of both leaders and artists face common stages. Otto Rank (1932) was one of the first to link these extraordinary contributors. He suggested that their accomplishment was the consequence of a shared, super-human urge to create fueled by a heightened quest for immortality.

Artists and leaders were similarly considered in Howard Gardener's (1998) book *Extraordinary Minds*. He proposed a set of traits shared by "influencers"—those truly great historic figures across professions. After studying such creative figures as Wolfgang Mozart, Virginia Woolf, Sigmund Freud, and Mahatma Ghandi, Gardener concluded that rather than actual base intellect, lucky circumstances, or even indefatigable energies, these figures possessed powerful skills at candid self-assessment of strengths and weaknesses, keen situational analysis, and the capacity to reframe past setbacks into future successes. A defeat merely energizes them to rejoin the fray with greater ardor. It is not the proportion of their losses that differentiates these "influencers" from the rest of us, it is how they construe their losses.

In teaching Harvard MBA students through their early career planning, I came to read over a thousand sixty-plus-page self-assessment papers. What was most stunning in this task—and what kept me wide awake through the late night, early morning pain of grading—was their remarkable self-awareness and their desire to confront horrible life tragedies as learning experiences. Whether the setbacks had been abusive parents, thieving business partners, deceptive romantic entanglements, false accusations, or even witnessing and explaining to mourners the catastrophic loss of innocent life during Peace Corps missions, these aspiring leaders saw some redemptive value in their experience.

It is, in fact, wrong to consider adversity a diversion off one's path toward greatness. The subsequent resilience from calamities has been revealed as vital to the character formation and differentiation of heroic figures. Anthropologist Joseph Campbell (1949) studied, across cultures and eras, religious and folk heroes such as Jesus, Moses, Mohammed, Buddha, Cuchulain, Odysseus, Aneas, and the Aztec Tezcatlipoca, and discerned a universal "monomyth" of the life stages of these heroes. One stage involved a call to greatness, which led to a separation from one's past to realize superhuman talent. This is followed by a series of continual trials and ultimately profound setbacks that are met with eventual triumph and reintegration back into society.

The apparent losses were reconstructed into assets. These visionary leaders were able to inspire others to join them through their own sagas of redemption. They gained the confidence for transformational leadership, in part, through their stunning transcendence over life's adversity.

Second Thoughts About Second Acts

Ironically, the very same assets of their past leadership, their re-nowned reputations and quest for immortal legacies, can become liabilities. My (1988) study of a generation of prominent CEOs leaving office revealed that reputation or heroic stature and the quest for lasting contribution or heroic mission can become daunting barriers. The loss of heroic stature compounds adversity because private losses are so public for these people. Literary scholar Leo Braudy (1986) suggested in his book, *The Frenzy of Renown,* that society generates a subset of people eager to live their lives in the public eye. They court fame and recognition in a grand fashion so that their prominence will allow them greater risk taking. These idiosyncratic credits come at a price. When a devastating career setback hits such superachievers, they feel greater shame because their loss of self-esteem, their loss of influence, and their loss of self-reliance are so very public.

In addition, seeing the passing of timely opportunities can be paralyzingly frustrating. The loss of heroic mission compounds adversity because the path to date has been so all-consuming that much else was sacrificed. Private dreams became public posses-sions, which were then cavalierly tossed away by an unappreciative, fickle society. F. Scott Fitzgerald's admonition that there are no sec-ond acts in American lives casts an especially dark shadow over the derailed careers of leaders and creatives.

Nonetheless, some do recover with their careers more ablaze than ever while others flame out into obscurity. Consider the resilience of John Irving, Mike Nichols, Robert Altman, Carlos Santana, and John Travolta against the retreats of Kurt Vonnegut, J. D. Salinger, Alan Jay Lerner, Judy Garland, and Orson Wells. Some were energized by their losses while others were forever haunted by the specter of their own early careers.

An examination of two recently departed prominent and wealthy fifty-eight-year-old California CEOs, profiled coincidentally in side-by-side articles in the *New York Times,* reveals how differently corporate leaders can also confront adversity. One article, "The Aftermath of a Powerful Chief" (Leonhardt, 2000), was an upbeat piece on former Hewlett-Packard CEO Lewis Platt's new life as a vintner running Kendall-Jackson Wine Estates—a workforce of

1,200 instead of his former 124,000. The adjacent article, "A General Whose Time Ran Out" (Barringer, 2000), conveyed the emotional outcry and frustration of Mark Willes, the CEO of Times Mirror, on his board's loss of faith in his strategy, and undermining him to sell the entire firm to media competitor, the Tribune Company of Chicago.

Platt, a popular engineer famous for his intelligence and honesty, was a thirty-three-year veteran of the "HP–Way," known also for his reinforcement of the firm's widely admired core values about people, service, product quality, and citizenship (Fisher, 1993). He had succeeded John Young as CEO and the legendary cofounder David Packard as chairman in 1993. After a great start, however, revenue growth and product innovation were seen as slipping by 1999 due to slow responses to falling PC prices, declining Asian sales, and vast Internet opportunities (Burrows and Elstrom, 1999). He announced new e-commerce strategies and broad restructuring while suggesting to his own board that he be replaced. Today he is enthusiastic about getting his hands dirty with direct product responsibility in the winery.

By contrast, Mark Willes seemed to many to be at war with the culture he had inherited at Times Mirror when he arrived from General Mills in 1995 (Alexander, 2000). He declared unattainable circulation goals and flouted journalistic conventions about the independence and objectivity of editorial versus commercial aspects of the papers. While this sparked a revolt by the *Los Angeles Times*'s journalists, ultimately he was undermined by his own chief financial officer, Tom Unterman, who negotiated with the Times Mirror board and the Tribune Company behind Willes's back. He emotionally addressed his employees the day the deal was announced lamenting the personal disappointment that he was not given the time to prove his strategies (Bannon and Deogun, 2000).

Bernstein and Bennis as Models for Leadership Resilience

The parallel lives of famed musician Leonard Bernstein and management scholar Warren Bennis provide complementary examples of career resilience and continuous creative contribution through late career. Their lives, in parallel universes, both crossed between teaching, performance, creation, and management. Bennis has written in his book *Organizing Genius* that Great Groups require Great Leaders. Bernstein, by all counts, was a visionary leader as music director of the New York Symphony, who always maintained his accessibility to all around him—never letting anyone refer to him imperiously as maestro. Bennis, as a college president, also avoided the trappings of hierarchy of authoritarian traditions, preferring instead to have open office hours for all in his community. These leaders, in turn, often require great acts of resilience.

The Call to Greatness

Having gotten to know both of these remarkable individuals, Bernstein at Harvard in 1973 over lunches before his Charles Eliot Norton Poetry Lectures, and Bennis in collegial circles and as a personal mentor since the early 1980s, I say with certainty that we should consider Warren Bennis the Leonard Bernstein of the management world and Leonard Bernstein the Warren Bennis of the music world. Seven years apart, both grew up as the sons of pragmatic Jewish merchants distant from the intellectual and aesthetic worlds that intrigued their sons. Bernstein was born in Lawrence, Massachusetts, to a beauty supply jobber who wanted his son to enter the business. Bennis was born in Westwood, New Jersey, to a soda stand and candy store operator who wanted his son to learn a skilled trade. Both had families who moved often during their early childhood, and they had few friends.

Early in their childhood, they distanced themselves from their surroundings and began to reinvent who they were. Bernstein changed his name from Louis to Leonard and demanded music lessons at age ten when a divorced aunt stored her upright piano in their home. He never heard a live symphony orchestra until age sixteen. Bennis found, at age fourteen, he could escape his origins by giving a compelling talk to his class about a hobby he had invented out of his imagination.

The Early Trials and Jedi Mentoring

During the 1940s, each of these men acquired both a taste of greatness and a strong bond with mentors who inspired them as leaders and even as Jedi-like surrogate fathers. In 1940, Bernstein met

Boston Symphony Orchestra's conductor Serge Koussevitzky while studying at the orchestra's newly created Tanglewood summer institute. He later became Koussevitzky's conducting assistant, protégé, and lifelong friend. On November 14, 1943, Bernstein, as an assistant conductor for the New York Philharmonic, was asked to substitute on a few hours notice for the world-renowned Bruno Walter, who was too ill to conduct a major concert. The concert was broadcast nationally to enthusiastic critical acclaim, and his prominence was launched.

In 1944 Bennis was the youngest infantry officer in the European Theater of Operations of World War II. There he met an Army captain—an inspiring leader who taught him the virtues of listening and patience that modeled many of the leadership qualities that he would appreciate just after the war at Antioch and MIT with his bold creative mentor Douglas McGregor. McGregor's "Theory Y" views on human development and leadership influenced Bennis's work.

Educating and Promoting Others

Both were profoundly influenced by their years in university life in Cambridge, Massachusetts, where they launched professional friendships and pioneering approaches to their fields. Bernstein at Harvard began a lifelong friendship with composer Aaron Copland and two other aspiring composers, Roy Harris and William Schuman. He became a leading advocate of American composers, particularly Copland. While studying under such greats as Walter Piston and New York Philharmonic Music Director Dimitri Mitropoulos, he also discovered the joy in teaching from the young musicians at his renowned master classes at Tanglewood to his fourteen seasons of televised Young People's Concerts with the New York Philharmonic.

At MIT and Harvard, Bennis began collaborations with fellow organizational development pioneers and social scientists like Douglas McGregor, Edgar Schein, Herbert Shepard, Richard Beckhardt, David Berlew, Charles Handy, Kenneth Benne, Philip Slater, and Ted Mills. He shared the group's collective skepticism over authoritarian leadership and rigid bureaucracy. His early work on temporary organizations, group dynamics, the more mobile workforce, and the convergence of knowledge and power was shockingly prescient and his writings remain current. It was also at this time when Bennis discovered his fascination with teaching new managers around the world. Bennis too has been a devoted and selfless mentor, like Bernstein, to many young professionals who have chosen to follow his path.

Crossing Boundaries

Bernstein and Bennis also shared a determination to live in multiple worlds. Far from slowing down as age advanced, they both increased their range and pace of activities. Bernstein was devoted to a hydra-headed definition of his careers. During his high-profile career he was a leader in a dozen fields including symphonic music, Broadway musicals, the ballet, films, and television. He wrote the popular scores for the film *On the Waterfront* and such musicals as *On the Town, Peter Pan, Wonderful Town, Candide,* and the smash hit *West Side Story.* His symphonic works included *Kaddish, Mass,* and *Symphony #1 Jeremiah* (coincidentally the prophet Bennis chose to discuss in his bar mitzvah speech). A dedicated teacher of rare communications skill, Bernstein regularly had to fend off critics who insisted he was spread too thin. Defending his restless and fruitful life he explained, "I don't want to spend my life, as Toscannini did, studying and restudying the same 50 pieces of music. It would bore me to death. I want to conduct. I want to play the piano. I want to write for Hollywood. I want to write symphonic music. I want to keep on trying to be, in the full sense of that wonderful world, musician. I also want to teach. I want to write books and poetry. And I think I can still do justice to them all" (Henahan, 1990, p. A-1). At his Norton Lectures at Harvard, he stressed that the best way to know a subject is in the context of other external subjects.

Bennis similarly explained his interest in writing for multiple audiences beyond pure scholars alone as well as to try his own hand as an institutional leader, as a provost and a university president, stating (in the chapter that forms the Postlude to this book), "I was tired of being Montaigne in the bleachers. . . . I wanted to be bold in the arena, to see if my written words could be embodied in the practitioners' world where deeds more than words counted. . . . Related to that, I suppose, is what all composers or playwrights must desperately want, getting their work performed, realized. How would a composer know how the music sounds without hearing it; how would a playwright know how the scenes actually play without seeing and hearing them."

Resilience Through Rededication and Support of Others

Both Bernstein and Bennis, however, had their share of setbacks. In 1950, Bernstein wrote a one-act opera called *Trouble in Tahiti* that was not popular. He immediately teamed up with Adolph Green to create *Wonderful Town,* which returned him to success at the same time that he was becoming a music professor at Brandeis and conducting on tour with Koussevitzky. While *Candide* in 1956 was not very successful, the premier of *West Side Story* a year later created some of the nation's most moving and lasting popular music, for which he will be most remembered. Bernstein's long-anticipated work with Alan Jay Lerner, *1600 Pennsylvania Avenue,* closed after seven performances in 1976 (Hurwitz, 1989). Nonetheless, his friend and collaborator, the playwright Arthur Laurents (2000), claimed that the only time he saw Bernstein defeated was when he was bedridden two months before his death.

Another friend, Ned Rorem, recalled Bernstein saying, "The trouble with you and me Ned is that we want everyone in the world to personally love us and of course that's impossible. You just don't meet everyone in the world" (Bennis, 1993, p. 32).

Ironically, Bennis has cited that same Bernstein exchange in reflecting on lessons from his own setbacks. Bennis left a full-tenure professorship at MIT to become provost at SUNY Buffalo, joining Martin Meyerson as president in launching an educational revolution. They failed. "We were sure that in this academic Great Good Place, creativity would count for more than traditional training and ordinary credentials. . . . Examining what went wrong at Buffalo altered forever the way I think about change. Martin Meyerson has the first thing every effective leader needs—a powerful vision of the way the organization should be. . . . But unless a vision is sustained by action, it quickly turned to ashes. The Meyersonian dream never got out of the administration building. . . . At Buffalo, we as newcomers disregarded history" (Bennis, 1993, p. 34).

Similarly at the University of Cincinnati as president, at age forty-three, he felt he learned some profound lessons, "Similarly my writing had implied a rather simple model of change, based on gentle nudges from the environment coupled with a truth-love strategy; that is, with sufficient trust and collaboration, along with knowledge, organizations would progress monotonically upwards and onwards along a democratic continuum. . . . You had to adhere simultaneously to the symbols of tradition and stability and to the symbols of revision and change. I was seen by many constituents as emphasizing the latter and tone-deaf to the former" (Bennis, 2000).

At the end of a speech at Harvard, he credited Dean Paul Ylvisaker with asking him if he still loved what he was doing. Realizing that he preferred the personalized power of a professor's voice to the positional power and minutiae of administration, Bennis accepted an invitation from James O'Toole of the University of Southern California and returned to academia to produce an extraordinarily productive portfolio of insights into leadership, making him the true intellectual dean of leadership study.

Both Bernstein and Bennis demonstrated five critical lessons for the recovery of great leaders. First, they believed in fight and not flight; they acknowledged and redirected the stress they faced. Second, they recruited others into battle with them for perspective. Third, they rebuilt their heroic stature by openly discussing the nature of their adversity. Fourth, they proved their mettle to regain trust and credibility; they plunged into their work deeper to produce even greater works. Fifth, they rediscovered their heroic mission; they cleared their past and charted a new future through the continuous reinvention of themselves.

Fight Not Flight: Acknowledging and Redirecting the Stress

We have long known that career distress can be one of the greatest sources of life stress (Cooper and Payne, 1988). Being fired, for example, has been ranked as number eight among the most stressful events in life—just after death of family members, jail, and personal injury or illness (Holmes and Rahe, 1967). Loss of title and social role ambiguity are powerful workplace stressors as well (Cooper, 1983; Golembiewski, Menzenrider, and Stevenson, 1986). Although the psychological and physiological symptoms of chronic stress can have a profoundly corrosive effect, many of the bromides of our therapeutic society are not appropriate stress responses for many creative individuals and leaders. Stress is the perception of helplessness in dealing with serious demands. There is no such thing as objective stress existing on its own. We only stressfully respond to people, places, and events, our response dependent upon our perceptions of the adequacy of resources to deal with the stressors (Matheny and Riordan, 1992).

Thus, since stress is an interpreted phenomenon based on one's feeling of competence and strength, it is unlikely that the vacations and retreats so often prescribed will yield creative individuals the sense of potency and connectedness they require to feel back in control. Research on psychological hardiness in responding to stress suggests that victims must regain control, make commitments to external events, respond to challenges, be willing to take a radical approach, and essentially become blind to their fears (Kobassa, 1979; Maddi, 1968). Coping with stress does not mean accommodating and accepting the stress. Often victims are encouraged to reduce the *importance* of stress through denial, avoidance, projection, and withdrawal or else to reduce the *effects* of stress through exercise, diet, meditation, and support groups, but it is also worthwhile to examine ways of reducing the *source* of the stress, perhaps through direct confrontation (Schuler, 1984).

Henry Silverman, the CEO of Cendant, was once a Wall Street darling, a dazzling deal maker, building a company called Hospitality Franchising. He assembled such brands as real estate brokerage Century 21, Ramada Hotels, Howard Johnson Hotels, Days Inns, and Avis Rent-a-Car to yield 20 percent plus growth rates and soaring stock prices. The stock jumped from 4 in 1992 to over 77 before the scandal hit. Following a presumed masterstroke merger with a direct marketer called CUC that led to the firm's renaming to Cendant in late 1997, his empire and reputation unraveled. A series of investigations revealed massive improprieties in the former CUC that led to inflated earnings of $700 million over three years. The subsequent stock meltdown cost roughly $13 billion in market capitalization.

Silverman, the son of the CEO of a commercial finance company, had been driven to emerge from the shadow of his father's success. "You want to be recognized for what you achieved rather than what your parents achieved" (Barrett, 2000, p. 130). After high-profile work with notorious corporate raiders and gilded investment bankers, Silverman had become a legend through his own empire building as well. In the wake of the CUC scandal, his diligence and management style came under attack. The anger and humiliation ate away at him. For Silverman, the personal toll was heavy. "My own sense of self-worth was diminished," he recalls.

Following suggestions from a psychiatrist he consulted a few times, Silverman found ways to direct his rage. He became a workout enthusiast, going to the gym daily with rigorous aerobics, tennis, and weightlifting. In a year, his bench press weight rose from 65 to 150 pounds. Such sublimation, however, was not sufficient for him—he was driven to regain his credibility. He clarified who he believed the villains to be as government investigators began their probe. In the meantime, Silverman replaced all of CUC's leadership and sued its accountants, Ernst & Young. To not have to constantly relive the situation, he and his family curtailed their social life, withdrawing to the comfort of friends such as financiers Leon Black and Darla Moore. Silverman sold non–core businesses to repurchase 20 percent of the outstanding shares to boost the stock price. He began eyeing smaller acquisitions, and finally, he began to form alliances with firms like John Malone's Liberty Media, building credibility and driving e-commerce traffic for his service businesses.

Recruit Others into Battle: Concern for the Collateral Victims

In addition to feeling the need to redeem himself before shareholders, Silverman felt responsible for the ways his situation affected his family, his coworkers, and his friends. His efforts to bring others into his campaign are not unusual.

By enlisting the assistance of others, it is possible to attend to the needs of the innocent bystanders who suffer from the victim's career crisis. This helps to show appreciation for and replenish the resources of one's support system, maintaining the system that is critical to coping with the stress. This reinforcement from trusted advisers is also of great value for candid feedback. Gardener's (1998) observation that resilient exceptional people have a talent for self-awareness is true, in part, because these people energetically use personal networks in both their ascent and in their recovery from setback. The trusted advisers the victim consults help through more than consolation alone; they hold up a candid mirror for self-reflection and help brainstorm the range of next steps.

Perhaps no leader's recovery from setback is more inspirational than that of Bernard Marcus, chairman of Home Depot, and his cofounder and current CEO, Arthur Blank. In 1978 Sandy Sigoloff, the CEO of their then-parent company, Daylin, fired them as the leaders of Handy Dan's Home Improvement Stores. Sigoloff, a tough turnaround manager, was often referred to as "Ming the Merciless." Marcus explained in his book that what motivated Sigoloff was that

> he really wanted credit for turning Daylin around, saving it from the creditors, saving it for the shareholders, saving it from bankruptcy. But the only Daylin division that had a great cash flow was Handy Dan—my division. . . . The day I knew I was finished with Sandy Sigoloff was the day the Daylin board of directors discussed succession. One Sigoloff-appointed board member said, "I don't know why there is any question about succession here, since you have your obvious successor right in this room, Bernie Marcus. . . . A quick glance at Sigoloff's ashen face told me that that was never going to happen. And the very notion that some on the board supported the idea made me a genuine threat to Sigoloff. The situation between us just went from really bad to dire [Marcus and Blank, 1999, pp. 32, 33].

While Marcus believed that he was the prime target of Sigoloff's wrath, when he was dismissed, so were his top lieutenants Arthur Blank and Ron Brill, in separate rooms and in rapid succession. "Ron, like Arthur and me, never knew what hit him." Sigoloff released a statement to the press at Friday afternoon's deadline so that the newspapers would promptly run the story. Marcus explained, "But it was far worse than just the loss of a couple of well-paying, high-profile jobs, or a few embarrassing newspaper stories. Sigoloff was primarily after me; for Arthur and Ron, it was more a matter of guilt by association. We all had painful experiences telling our family and friends what happened" (Marcus and Blank, 1999, p. 34).

Marcus charged that subsequent to this termination, Sigoloff tried to vilify the victims further by suggesting to the authorities retrospectively that there had been some infractions in labor-organizing efforts. Marcus and Blank (1999) say these allegations were trumped up and never found to have merit by the authorities but invented to humiliate and wound them sufficiently to keep them from fighting back.

Now, however innocent, Marcus had his loyal coworkers with him. Another close friend, the financier Ken Langone, joined him, saying, "This is the greatest news I have heard. . . . You have just been kicked in the ass with a golden horseshoe" (Marcus and Blank, 1999, p. 37). Langone encouraged Marcus then to open the novel sort of store he had dreamed of and offered to help Marcus. Similarly, when he confided in his friend Sol Price, cofounder of the Price Club, he found feedback beyond solace. Price asked Marcus if he believed he had talent and if he thought that he had "the ability to build something, to create, do you feel good about yourself?" (Marcus and Blank, 1999, p. 40). He then realized for certain that it was time to get on with his life.

These colleagues and friends believed in Marcus and joined him in battle, encouraging many others to join as well. The stores he envisioned were immense warehouses for do-it-yourself home repair enthusiasts, with greater selection, superior customer service, a highly trained staff, and direct purchasing from the manufacturer. The group relocated from Los Angeles to Atlanta and opened their first store in 1979. By 1990 they had 17,500 employees with sales of $2.7 billion; today, Home Depot has sales of $35 billion and 160,000 employees. It has roughly eight hundred superstores with each store stocking more than forty thousand types of home improvement supplies. The founders have stayed together to become some of the wealthiest people in the world. They still rally around the motto born in crisis, "We Take Care of the Customer and Each Other."

Rebuild Heroic Stature: Spread the True Nature of the Adversity

Thus we see that Bernie Marcus did not just take up with syco-phantic supporters to assuage his hurt. Instead, his friends and col-leagues challenged him, inspired him, and joined him. Great leaders acquire a heroic persona that gives them larger-than-life presence. When that is removed, the audience disappears, the coworkers are no longer around, and leaders can lose their identity. They are not comfortable merely being one of the crowd. Great leaders like great artists develop a personal dream that they offer as a public possession. If it is accepted, they become renowned, but should it ultimately be discarded, they suffer the loss of both a private dream and a public identity. As people rallied around Marcus, they allowed him to regain his familiar role. They rallied because they still believed in him and in his heroic identity. They were able to rally because Marcus told them the truth and gave them something to believe in. When a hero stumbles, the constituents are confused as to how that happened given the larger-than-life presence the hero held.

Just as Marcus took his story to friends, investors, employees, and now to countless readers, so have others who have discovered the need to repair their armor. John Eyler, the chief executive of Toys "R" Us and previously of FAO Schwarz, was terminated at a large clothing retailer on Christmas Eve. He feels what was critical to his resilience was that he did not let the situation define him to others, because if it did, "I might have started to doubt myself as well." Scholars of reputation management have long recognized the value of reputation as a corporate and a personal asset. It is built through experience, performance, and affiliations (Fombrun and Shanley, 1990; Staw, McKechnie, and Puffer, 1983; Elsbach and Sutton, 1992).

New accounts that one circulates must embrace several critical elements for successful image restoration: clear denial of culpability, or a shift in responsibility for the mishap; reduction of the offensiveness of the act; the appearance of reasonableness of behavior (Jones and Nesbitt, 1971); and acceptable motives (Scott and Lyman, 1968). Marcus's explanation of the Handy Dan termination easily satisfies these dimensions.

Yet another great retailer, Leonard Roberts (CEO of Radio Shack Corp.), was fired previously as CEO of Shoney's restaurants. Known throughout his life as a maverick, he married at age seventeen while in high school and became a father at nineteen. He gained several food processing patents and a law degree. In 1985, Roberts left as head of the food service division of Ralston Purina to become CEO of the troubled Arby's roast beef restaurant chain. Roberts engineered a profound turnaround there through a combination of team management, aggressive marketing, and new product development. In 1989, he left behind a difficult controlling owner who faced his own legal challenges to run the $1.5 billion Shoney's chain of 1,600 restaurants. Roberts produced dramatic improvements in customer service and franchise relations. Store design, purchasing, and marketing were overhauled quickly. In three years, Shoney's profits went from $15.5 million to over $50 million.

Yet Roberts was the first CEO to be recruited from the outside and some see his exit as a political revolt of the old guard against Roberts's style (Romeo, 1993). The *Wall Street Journal,* however, carried a report that some board members felt Roberts had gone too far with his affirmative action efforts just six weeks after Shoney's settled a $105 million racial discrimination lawsuit. The founder, Raymond Danner, is said to have told one manager, "You've got too many niggers here. If you don't fire them, I'll fire you" (Pulley, 1992, p. A-1). Roberts was unable to offer public comment as part of his $2.9 million severance package but word of his skills got around. Some recruiters thought that his battle at Shoney's made him too controversial. However, when in 1994 Tandy CEO John Roach went looking for a successor, he was so impressed with Roberts's courage as well as his general management skills that he made Roberts, a lifelong restaurateur, president of the seven thousand–store electronics retailer. In 1998, Roberts succeeded Roach, and has pioneered creative store-within-a-store partnerships with suppliers like Sprint, RCA, Compaq, and Microsoft (Palmeri, 1998).

Proving Your Mettle: Regaining Trust and Credibility

Artists and performers need audiences for their work, but they often find others controlling access to potential viewers. Regularly, actors hear that they are too old, musicians that they are passé, and artists that galleries will no longer present their work. Similarly, even chief executives face gatekeepers to showcase their skills.

Tarred with the brush of controversy and the ready pool of rising stars, it is easy to be cast aside as last year's model. After setbacks, leaders have had to demonstrate that they still have the skills that made them great. Roberts, Marcus, and Silverman all eagerly jumped back into action to prove they retained the talents that built their careers.

The name Trump could easily have gone the way of other real estate titans of the 1980s, such as the Reichmann brothers and Robert Campeau. Donald Trump joined the family real estate business after graduating from Wharton in 1968. In his twenties he was already considered New York's paramount developer, his name whispered in the same breath at the legendary William Zechendorff. At the age of thirty-six he put up his Trump Tower, the tallest, most expensive reinforced concrete structure in the city. Trump's name appeared garishly on his building projects, but by 1990, he was caught in a real estate crunch with a crushing $975 million debt (Rutenberg, 1996).

A few years later, his net worth was reportedly back to $3.5 billion, his casinos were booming, and he was wheeling and dealing in real estate development just like before. Both he and financial analysts consider the resurgence of his Atlantic City casinos, Trump Plaza, the Taj Mahal, and Trump's Castle, as the source of his comeback (Thomkins, 1994). In addition to the disposal of personal assets, however, he made his much-derided ego and celebrity a bankable asset. His 1997 book, *The Art of Comeback,* was a proud follow-up to his brazen *Art of the Deal* from a decade earlier. With $7 billion in sales and twenty-two thousand employees, his empire has continued to grow. He has acquired the GM Building and half of the Empire State Building, and is building the world's tallest residential building (scheduled for completion in 2000), the ninety-story Trump World Tower.

Even more impressive a comeback is that of the 1980s iconic financier, Michael Milken. Many have seen Milken's life as the essence of American myth. He was born on the Fourth of July 1946 to a modest California family, and by the mid-1980s, he was a billionaire and one of the most influential investment bankers in the world. He bypassed Wall Street snobs by building the moderate-sized, stodgy Drexel Burnham Lambert into the capital of high-yield (junk bond) debt. By 1987, the value of junk bond debt rose from almost nothing to about $200 billion. The Justice Department's investigations, led by Rudolph Giuliani as U.S. Attorney, led to Milken's plea of guilty to six breaches of securities law. He was fined over $1 billion and sent to prison for two years, his reputation shattered—a lifetime ban prevents his return to the securities business. Many of the institutions holding the junk bonds went into financial distress. This negative press overwhelmed the image of the enterprises junk bonds helped create, such as CNN, FedEx, and MCI. To make matters worse, soon after leaving prison, Milken was told he had prostate cancer and had eighteen months to live.

Nonetheless, Milken is alive and well. His cancer is in remission and he has written several cookbooks for fighting cancer through diet. He is growing a cradle-to-grave-learning company he founded in 1997 with his brother and Oracle chief executive, Larry Ellison. He has a consulting firm called Nextera and funds an economic institute called the Milken Institute. His CaP CURE charity has raised over $63 million for research into prostate cancer.

Milken was unwilling to wallow in grief, to accept any of the externally imposed constraints on his desire to create and regain prominence. As he returned to demonstrate his business acumen, old and new partners rushed to join him.

Rediscovering the Heroic Mission: Clearing the Past and Charting the Future

The quest for immortality that drives artists and leaders requires that they see a lasting legacy through their work. Even more than the externally imposed barriers that confront exceptional people after setbacks are the self-imposed barriers of shattered confidence or a lack of replenishment of their ideas and their energy. In many of the cases discussed here, this meant lowering the image of where they left off. Marcus and Milken had to start over from scratch. Silverman and Trump had to rebuild their own wrecked empires, while Roberts assumed a challenging environment that required learning new skills.

Michael Bozic, now the vice chairman of Kmart, found that a career crisis can be liberating. In 1990, he was thrown out of the chief executive's throne of the Sears Merchandising Group—all that remains of Sears today—after twenty-eight years at the company. Many believed he had not been given full credit for his innovative triumphs at Sears such as his Brand Central merchandising concept, and in fact he was assumed to have taken a bullet for his boss, the chairman, Edward Brennan.

Following many months of job hunting, Bozic became CEO of Hills Stores, a bankrupt discount retailer in Canton, Massachusetts—

quite a comedown from the world's largest retailer. After bringing Hills back from near death, Bozic lost control of the company in a wild proxy battle of competing value-investors (Rouvalis, 1995). Thus after a successful turnaround there, Bozic left for Florida to lead the turnaround at Levitz furniture. Bozic left for Levitz with his world-weary wit intact, announcing, "No good deed goes unpunished." In November 1998, Bozic became vice chairman and CEO-contender at Kmart (Coleman, 1998).

In the world of communications, Michael Bloomberg has become a legend nearly overnight. He was fired as a Wall Street broker and went on to build one of the fastest-growing media empires in the world. His TV stations broadcast twenty-four hours a day to forty counties in seven languages. His radio networks, publishing empire, online businesses, and wire service approach a $2 billion empire with four thousand workers. He calls himself the David who challenged the Goliath of financial news. In 1981, Bloomberg was fired by Salomon Brothers, the elite investment bank and the only employer he ever had, where he had flourished for fifteen years. The night he was fired he bought his wife a sable jacket, saying, "Job or no job we are still players" (Bloomberg, 1997, p. 17). The next morning he settled down to work at his customary 7 A.M. to launch Bloomberg with his $10 million severance payment.

Finally, no reflections on resilience can be complete without acknowledging the fabled return of Apple founder Steve Jobs. At age thirty-two, two years after being forced out of the firm he created at age twenty-one, he founded Next with five devotees from Apple to build a powerful computer to be used in university instruction. He ultimately sold the company back to Apple for $425 million and persuaded the then–Apple CEO, Gil Amelio, to bring him back as a "consultant" as part of the deal. Jobs showed open disdain for Amelio around the office and derided many of his management team members (Carlton, 1997; Pollack, 1997). After Amelio resigned in July 1997, Jobs agreed to become interim CEO. He cut many of the projects he had inherited and introduced triumphant new products like the iMac, G3 desktops, and Powerbook laptops that helped increase Apple market share by 10 percent.

Not every accomplished, creative person can drop back and start anew. In his late twenties and thirties, Alan Jay Lerner wrote or cowrote great Broadway classics like *Brigadoon, Paint Your Wagon,*

Gigi, *My Fair Lady*, and *Camelot*. By his fifties and sixties, he felt his creative genius suffocated by his own creations. "The older a writer gets, the harder it is for him to write. This is not because his brain slows down; it is because his critical faculties grow more acute" (Freedman, 1986, p. 1).

It was not his public that held Lerner to punishing standards, it was himself. In contrast, many we have profiled optimistically believe what Nietzsche said, "what does not destroy me, makes me stronger." Through heavy life demands, these exceptional people are actually strengthened rather than weakened by triumphing their adversity.

When Bad Things Happen to Good Leaders: Final Thoughts for Future Heroes

It has been observed that if you want to be successful in life, you should first select great parents. Much of life is out of our control. Rising leaders, however, can anticipate that they will experience a wide array of life's adversity. The nature and timing of setbacks will never be convenient. The costs may include derailed career momentum, personal humiliation, the draining of finances, strained personal health, the shattering of personal dreams, and the suffering of innocent family and associates.

At the same time, these occasions of distress are potentially clouds with silver linings. It is through such loss that we often discover what we truly value. It is through such loss that we discover whom we can really trust. It is through such loss that we reveal new dimensions of our own character. The heroic persona is one that emerges only through triumphant battle over sadness and adversity.

As new leaders see that their success spiral has just smacked into a wall, they should step back, catch their breath, and then embrace the obstacle itself as a fresh opportunity to meet unfamiliar challenges. At the same time, they must realize that their mission cannot be accomplished alone. They will need to draw on the full reservoir of their early career experiences and relationships. Once a devastating crisis hits it is too late to make friends, too late to establish professional credibility, and too late to build a reputation for integrity. As the French scientist Louis Pasteur intoned, "Chance favors the mind that's prepared."

Part Five

Insights from
Young Leaders

Chapter Sixteen

Where the Leaders Are
The Promise of Youth Leadership
Tara Church

I am a morning person. The hour or two between getting out of bed and leaving for work is sacred time that I use to reflect on myself, the world, and the day ahead. This morning while I sat at my dressing table with a giant mug of coffee, humming the last notes of "Unchained Melody," a radio commercial for some new dot-com and the rather loud voice of Tom Peters jolted my serenity: "We need your youth! We need your enthusiasm! . . . Be CEO of your own life!" I chuckled to myself as I headed out the door to my office at Tree Musketeers—a place where kids gain the tools and the power to be CEOs of not only their lives, but of national movements as well.

While Peters may not envision middle-schoolers "in search of excellence" answering his call to action, I do. In fact, the best way I see to secure a healthy future for our rapidly changing business, political, and social institutions is to engage youth directly in the dialogue and practice of leadership. Forging a path for young community activists and, in turn, empowering all youth as leaders of social and environmental change is what I do at Tree Musketeers. I cofounded Tree Musketeers at age eight to fight pollution in my hometown suburb of Los Angeles. Unlike most youth groups—run by adults for kids—we created the nation's first nonprofit corporation actually administered by kids with support of adult partners. While working for a healthy future and inspiring other young people to be leaders of social and environmental change, we proved, as a by-product, that young people do have the power to change the world.

In the past thirteen years I have seen scores of young lives redirected, environmental and economic quality of life improve, enterprising partnerships create powerful community solutions, and precedent-setting opportunities emerge for young people to make a difference. I derive intense gratification from the dynamic young executives I mentor; those of us concerned with leadership will ultimately measure our success by how creatively and effectively we can implement this model on a societal scale.

In his recent masterpiece, *Managing People Is Like Herding Cats,* Warren Bennis tells us that "we need some fresh faces and voices to renew organizations and regain advantage, but we can't seem to find any." His big question is: "Where have all the leaders gone?" (Bennis, 1999, p. 25). I am quite certain that they are in school or on the soccer field. I further suggest that it is not fresh faces but mentors and resources to nurture a new crop of leaders that are in short supply. The future of society depends upon healthy, productive young people prepared to become competent, ethical leaders; the Tree Musketeers story is but one indication that we can do this. But before every young person has the drive and opportunity to make a difference as I did, we must alter some of our fundamental assumptions and practices about leadership.

- Inspire, empower, and support youth leaders—share, don't patronize; coach, don't teach; mentor, don't lead.
- Take youth seriously as leaders—allow them to lead.
- Trust the youth-led process—lose the traditional thinking that leadership belongs to gray-haired men with positional power.

The most vibrant and powerful leaders among us may be the smallest. From grassroots social services to national movements, kids can accomplish remarkable feats. But adults are charged with the most solemn duties of all: providing opportunities, mentoring, and allowing young people to become active leaders in creating their futures. The unfamiliar process of allowing youth to lead social change can begin quite simply.

The Tree Musketeers Story

I was eight years old when the world and my place in it turned inside-out. It was a lovely Friday afternoon in 1987 that my Brownie Girl Scout troop met to discuss an upcoming camping trip. This was not Brownie business as usual, however, because severe drought assailed California at the time and we faced the difficult decision of whether to use paper plates or our traditional tin dishes on this outing. Since water was going to be difficult to come by at the campsite, paper plates seemed like the natural choice. My mother, our Girl Scout Leader, wanted us to make an informed decision as we laid out the pros and cons of disposable and reusable. She mentioned, almost off-handedly, that using excess paper wastes trees.

"Wastes trees?" someone asked. "What does that mean?"

"Don't trees just grow back?" another demanded.

My mother was not a scientist or an environmentalist, but she told us what she knew about rainforest and old growth deforestation. Searching her memory for bits of information about the effects of forest destruction, she related a conversation she had had with someone on a plane about the hole in the ozone layer.

"If there aren't enough trees to fight pollution, it will all go up into the atmosphere and eat away the ozone layer. If the ozone layer isn't there to block the harsh rays of the sun," she concluded, "then the surface of the Earth will get very hot. Someone told me that scientists are already looking for ways for the human race to live underground after the atmosphere is gone."

It was as if a dark cloud had settled upon our little circle. Stifled by despair I looked around the room at twelve brows furrowed just like mine as each of us created a mental picture of dark underground caverns beneath the burning surface of the Earth. One of the girls cleared her throat and finally asked the question:

"Can you play soccer underground?"

We all agreed that it seemed unlikely. I sunk back into my gloom until a brilliant idea cut through like a sunbeam:

"We should plant a tree!"

On May 9, 1987, thirteen of us sat around the freshly planted Marcie the Marvelous Tree, dreaming up a plan to save the environment. A skinny, rootbound sycamore planted in the middle of a barren strip of city land, she was our hope for the future. Marcie had only a dozen or so leaves at the time, but I remember envisioning how majestic she would grow, how much good this tree would do for the environment, how she would inspire people around the world to protect our Earth.

Planting Marcie was my first political act and the single most empowering experience of my life. I felt, facing the global menaces of deforestation and ozone depletion, that my actions could make a difference in spite of the fact that I was just a little girl. I did not consciously recognize that I had discovered my mission; I rather sensed that there were no limits to what our passion and drive might accomplish.

My friends and I called ourselves Tree Musketeers and launched a crusade to heal our local environment that carried us to the White House to accept an award from President Reagan in little over a year. In 1990 my eleven-year-old colleagues and I incorporated Tree Musketeers as the world's first youth environmental organization and drafted bylaws and policies that ensured that people under age eighteen would forever sit in the driver's seat. With an increasing volunteer force and the tenacity of kids we took our urban forestry program to national dimensions in under five years. Journalists heralded the marked decrease in pollution and increase in property values that accompanied our activities, and word of how the Tree Musketeers' innovative youth-led programs were changing our community spread across the country. I was invited to make speeches at major events about youth leadership and activism and my message was usually the same: "Don't ever let anyone tell you that you can't make a difference. If we all work on our own little parts of the planet, then neighborhood by neighborhood, state by state, nation by nation we *will* change the world."

By 1997, when I attended the President's Summit for America's Future as a nonprofit delegate, we had developed a worldwide network of over two million young people. The President's Summit inspired us to dream of a massive, concerted effort to unify and quantify their work. The result was One In A Million: a campaign to empower a million kids to dedicate a million volunteer hours to planting a million trees by the end of 2000. The power of One In A Million was the simple act of planting a tree. A sycamore named

Marcie changed my life and I have been blessed with the opportunity to share that magic with millions of kids.

The Need: Inspire, Empower, and Support Young Leaders

I feel fortunate to have found my mission early because I got a head start on leadership, so to speak. Most young people, however, are not given the opportunity to make a difference, much less develop a cohesive vision of their roles in creating a healthy future.

It seems that everyone these days is talking about a leadership crisis whose tentacles extend to business, politics, criminal justice, education, and social services. Some say it is due to the human isolationism or narcissism of the technology age; others say apathy, corruption, unresponsive government, or increasing centralization of wealth and power in the hands of a small elite (Tolchin, 1996, chapter 1). Adherents to bootstrap empowerment claim that today's young people have it too easy. These are myths, or at best half-truths. The real problem with leadership today is the squandering of our most precious natural resource: our children. Youth are not engaged in the public discourse that breathes life into democracy, nor are they stakeholders in meaningful decision-making processes. Yet they have the most at stake.

The way that we in the social sector account for human time and talent offers an interesting perspective on the position of young people. Robert Putnam popularized the notion of social capital as an investable product of voluntary citizen action. Putnam warns that social capital has plummeted in recent decades as meaningful avenues for connectivity become increasingly endangered—impoverishing us as communities even as the economy booms (Putnam, 2000). Similarly, leadership educators rally around human capital as an organization's richest asset. Nonprofit organizations literally account for human capital, which translates into social capital, in the form of volunteer hours for which the Independent Sector each year assigns a standardized value. The dollar amount—$14.83 in 2000—is the same for black or white, thin or fat, small or tall, because every human being has the capacity to make a valuable investment of personal capital. But human capital is valuable only insofar as it is valued. Young people are not valued as leaders but as obedient followers. They are not nurtured as liquid assets but more often as liabilities. This is the leadership crisis.

The only viable reaction to Bennis's question, "Where have all the leaders gone?" is to nurture civic duty and social action in the grass roots by actively drawing young leaders into public dialogue—empower, don't lead. As it stands now young people have very few opportunities to make a difference in the world. They are, literally by age and figuratively by social attitude, alienated from the most fertile training grounds for leadership: business, politics, and social activism. In many cases, failure to develop leadership ability results from a sense of impotence that generates a reaction against a social system that is perceived as so autonomous and exclusionary that young people feel powerless to control and direct it. As we often say at Tree Musketeers, solving global problems seems to most kids like trying to put out a forest fire with a squirt gun.

I view America's appalling voter turnout rates as one of the most serious indications of a profound malaise implicating aspects of society far beyond politics. Alienation is not something that happens to people on their eighteenth birthday, it is a culture learned through the formative years. Using my work with young people as a measure, I believe that around the age of eight or nine, children start to realize that their world is larger than their home or school. They begin to understand that a mixing of people—parents, teachers, religious leaders—is a "community," and children want to be recognized as a part of that community. Instead of opting for volunteer service or other positive steps, kids without a support system may make their presence known in counterproductive ways.

Also at age eight or nine, the social and environmental perils spelling potential doom for life on Earth catch the attention of children. Such global crises are more overwhelming today than ever in human history, with the advent of threats such as global warming and nuclear world war. The menu of problems so daunts most adults that they leave the solutions to a handful of "radical" activists—imagine the paralyzed fear of children assured that they will "understand when they are older," watching as adults helpfully point fingers of blame. It should not surprise us that many young people feel powerless and lose hope.

An absence of hope for the future, meaningful outlets for social consciousness, and supportive role models are significant reasons today's youth opt for antisocial behavior. In our busy families and underfunded schools, mentoring is often insufficient to empower kids with the skills to become leaders. The need for leadership development for kids and society at large is underscored by the findings of a study (Search Institute, 1997) of 254,000 eleven- to eighteen-year-olds across the United States:

- 65 percent of seven- to fourteen-year-olds report they would like to connect with an adult they can trust and who respects them.
- 60 percent of 6th to 8th grade youth spend two or more hours per school day at home alone; 22 percent of violent juvenile crime occurs between 2 and 6 P.M. on school days; and 51 percent of middle school youth say available after-school programs do not interest them.
- 85 percent of high school students report little or no knowledge of how business works, while 69 percent want to launch their own business.
- 63 percent of middle and high school youth report not engaging regularly in volunteer service while 27 percent of high school seniors have never volunteered.

Although the realities of youth alienation may sadden or frighten us, that must not be all they do. We must change our definition of leadership to include young people. The bulk of contemporary leadership scholarship has centered on turning managers—maintainers of the status quo—into innovative leaders. The subject is important enough to warrant Tom Peters's call to action in his 1987 foreword to Jim Kouzes and Barry Posner's *The Leadership Challenge:* "The manager-to-leader revolution is not optional if you are interested in your children's well-being" (Peters, 1987, p. xiii). There is no question that we need to revolutionize the status quo to inspire leadership in all people, at all levels. But our children's well-being rests more squarely and urgently on their own empowerment as leaders with the capacities and resources to make a difference. The future of leadership centers around the question: Can we use this period of shifting economic and political paradigms and their concomitant uncertainty as a creative force for healthy change? Kouzes and Posner write that "people do their best when there's the chance to change the way things are" (1987, p. 29). Is this not the ideal time to inspire and nurture a new generation of leaders?

Overcoming Obstacles: Take Youth Leaders Seriously

The Disney Institute recently released a poll of eight- to fifteen-year-olds in which respondents were asked to define "the biggest challenge you faced in making a difference in your community." The top answer by an overwhelming margin was that kids are "not taken seriously by adults" (Disney Institute, 2000). Young leaders *need* grown-ups to take them seriously in order to make a difference. Most leaders with even a modicum of modesty recognize that leadership is not a solo performance and credit others—family, friends, colleagues, funders—for their success. Adult support in proper measure is the key ingredient to youth leadership. When I say "proper measure" I mean not so much as to be overpowering or the driving force, but not so little that kids are left to fend for themselves. Such a banal fact would be easy to translate into practice were it not for an acquired affliction that has yet to receive due attention from the psychiatric establishment.

I call it Adult Superiority Syndrome (ASS), and with a few years of adulthood under my belt I feel comfortable speaking frankly about its harmful effects on developing young leaders. These are the most salient symptoms:

- Imagining that capacities for vision, drive, passion, and social consciousness are directly proportional to candles on a birthday cake.
- Supposing that kids have vicarious intellects dragged around on parents' leashes waiting to be instructed.
- Assuming that kids are simply students—empty vessels sitting with hands folded in a classroom waiting to be filled with teacher's wisdom.

- Forgetting that in a short time young people will be mature people acting on the skills and principles developed during formative years.
- Not taking youth leaders seriously.

Jim Kouzes brought to my attention the most severe case of ASS yet reported. During a recent lecture he used my story as an example of how "Leadership Is Everyone's Business." After he related Tree Musketeers' history and my leadership accomplishments, a woman in the audience remarked: "I bet her mother drove her to do it." He was somewhat surprised at the choice of the word "drove," so Jim asked if he had heard the woman correctly. She said that he had. Jim replied: "My sense is that her mother supported her, but didn't drive her. I think Tara's drive comes from inside Tara."

When Jim told me that story I was hurt, but not surprised. I have come to take for granted that most adults find vision and initiative at such a young age incredible. I would make fun of that woman's attitude were it not so common and destructive. In a very real sense she sought to invalidate the work to which I dedicated my childhood, and it is that disregard for the potential of youth activism that bodes ill for the future of leadership. As long as adults are unwilling to recognize that young people can have tremendous capacities for social consciousness and service, those capacities will not be nurtured.

ASS affects all young people in a less visible but equally harmful way when every kid's need to be useful and contribute to the community is suppressed. That every person is driven in some sense by this need to "do something" we know from the common symptoms of at-risk or antisocial behavior. Traditionally, a child's only opportunities to excel on personal merit were through school or sports. But what of the millions of kids who master neither? A few will use their initial stumbling blocks as launching pads to tremendous success. It is up to us to provide the same inspiration and opportunity to the rest.

The only significant difference between empowering youth and adults as leaders is age. Just as grown-up leaders must be self-directed, create a compelling vision, and inspire others to be stakeholders in the mission, so must a young leader's drive and energy come from within to be at all effective. The Disney poll and the Tree Musketeers story challenge conventional wisdom that young people are apathetic and uninformed. Rather, they want to make a difference and adults fail to take them seriously. What could be more serious than an energetic, inspired person driven to change the world?

The Challenge: Trust the Youth-Led Process

Tree Musketeers was the first youth-led organization, but we were not alone in our passion to change our community. During the few years following our 1987 founding, unbeknownst to each other, children in far corners of the country launched similar efforts. A terribly exciting vision struck me while volunteering at an adult conference at age twelve. I wished out loud for just such an event for kids, and my words fell into the ears of someone with the USDA Forest Service. The government commissioned us to perform a feasibility study after which it invested in a huge experiment in youth leadership.

The prospects of this opportunity were at once thrilling and frightening. While we at Tree Musketeers had practiced pure youth leadership successfully for five years, this would be the first time we had taken the show on the road, so to speak. Would the concept be transferable, or had some sort of magic taken place in 1987 in El Segundo, California, that made it possible for youths to surface as effective leaders?

Undaunted by the importance of the answer to that question, we set the wheels in motion. With little or no knowledge about Tree Musketeers, twenty-nine people representing fourteen adult-youth teams accepted a telephone invitation to serve on the steering committee. The diverse group of people reflecting gender, age, ethnic, geographic, program, and organizational size diversity met for the first time only eight months before they would present the first "by and for kids" National Youth Environmental Summit. I cochaired the steering committee, and the only predetermined parameter was that youth leaders would make all the decisions.

Some adults in the group had almost no experience working with kids, and most were accustomed to leading young people rather than mentoring. Nonetheless, adult partners shared wisdom and opinions, and then sat back during decision-making sessions. Youth established group ground rules, determined the location, date, general format, and assumed chairmanship of empowered subcommittees to handle various aspects of the conference. With support of adult partners, they created budgets, timelines, and generally took charge of their areas of responsibility.

Achieving broad diversity among the leaders meant that some had never ventured out of their neighborhoods before families put them on airplanes for Los Angeles. Experience with meetings, teamwork, and being taken seriously by adults was indeed spotty. One boy who left an indelible impression came from New Haven, Connecticut, where he lived in a group home without a telephone. Joseph's adult partner revealed later that she had had to buy him shoes for the trip.

On the second day of our meeting I talked the group through the steps of developing a project plan, starting with the vision and finishing with assigned tasks. Midway through the discussion an adult partner who was executive director of a nonprofit raised her hand with a suggestion for a goal. The twelve-year-old Joseph corrected her: "Since that deals with specific numbers, it would make a better objective." Anyone who has ever served on a board of directors knows that months can be spent developing just a mission statement. Much to the amazement of adults present, the youth steering committee not only grasped the concepts but marched right through the entire planning process in half a day!

At age fourteen, I delivered the Youth Summit closing address before six hundred delegates from as far away as Guam and Russia. The media kept reporting that my dream had come true, but at that moment I realized that it was the vision of all those kids that had become reality.

By all measures, the Summit was a smashing success and the "Partners for the Planet" theme became an ongoing relationship between kids, adults, government, environmental groups, the private sector, and forestry professionals. Youth delegates pledged to lead projects at home in the environmental field of their choice. Kizzie, a young girl from Pennsylvania, provides one of the more poignant case studies of participants in the 1993 Youth Summit, and clearly answers the question as to whether inclination and ability of youth to lead is a transferable concept.

Kizzie had long worried about both the environment and the knowledge that some people in her community suffer lives of malnutrition and constant hunger. At one time she did not think she could do much about the problems that worried her. National Tree Trust grant funds bridged economic barriers and made it possible for Kizzie to attend the Summit, where she realized a sense of power: "I was amazed that kids could pull all that together. That summit really did something to me. It made me think, and now that I know other kids are doing all these projects, I feel different knowing I am not doing it by myself, that they are working with me." She went on to say, "I feel better about myself as a person. I see now that I can do more than I thought I could before. I now feel I have great power to change the world."

Kizzie and four other students comprising the Pulaski Middle School delegation brought the "Partners for the Planet" theme home to a community described by science teacher Bobby Stewart as "impoverished, with a bleak future, and an abundance of despair." Inspired by the National Summit, the young leaders committed to hosting a Regional Youth Summit.

Adults associated with delegate groups demonstrated that by supporting children in their own initiatives, or by creating a framework whereby children can channel and pool their efforts, they can facilitate youth leadership and empower kids to make a difference. It seems to me that children are visionaries by nature. To translate those visions into effective leadership, adult supporters need to polish their managerial skills.

My professor and mentor Warren Bennis writes famously about the differences between a leader and a manager. "The manager administers; the leader innovates." "The manager has his or her eye on the bottom line; the leader has his or her eye on the horizon." "The manager maintains; the leader develops." "The manager asks how and when; the leader asks what and why" (Bennis, 1999, p. 63). Putting aside the negative distinctions (we would not, for instance, want the adult partner to be a "copy" or someone dedicated to the status quo!), this model applies perfectly to my business relationship with my mother at Tree Musketeers and to the larger project of empowering youth as leaders.

In her own right my mother, Gail, is a leader—one of the best I have known—who has been well recognized for her accomplishments among peers. But when it comes to supporting my work and that of our younger executives she slips comfortably into a managerial role. The young leader is first and foremost the visionary, the inspiration, the person with the "big picture," the driving force without which a fledgling organization cannot survive. The manager deals in rudiments and competency, ensuring that the leader's vision fits with the bottom line and that the supply shelf is stocked. I certainly could not have incorporated Tree Musketeers, drafted a municipal waste management plan, or raised $500,000 for our national youth summit without my mom's support. But never in a million years would she have done those things without my urging. For years she thought Tree Musketeers was just a phase I would grow out of so she could return to business as usual. But as I felt a meaningful sense of accomplishment, my passion and drive—and my mother's commitment to the vision—only intensified. It is a testament to her leadership abilities that she has been such an effective manager.

I can count stories like mine on my fingers—so short is the supply of youth leadership resources—but at least there are that many. I was not unusual for my concern and determination to make a difference. Almost every day I get a letter or call from a child expressing a sophisticated understanding of the environmental perils facing us and asking how to go about making a difference. I personally coach dozens of these young people and attempt to put them in touch with the resources they need to succeed. Some of them launch very impressive programs or start their own nonprofits. Some of them fall by the wayside for lack of support or as the usual demands of adolescence consume them. The young participants in the Disney poll cited earlier had already taken on leadership roles, had already learned that every small or tall person can be a force of one, had developed some sort of vision. If we think about the nature of their biggest challenge, not being taken seriously, it is amazing that they accomplished what they did. I am still amazed that I was fortunate enough to have all of the ingredients for successful activism at my fingertips: an urgent environmental need, a clear vision, a strong adult support system, a community that loves to invest in its children, an army of enthusiastic peers, and a story that drew media like a magnet.

I use my story as an example because it is the one I know best. The point, however, is not the environment, nor is it to run out and start a youth leadership organization. The point is that we, as leaders, must plan for the future by investing now in the freshest, richest pool of human capital: our young people. Leadership can be learned. And if leadership ability generates vision, competence, virtue, credibility, authenticity, and innovation, don't we desire those qualities in our young as well as our old? Don't we owe it to them and to our own legacies?

Joseph and Kizzie are but two examples of how becoming a leader can redirect the lives of children from all socioeconomic backgrounds. I firmly believe that the Tree Musketeers kids who have assumed my role at the helm of the organization are all but immune from the negative pressures which destroy many a young life . . . all because they are leaders whose place in society is defined by their passion and mission. I am also convinced that empowering our youth with the knowledge and tools to effect change in volunteer service, business, and politics will diminish juvenile crime, dropout, and pregnancy rates while infusing communities with investable social capital. Politically we can expect to rejuvenate voter turnout and expand the public discourse in integrity, vitality, and scope.

The question is how we will empower our young people to lead. Although I do not have comprehensive answers, I do have some ideas:

- Develop a new definition of leadership that includes young people.
- Create a new conception of young people that includes leadership.
- Offer youth meaningful opportunities to become leaders through education- and action-oriented roles in the civil, political, and business sectors.
- Recognize young people as valuable stakeholders and active members of communities with decision-making power.
- Take kids' dreams seriously and offer them personal and institutional support.
- Be a mentor and a manager—not a teacher or a leader—of youth initiatives; remember that empowerment comes from a sense of accomplishment embraced by children as their own.
- Trust the youth-led process—it may look and feel strange but the results will be phenomenal!

I will leave you with the story of Ryan, Tree Musketeers' immediate past president. He is my inspiration and hope for the future. Twelve-year-old Ryan came into my office by order of his middle school principal, with ten hours of "volunteer" service as a last-resort punishment for chronic misbehavior. Within a couple of weeks he decided he liked working in an office for kids, and set up a regular schedule to volunteer—voluntarily. We have since worked closely together on letter writing, public speaking, and leadership skills. A year and a half ago he made his first speech to the City Council, broadcast for all of El Segundo to watch. As I sat in the audience watching him deliver the speech we had rehearsed over and over, I was overcome with admiration and pride. He was so good! When he finished, everyone cheered, and Mayor Mike Gordon lauded him as the "future Mayor of El Segundo"—Ryan just beamed. This is a boy who had never done well in school, who was labeled as a bully and a troublemaker. Ryan became the chairman of Tree Musketeers' Youth Management Team, a dogged volunteer recruiter, and eventually president of the organization.

Ryan's story is so powerful because it is evidence that we can indeed change the direction of young lives. Their futures sprawl before them, and there are as many healthy paths as there are pressures to lead a child astray. Failing to empower bright, eager young people to be leaders is one of the surest ways to discourage them. I am gratified to have created a forum that allows kids to succeed on their own terms. We must all commit to create opportunities that invite children like Ryan to simultaneously achieve personal success and contribute to the public good. Most of the kids I mentor would not have started their own nonprofit organizations—it is a strange child indeed that would take interest in bylaws and employee benefits packages! But each and every one of our youth directors began volunteering because they wanted to do something important for the world. What we do is provide the place, the tools, and the vehicle for them to develop as leaders.

With kids like Ryan bursting with untapped potential, the future of leadership is bright. We know where the leaders are. Now we must live up to the promise of youth leadership.

Chapter Seventeen

Seeking a Newer World

Edward W. Headington

There is an old Chinese curse that runs, "May you live in interesting times." Whether we choose to believe it or not, we live in interesting times. We live in a time of incredible economic growth and rising globalization. We live in an era of increased personal wealth and the rising tide of democracy. Finally, we live on the verge of new frontiers—searching for life on Mars, completing the genome project, and exploring the darkest depths of our oceans. But while we pause for a moment to take inventory of how far we have come, so we also remind ourselves of our unfinished work—improving the human condition. Global warming is no longer a theory. AIDS is ravaging the African continent. Nuclear tension continues to mount in Kashmir. Old hatreds simmer in the Middle East. The duality in which we live—a time of unparalleled uncertainty coupled with unprecedented creativity—leads some to action and others to apathy. Will Generation X meet these challenges and assume the mantle of leadership? What will be the catalyst? Indeed, future generations will judge us on how well we seized the good times and progressed along the great democratic journey. We cannot solve all the problems of the world, let alone the many that plague our nation. But we can take comfort in the fact that action can be taken on many and a few might be solved. And we remind ourselves, as Albert Camus once observed, "Perhaps we cannot prevent the world from being a place in which children are tortured. But we can reduce the number of tortured children. And if you don't help us, who else in the world can help us do this?"

For students of history and those inspired by political leaders alike, the life and legacy of Robert F. Kennedy stands as a testament to what is possible to a transforming leader. Throughout his life and especially in his later years, Kennedy chanted the activist mantra: "This is unacceptable. We can do better." His ability to take action, hold others accountable, and commit himself to standards no one else of his era could possibly match still inspires. He put his creed in his deed and paid tribute to Henry Ward Beecher's adage, "Hold yourself responsible to a higher standard than anybody else expects of you." In 1967, he released *To Seek a Newer World,* a collection of speeches that served as summation of where he had been, what he had seen, and where he could take the nation. What is important for me was his effective use of Tennyson's refrain "'Tis not too late to seek a newer world." Like Kennedy, I see value in the refrain and use these words as inspiration and also as the theme for my meditations and ruminations on Generation X.

As we look at the dawn of the twenty-first century, we can hardly resist taking a step back and reflecting on the evolution of our society—especially in the field of leadership. From Max Weber's charisma to James MacGregor Burns's moral leadership to Ron Heifetz's adaptive leadership, we have seen immense change not only in how we view our leaders but also in what we expect from them. For many, the study of leadership is both a private and a public journey. We learn much by poring over what has been written and said on the subject and by speaking with those who are knowledgeable. In a sense, the private journey is potential energy. It gives one the potential to see things differently and sheds light on the destiny that awaits us all. But only by action in the public sense does this potential turn into kinetic energy and we truly become full-fledged practitioners of leadership.

At the beginning of my academic journey, I was fortunate to study at the feet of two masters, Warren Bennis and Steven Sample. Indeed, while my tenure with them was brief—only a semester—they gave new meaning to William Butler Yeats's notion that "Education is not the filling of a pail, but the lighting of a fire." The fire that they helped ignite led me to further my study of leadership and it continues unabated to this day. One of the primary texts of the course was Bennis's own *On Becoming a Leader* (1994). Two major points drawn from the book were that leaders are made, not born, and that leaders are people who can express themselves fully—who they are, what their strengths and weaknesses are, and how to maximize their strengths while compensating for their weaknesses. Also drawn from the text was the metaphor of mountain climbers—that is, mountain climbers map out their strategy from the top and work their way down, not the other way around. This metaphor, coupled with exposure to Garry Wills's notion of certain trumpets, accounted for my approach and abiding interest in politics and the study of leadership. The course itself showed me how to tailor ambition, favor boldness, and develop latent leadership skills.

Following my studies at the University of Southern California, I went to work in the public sector—first for Los Angeles Mayor Richard Riordan and then for California Assemblymember Scott Wildman. In the spring of 1999, I left Los Angeles for Washington, D.C., to attend George Washington University's Graduate School of Political Management (GSPM) and further my study of leadership and love for politics.

At the GSPM, I began my study of leadership with earnest. After reading Ron Heifetz's *Leadership Without Easy Answers,* James MacGregor Burns's *Leadership,* and others, I reevaluated my interest in running for office. Simply wanting to run was not enough. I realized one must understand the why: to effect change, to mobilize a community, to fight for a cause, and so on. I was also moved by the work of Bill Shore in *Revolution of the Heart* and *The Cathedral Within.* Beyond the terrific metaphors of his book titles, Shore shares wonderful anecdotes and leaves his reader with the desire to build on what he has written. With respect to my preconceived notions of leadership and its relationship to holding office, he really opened my eyes to the concept of being an agent for change without holding office—the servant leadership model. Simplistically, I had always thought of elective office as the engine of change in society. From his description of what is being done with community-wealth enterprises, I was inspired to go out and do something on my own or aid in the efforts of those who were already out there on the front lines.

Defining leadership is a generational endeavor. While the traits and attributes can be timeless, each generation has to filter the meaning through its own experience and collective anchors. Take for example, the anchors between Generation X and the three generations that preceded us. According to a study done by the Pew Research Center, the five most common anchors for Generation Xers are the assassination attempt on President Reagan, the explosion of the *Challenger* space shuttle, the fall of the Berlin Wall, the Gulf War, and the Oklahoma City bombing. Contrast these five with those of the baby boomer set and higher. For the most part, they are World War II, the assassination of President Kennedy, the assassination of Martin Luther King, the landing on the moon, and the *Challenger* explosion.

Many thinkers and social critics decree that today's young adults—Generation X—are perhaps the most disengaged in U.S. history. Where the generation before us is estimated at 80 million, we comprise about 50 million. From the years in which we were born—1965 to 1979—we have witnessed a government that has neither undertaken bold initiatives nor defined our long-term purpose as a nation. Many point out that not only are we less civically and politically inclined, we are also more apt to find self-fulfillment in the private sector rather than the public sector. In a similar vein, the social activism that marked our parents' coming of age is believed to have atrophied with ours. We have no leadership icons and are perceived to have less allegiance to our country or either political party. Where previous generations had Roosevelt, Truman, Eisenhower, and Kennedy to admire, Generation Xers have Nixon, Ford, Carter, Bush, and Clinton—leaders known more for their weaknesses than their strengths. But just as a 1960s-era leader reminds us, we should think anew as the case is new. Rather than accept traditional measures of civic responsibility, Generation Xers seek other ways to effect change and define leadership. In the past, community service was done through institutions. Now we see that Generation Xers want more direct action and one-on-one service that allows us to practice our ideals every day. In a 1998 survey by Peter Hart, it was noted that young people have built a vision of leadership that reflects our principles—sensitivity and cooperation over charisma, individual empowerment over institutions, inclusive and bottom-up decision making over top-down. This new vision of leadership means working with others to offer our services directly and reaching out to others from diverse backgrounds to find new solutions. What's more, we seek to begin with these solutions at the local level rather than wait for institutions to respond.

E. J. Dionne Jr. (1998) of the *Washington Post* also has noted the changed emphasis of today's young adults and has called us the "Reform Generation." Dionne also underscores that we value both community and self-reliance and try to balance the two. The question he poses, though, is whether our community-mindedness will transfer over to the political arena. To date, we have viewed politics as selfish and government-led efforts to respond to societal problems as ineffective. However, he argues that to become engaged citizens, which is the ideal of our democracy, we must marry the world of service and politics.

For the moment, the focus of Generation Xers is on community service and away from conventional politics. Ideology and partisan wrangling in our political system turns many away from the political arena and young people have chosen to "live their politics" by going into the streets of their neighborhoods and volunteering their time and effort. Incidentally, the first presidential election to see eighteen-year-olds vote was 1972 and there was a turnout of 42 percent among adults between the ages of eighteen and twenty-four. By 1996, the number had dropped to below 30 percent and many pundits and scholars suggest the number will dip even further in the 2000 race. The Center for the Study of the American Electorate has noted that overall voting for voting-age adults dropped from 55 percent to 49 percent. But as a voting bloc, our nation's youth has declined the most. Nevertheless, when there are more reasons to vote (that is, change versus status quo, viable third-party candidates), Generation Xers do turn out to vote as they did in 1992—about 38 percent.

Ted Halstead (1999), president of New America, notes that there is a general decline in social trust among Generation Xers and more exhibition of materialistic and individualistic tendencies. The result of these tendencies may contribute to social incohesion, and Halstead suggests that we should not forget Alexis de Tocqueville's prophetic lament that these isolating tendencies will weaken our communal bonds—the same bonds that offer meaning and force to our notions of national identity and the common good. Generation Xers see challenges in the fiscal, social, and environmental areas but do not see any leadership provided in the political arena. There is no reasonable expectation that the political establishment will address this agenda—fiscal prudence, economic populism, social investment, campaign reform, shared sacrifice, and environmental conservation—so we attempt to do them in our own individual way.

Halstead points out that the introduction of digital democracy may serve to further engage Generation Xers, but that until we flex our political muscles many of the issues on our agenda will not be addressed, let alone fixed. He also points out that if we look at the cyclical view of America's political history, we can see patterns whereby the demise of civic responsibility and political activism has been coupled with widespread individualism, weakened institutions, and political disengagement. The upshot of this cycle is that such periods have also brought forth new political agendas that forced our political parties to focus on new priorities. Focusing on different priorities forges new coalitions—and this could go a long way toward reinvigorating our political system. The question is whether or not we can develop enough critical mass to have our agenda recognized and prioritized.

If the Annual UCLA Freshman Survey performed by the Higher Education Institute is any indicator, this mass may take some time to build. While volunteerism has continued to climb in high school years—currently 75.3 percent of freshmen said they did volunteer work in their senior year—long-term goals for activism are on the decline. The percentage of those who felt it was important to "influence social values" dropped to 35.8 percent. Furthermore, the percentage of those who want to participate in community action programs has fallen to 21.3 percent, the lowest in a decade. The founding director of the survey, UCLA education professor Alexander Astin, suggested that an expansion of "service-learning programs" might be the prudent course of action for college officials to take.

Former congressman, White House chief of staff, and Panetta Institute director Leon Panetta has also noticed these trends. Panetta (2000) says that although "students are very tuned in to public issues and community involvement, they're just not expressing that interest through participation in electoral politics." This was in response to a study done by the Mellman Group for the Institute that found that college students have little interest in politics or political careers but nonetheless are remarkably civic-minded and public-spirited. Unlike Halstead and others, who note that Generation Xers' lack of engagement stems from a greater sense of cynicism, alienation, and other causes, the survey suggested that this was not the case. To be sure, students are less likely to vote or to follow political news than adults overall, and less likely than earlier generations to pursue a career in politics or government, this is because their interests lie elsewhere. For many, it is simply irrelevant to their lives and the issues of concern. A career in "public service" tends to be seen in terms of work in education or with nonprofit organizations.

In a recent issue of the *California Journal,* Noel Brinkerhoff (1999) reflected on the unknown quality of Generation X. Generation Xers are reaching a time of political maturity as thirty- and forty-somethings while at the same time remaining more detached from politics than any preceding generation. Brinkerhoff notes, as others have, that Generation Xers emphasize that volunteerism helps refute the notion that we are a lost generation and that California, as the third-youngest state, will be the political trendsetter for our political engagement.

Mary McGrory (2000) of the *Washington Post* found similar findings in her exploration of Generation X and its involvement with the McCain 2000 presidential race. In trying to discover the attitudes of the potential 25 million Generation X voting bloc, McGrory spoke with students about their involvement in politics. She found that while young people can get instant gratification by helping to feed the disadvantaged, they cannot by turning to the ballot. While other groups had big increases this year in the presidential primaries, turnout among eighteen- to twenty-nine-year olds remained low—effectively demonstrating that young people still have little interest in presidential politics.

There is reason to believe, however, that young people would turn out to vote if candidates made the effort to reach out to them—as Clinton did in 1992—donning shades and playing the sax on the *Arsenio Hall* show, appearing on MTV, and so on. For the foreseeable future, the target of campaigns will be seniors and aging baby boomers because they have the highest turnout numbers. Third Millennium (TM), an advocacy group for Generation

Xers, also noted this trend in a recent research project called "Neglection 2000" (Bagby, 2000). Richard Thau, TM's executive director, noted the irony of political targeting. Candidates ignore young people because they don't go to the polls; young people feel they are ignored, so they don't go to the polls. What this means is that issues important to seniors—Social Security, prescription drugs—will be given a higher priority than those of Generation Xers who have no political voice. According to the National Association of Secretaries of State (NASS), 25 percent of Americans aged eighteen to twenty-four cited lack of information for not deciding to vote, while only 10 percent cited no interest at all (Thornburgh, 1999). To those candidates like Jesse Ventura who can mobilize that 25 percent—nearly 80 percent of the eighteen-year-olds who registered voted—victory may be within reach.

Many cite the lack of life-or-death issues like civil rights and the Vietnam War as the major reason for Generation Xers' disengagement. To be sure, that is one factor. But another factor to note is the presence of high-profile political scandals in recent decades. Combined, they account for two powerful forces in moving Generation X away from the public service model. As has been stated earlier, another reason is that Generation Xers want to see tangible and timely results for their efforts. Paul Light (1999) notes in his recent book, *The New Public Service,* that even for students who wish to pursue a career in public service, it is no longer their first choice. What's more, there are reports from leading public policy and administration schools that suggest that recruitment from private contractors has increased significantly. As Light points out, with signing bonuses, better entry-level pay and benefits, and more opportunity for rapid advancement offered from these contractors, the allure of public service has considerably dimmed.

The Oracle at Delphi is not available to today's young crop of leaders. There is no "leadership Shangri-La" we can go to, as Bennis reminds his students and readers. Shying away from political careers, Generation Xers are living their politics. We effect change by volunteering and involving ourselves in the community. The model for this type of leadership appears to be what social entrepreneur Bill Shore (1999) calls the servant leader. It is servant leadership and community leadership that is supplanting national leadership. Shore notes that it used to be that young people went into politics to change the world and now are going other places to do it. It does not have a name yet; rather, it has many names. This will likely be the trend in the years ahead until a major event draws us back into the political system. The current shift from political activism to direct community service causes many observers to question our commitment to a robust democracy. But perhaps our servant model will take our nation in a new political direction. The present situation is like that of the qawwal music of Nusrat Fateh Ali Khan. It starts off slow and simple, gradually intensifies, and then works up into a crescendo that overwhelms the listener.

If we believe that times are interesting now, what the future portends is breathtaking. We will face uncertainty and even danger, but then we will also bear witness to the greatest burst of creativity our civilization has ever seen. What is important, however, is that we demand of ourselves the same high expectations other generations raised for themselves. Following are just a few of the challenges and new frontiers.

Global Warming. Despite a shrinking chorus of naysayers, global warming is a reality. Coastal cities and nations like Bangladesh stand to suffer the most. The causes are not in doubt, but the solutions are problematic—especially here in the United States. The ubiquitous sports utility vehicle is indicative of our irreverence to the effects of fossil fuel consumption. No one wants to make the hard choices and demand more stringent emission standards. Standards that do emerge are introduced incrementally and are a far cry from what needs to be done. The bottom line is that we need to move beyond the internal combustion engine and live more efficiently. If we do not, things will continue to get worse. Of course, ingenuity will intervene and new technologies will lessen the effects. But they are a Band-Aid approach to a problem that goes unresolved. We will need leaders who are willing to take unpopular stands and do what is right for the common good.

Vegetarianism. More and more people are making educated decisions when it comes to their food intake, but the sheer number of people who eat animals is staggering. In the twenty-first century, we are going to see a major shift from a flesh-based diet to a plant and grain–based diet. Without going into the cruelty-to-animals argument, our choice to eat animal flesh—meat—is entirely irresponsible. First, the waste produced from slaughterhouses is polluting our streams and rivers. Second, like cigarettes, drugs, and alcohol, meat is toxic. We will not die immediately—notwithstanding breakouts of *E. coli* variants—but over a lifetime our life span will be shortened and our quality of life diminished. Third, there would be no food shortage if we moved off the flesh-based diet. To be sure, there is the political aspect to contend with, but grain would be far more abundant. If people still wanted flesh as a staple of their diet, perhaps a "human resources" cue from the 1970s sci-fi movie *Soylent Green* might be appropriate. Finally, and perhaps the most important, we are tearing out the lungs of our planet—the rainforests, to make room for cattle grazing.

This assessment is clearly out of mainstream thinking, but it will take patience, persistence, and articulation to remove the blindfold most people have when it comes to their eating habits. With the Internet to increase awareness, growing concern for personal health, and leadership, vegetarianism will continue to grow.

Deep Sea Exploration. Space exploration captures the hearts and minds of Hollywood and addicts of the Discovery Channel, but the planet still offers a frontier we have yet to fully explore—our ocean depths. As we develop new technologies, the secrets of our blue planet are being unearthed. Incidentally, only 5 percent of the ocean is even penetrated by light from the surface—and most of the fish and other creatures we are familiar with come from this region. A whole new world opens up as we descend toward and to the ocean floor. In fact, more life actually exists below the ocean surface than on land—some scientists suggest around 100 million species. Lying deeper than Mt. Everest is tall, the deep sea is still virtually unknown. The discovery that giant tube worms living around hydrothermal vents can survive through chemosynthesis, as opposed to photosynthesis, has made the search for life on Mars and Jupiter's moon Europa all the more invigorating.

Deep Space Exploration. Until the Hubbell space telescope sent back stunning pictures of our universe's origins and the Mars space probe captured new shots of the red planet, funding and interest in NASA had been lagging. The debate between using resources for domestic problems versus searching the stars is an important one. We must never lose sight of the government's role and ability to alleviate suffering, but we must also commit ourselves to searching the stars for life and local planets for answers.

Although it may not happen in the lifetime of Generation X, or even their children for that matter, we will discover that we are not alone in the universe. When looking at the conditions necessary for life—life as we know it—it is a virtual mathematical certainty. Discovering water on a nearby planet or moon is only the beginning. What will be interesting to behold is how marginal our national squabbles will become when compared to meeting an entirely unknown extraterrestrial life. The internecine fighting might subside and the commonality of humankind could rise. Perhaps then, a world federation, a world congress, or a revitalized United Nations—a suggestion anathema to many America-Firsters—will not be such a utopian idea and the world's many civilizations will unite.

The foundation for understanding leadership has already been laid by Burns, Bennis, Heifetz, and several others. We study them, and the past for that matter, to understand the present and help shape the future. The demands of the twenty-first century will be different from those of the twentieth. But that does not mean we molt our previous assumptions. We should hold ourselves to the candle of Eugene Delacroix's words on what inspires great artists: "It is not new ideas, but their obsession with the idea that what has already been said is still not enough." Value-laden and transformational leadership will always be in demand—just not always in the political context. As James MacGregor Burns (2000) notes in a recent piece in the *Washington Post,* leaders in science, technology, education, entertainment, finance, and the media are pursuing their own transforming visions. Perhaps the route taken by Tufts University will become the new standard of measurement. The Tufts University College of Citizenship and Public Service degree was created in the hopes of creating responsible citizens rather than offering mere job training. It is not unconceivable that the cadres of service leaders the program produces can match Bill Shore's idea of the servant leader.

As Generation X commentator Ted Halstead suggests, America's next major political cycle will begin with some sort of galvanizing event. Whether this comes in the form of economic recession, widespread social disruption, or a foreign policy crisis, no one can foretell. This may lead to increased political activism and social engagement. For the time being, we can take solace in the fact that as much as we may be turned off by national politics and cynical about the role of government, we do care about the world and the communities we live in. We embrace a new style of leadership that connects and engages people rather than divides them, that emphasizes the "we" over the "I."

To meet the aforementioned challenges and new frontiers and avoid other potential crises, we have to find ways to marry our want for wealth with our desire to serve the common good. The extent to which we build that bridge will determine how effective Generation Xers will be in chanting the activist's mantra and meeting our responsibility to improve the human condition. All of us want to build the cathedral within, and Shore has outlined the way to do it. We can become part of something larger than ourselves and meet our material comfort level. The servant leaders of the future will take us to places we have never gone before as a polity; perhaps by recognizing that we must *be* the change we wish to see in the world, we can lead by example. The road will not be smooth and breaking out of the shackles of contentment and mediocrity will not be easy, but it can be done. A galvanizing event may do it for us or we might do it ourselves. The key will be to stay committed to this new ideal and bear in mind the words of Robert F. Kennedy, who once observed, "Few will have the greatness to bend history itself. But each of us can work to change a small portion of events. And in the total of all those acts, will be written the history of this generation."

Part Six

Some Closing Thoughts

Chapter Eighteen

The Leadership Challenges of the Next Generation

Gretchen M. Spreitzer
Thomas G. Cummings

What if Warren Bennis is right, that the future has no shelf life? What if what worked yesterday will no longer work tomorrow—what can we do? Some are likely to respond with paralysis. Others, like the leading thinkers in this book, view this inevitability as a challenge—an opportunity for personal and organizational growth and change—engaging our imaginations and getting our creative juices flowing. Those who can foresee these challenges and respond to them confidently and creatively will have a huge competitive advantage over those who hide their heads in the sand or remain indifferent.

The leading thinkers in this book give us reason for optimism. Inspired by Bennis's uncanny ability to predict important shifts in our environment almost a generation before they happen, they do the same for the next generation of leaders. They provide important clues about how leaders in the twenty-first century can maintain or even increase their shelf life. In this concluding chapter, we synthesize across the chapters to evoke some wisdom for leaders of the new millennium.

Setting the Stage for Leadership: Making Sense of the Context

All of the authors agree on the importance of context. Today's leaders face an environment characterized by uncertainty and unpredictability. The specific context a leader faces is hard to grasp because it's like stepping into a river—you can never step into the same place twice because its flow is constantly changing. So an important job of the leader will be to continuously scan the environment and try to make sense of it. Leaders who find comfort and security in stability will have difficulty surviving. Instead, tomorrow's leaders must find comfort in the mantra, "change is a constant." Of course, not all contextual changes will have implications of the same magnitude. Some are more critical to the next generation of leaders than others. Drawing from the chapters, we identify several particularly impactful contextual influences.

The Global Village

Today, not only do Fortune 500 giants like Ford and Coca Cola span the globe, increasing numbers of middle and small organizations also have markets, if not operations, in distant corners of the world. The fall of communist and totalitarian regimes around the world has led to more open competition and free trade. North American and European companies are taking advantage of cheaper labor markets for manufacturing and production.

The globalization of the marketplace also has implications for how work gets done. Global leaders must learn how to manage virtually with direct reports who work and live around the world. For example, high-tech product development often relies on virtual teams operating in 24/7 mode, taking advantage of time-zone differences around the world. At the end of their work day, American engineers hand over their work to Indian engineers, who then at the end of their work day hand their work to Israeli engineers so that the team literally never sleeps.

Global leadership challenges include how to manage the inevitable cross-cultural differences that surface as employees with different cultural values and native tongues attempt to work closely together. And global leaders must learn to mesh different international business models and political systems. For example, the merger of the German company Daimler-Benz and the American company Chrysler meant that executives had to come to terms with dramatically different pay practices (with Americans making more than double what the Germans were making) and regulatory environments (German law requires six weeks of annual vacation and labor representation on the Board of Directors). One advantage that leaders of the next generation may have is that they have grown up in a global business environment, making it more nearly second nature for them to deal with.

Demographic Diversity

In addition to the ethnic diversity that comes from globalization, the aging of the workforce and increasing numbers of women in the workforce are dramatically changing the face of tomorrow's organizations. Caucasians are predicted to be a minority in the United States in the next twenty years. Moreover, tomorrow's leaders of the next generation are more likely to be women or minority members themselves. Headington argues that generational differences between Generation X employees and baby boomers will exacerbate the potential for conflict between different groups in the workplace. Greenberg-Walt and Robertson acknowledge that these dynamics become particularly dicey when Generation Xers are leading baby-boomer employees.

Tomorrow's leaders will need to come up with innovative ways to satisfy the differing needs and preferences of a diverse workforce. They will need to go beyond the kind of cafeteria rewards systems that are popular today. Diversity also increases the potential for conflict in the workplace, so leaders will need strong conflict-management skills to create the teams that are so important in the contemporary work environment.

Technology, E-Commerce, and the Information Superhighway

Most of the authors touched on the critical impact of technology. Because of technology, Davenport notes, an increasing percentage of today's workers are "knowledge workers." From the ubiquity of cell phones, pagers, e-mail, and faxes, leaders are literally never out of touch with the workplace and people—for better or worse. This may increase the flow of information but may also reduce the time available for renewal and reflection, which are critical for effective leadership.

Though computers have been around for decades, their potential is only beginning to be tapped through the Information

Superhighway. Through the Web, employees have cutting-edge knowledge at their fingertips twenty-four hours a day, around the world. This makes sharing knowledge across the organization easier. And the World Wide Web opens up new business models and opportunities. As Kerr notes, General Electric—perhaps the most successful traditional organization in history—is reinventing itself as an Internet company, becoming truly boundaryless across divisions and functions and with customers.

The New Employment Relationship

As Bennis prophesied many years ago, we are seeing the beginnings of a new social contract in our temporary society. Lawler refers to this as the "era of human capital." Skilled workers are in high demand, and companies are scrambling to hire and retain them. Yet, at the same time, job security and lifetime employment are historical artifacts. Employee loyalty and commitment are being challenged in an age where downsizing is the norm, even for companies trying to grow. Taking their place is the notion of employability, giving employees training in cutting-edge skills so they will be marketable should they need or desire to find alternative employment. The challenge for contemporary leaders is how to retain and motivate top talent.

Continuing Business Consolidation

In many industries today, consolidation through mergers and acquisitions is the name of the game. Kerr mentions how General Electric acquires over a hundred companies a year. Who would have predicted that household names like AlliedSignal, GTE, and J.P. Morgan would literally vanish from the radar screen as they have merged with or been acquired by competitors? In some industries, consolidation has left only two major competitors—like Boeing and Airbus in large aircraft productions.

Leaders must be savvy in the skills necessary to integrate organizations—bringing together distinct organizational cultures and business systems to work as a coherent whole. Handy suggests that leaders must work hard to keep the entrepreneurial spirit alive even as start-up "fleas" are acquired by large-scale, traditional "elephants." Even in cases of mergers of alleged equals, we are increasingly likely to see what Greenberg-Walt and Robertson refer to as "shared leadership and the devolving CEO." In the wake of public failures of co-CEOs such as Sandy Weill and John Reed of Citigroup or Jurgen Schremp and Robert Eaton of Daimler-Chrysler, a big question is whether shared leadership is sustainable.

According to Weick, all these contextual changes mean that tomorrow's leaders will need to spend more time making sense of an uncertain environment. They must keep in close touch with their context and actively engage it if they are to learn and increase the complexity of their understanding. The safety of the executive suite is not the place for future leaders to spend their time; they need to be visible on the production floor, talking with customers, and interacting with other key stakeholders. Leaders need to be humble, admitting they often "do not know" all the answers themselves, and consequently they need the brainpower and insight of all employees. Saying "I don't know" is the beginning of a powerful discussion to engage others in the sensemaking process, not a sign of personal weakness.

Who Is the Leader of the Future?

Will the next generation of leaders look the same as successful leaders today? Not necessarily. As the glass ceiling shatters, tomorrow's leaders are more likely to be women or minorities—quite different from the demographic makeup of today's top leaders. Fortune 500 CEOs currently include women and minorities in the single digits. The authors in this volume note some important changes in the nature and capabilities of successful leaders of the next generation. These differences are discussed in subsequent sections.

Leaders Are Ubiquitous

Traditionally, leadership has been viewed as synonymous with the executive level of the organization. But there are many examples of senior executives who are not leaders. Lipman-Blumen discusses the case of Chainsaw Al Dunlap of Sunbeam, whose ego and ineptitude practically broke the organization—he certainly is not what we think of as a leader. At the same time, there are many examples of leaders who operate in the bowels of the organization or even outside of the formal chain of command. Church provides the compelling example of how even small children can be leaders. According to Kouzes and Posner, leadership goes beyond the size of one's budget or title. Many of the authors note that in today's complex business environment, leadership must come alive throughout the organization, not just at executive levels.

Leaders Act

Leadership is less and less a state of being (O'Toole refers to this as a trait) and more and more a process of doing—a set of actions. Weick shows how in today's business environment there is less time for reflection and processing. By acting, leaders discover and grow. Tomorrow's leaders will have less time for planning and forecasting. They will need to build the bridge as they walk on it. As Peters says, leaders "just say yes." Leaders don't make excuses for inaction. They are first movers and early adopters. They make things happen. Slater goes further to say that leaders need to get beyond protecting their own ego and allow themselves to experiment and explore. The rigidity that comes with ego protection keeps leaders from adapting to change. Csikszentmihalyi notes that leaders question everything and are dissatisfied with the answer, "but this is always how things have been done." They bring an element of creativity to a system. Most important, leaders get others to act—one of their most important jobs is to get members to act, test, argue, persist, innovate, and learn. They must model the behaviors they expect of others.

Leaders Fail

Next-generation leaders will need to fail frequently. If leaders aren't failing often enough, then they probably aren't stretching themselves enough. Given an environment of uncertainty, leaders learn through a process of trial and error. Weick and O'Toole both argue that leaders must admit they don't know all the answers and must seek the help of others. Effective leaders need to have many different experiments running simultaneously to see which ones will pan out, realizing that some—even most—will fail. Failure is perceived as inevitable and expected—as an opportunity for learning.

Leaders Are Agile

Traditional models of leadership emphasize the importance of creating a vision and setting direction. O'Toole agrees that contemporary leaders still must create vision and set direction but they must also be agile—recognizing the need to shift and adapt as needed. Weick argues that like fire jumpers, leaders need to travel light, avoiding the tendency to get weighed down by a lot of baggage or constrained by a history or tradition of doing things a certain way. Leaders need to be on their toes, to react with barely a moment's notice. In August 2000, Ford Motor Company's CEO Jacques Nasser was launching a process to reinvent Ford as an e-commerce company. But in a matter of days, he delegated this task to key VPs and turned his whole attention to the recall of Firestone tires on the popular Ford Explorer. He realized that Ford's quality reputation was at risk, and he reacted swiftly.

Leaders Aren't Always Popular

Some parts of leaders' jobs are apt to make them unpopular. Leaders make tough decisions, with the input of all stakeholders who are affected. Sometimes they may have to downsize a part of the business that has not responded to turnaround efforts; other times, they may have to institute an unpopular change in policy. Leaders can't be afraid to tackle sensitive issues. Peters argues that effective leaders often make people uncomfortable—they push them beyond their comfort zones by asking them to learn something new, to give up something they have come to expect, or to change the status quo. Leaders stretch followers to reach for their full potential. Unpopularity is one of the most difficult things about being a good leader. Leaders put the collective good beyond their personal self-interest.

Organizing for the Future

Leadership and organization are difficult to separate as O'Toole cogently argues. Many of the key tasks and responsibilities of leadership are institutionalized in the systems, practices, and cultures of the organization. Leadership is about creating context that enables and supports leadership. The authors in this book identify several organizational forms that will enable and support leader-ship in the new millennium.

Organization as Partnership

Organizations are seeking to build more of a partnership with employees, particularly with the rise of knowledge workers. Daven-port suggests that more than ever before workers bring critical resources to the workplace—oftentimes they know more than their leaders about how the work is done. In this era of human capital, says Lawler, employees are expected to bring their creativity, ideas, and initiative to the workplace in exchange for a share of the orga-nization's gains (through rewards such as stock options for even the lowest-level employee). The result, according to O'Toole, is an organization where workers act more like owners or entrepreneurs, taking the initiative and acting with a sense of accountability.

Organizations Without Boundaries

Kerr makes a powerful case that in the age of globalization, con-solidation, and diversity, integration becomes ever more important but also more difficult. Integration is necessary for the parts of the organization to work together, particularly in teams. Integration comes through moving money, people, and ideas across the boundaries of the firm. Slater calls this the miracle of coordina-tion. Kerr describes how General Electric breaks down the floors of the organization (that is, the levels of hierarchy) through its Workout program. It also makes the inside walls between functions and divisions more permeable and does the same with the outside walls with customers, suppliers, and regulators. The networked organizations that Stewart describes also create integration because they connect everyone to everyone.

Relationships Based on Trust

As organizations become more boundaryless and networked they require the abandonment of traditional hierarchies. Creating a context to enable trust, according to Stewart, requires high levels of competence, strong communities of practice, the free flow of communication, and alignment to the organization's vision. Moreover, Kouzes and Posner describe the depth of relationships inherent in a leadership-enabling organization—relationships based on trust, mutual respect, and caring.

How Leaders Stay On Top of Their Game

It is difficult to pick up an issue of *Fortune* magazine or the *Wall Street Journal* and not see a story of a leader who has derailed. Stories abound of executives such as Douglas Ivester of Coca Cola or Durk Jager of Procter & Gamble who are fired after disastrous starts as CEO. Unfortunately, it is all too rare to profile a CEO like Jack Welch, who has stayed at the top of his game for close to two decades. The authors in this book suggest a number of ways that leaders can sustain and energize themselves for the long term.

Focus on What Energizes

Sustainable leadership involves knowing what you love to do and what you are good at—the intersection of passion and capability creates energy. Peters argues that if you aren't doing what you love, if your work is passionless, you aren't going to devote enough energy and perseverance to achieve excellence. Likewise, if you are constantly struggling to build your competency in a given area, if you feel overwhelmed, you will waste critical energy. Both passion and competence are important. Consider the example of Herb Kelleher, CEO of Southwest Airlines. He knows exactly what he is good at—developing a vision, creating a culture, and touching people. He is lousy at administrative tasks and details. So he has a COO who loves that side of the business. Together, they make a perfect team. For leaders to stay on top of their game, they must spend time on those things that excite them and delegate what's left to people they can trust.

Be Resilient

As we described in the preceding section, leadership is all about failure. Leaders who are at the top of their game learn to quickly pick themselves up and get back in the race after failure. Sonnenfeld, speaking from his own experiences, suggests that real leaders turn failure to their advantage—creating triumph from tragedy. They learn from their experience and find redemptive value in it. In fact, Sonnenfeld goes so far as to say that adversity smoothes the path to leadership greatness—life's calamities contribute to character formation and empathy for others.

Reinvent Oneself

In the festschrift conference that stimulated these chapters, there was discussion of balance. Interestingly, almost all of the contributors to this volume questioned whether balance was really possible or even desirable. Most felt that they didn't have balance in their own lives. They were so turned on by what they were doing that they were almost obsessed by it. To keep from burning out, they didn't seek balance per se, but rather sought to continually renew themselves. Peters describes how to do this most eloquently, "Surround yourself with books of all sorts. Pal around with folks of all stripes and ages. Just say yes." Leaders must take advantage of opportunities to reinvent themselves or better yet, they must create new opportunities themselves. Bennis is a great example of this—as demonstrated in the memoir that closes this book, he has continually reshaped and reinvented himself throughout his career.

What Young Leaders Have to Say: Hearing from the Generation Xers

The two young leaders who contributed to this volume, Church and Headington, fit squarely into the Generation X cohort. They *are* the next generation of leaders. So they speak from their experience—and from their heart. They are impassioned about what they do and what they want to achieve.

Generation Xers Seek to Make a Difference

Both of our young leaders argue that the next generation of leaders wants to make a real difference in the world—to effect change, to mobilize community, to fight for a cause. Church is seeking to make a difference through her "One In A Million" campaign to inspire a million kids to plant a million trees. Headington is working to make a difference through his founding of the Robert F. Kennedy Forum, an educational forum on the life and legacy of RFK. Both put less emphasis on shareholders and profits and more focus on service to the community. In their worldview, leaders are activists who want to make the world a better place, and who don't take no for an answer. They hold themselves to the highest standard, following the servant-leader model. They like to think of themselves as driven by a set of higher principles that can't be compromised.

Is their perspective on leadership any more service or activist oriented than generations before them? The baby boomers in the 1960s surely said many of the same things. Regardless of whether the next generation of leaders are really different from current leaders, we can agree that this will be an important goal of every leader in the new millennium—to make a significant difference in one way or another.

Generation Xers Are Unconventional

Consistent with the literature on Generation X, both Church and Headington admit their disenchantment with authority. They describe how young people distrust the political system and its leaders. Generation X leaders seek other ways to effect change and define leadership. In their eyes, leadership is less directive, top-down, and charismatic and more empowering, bottom-up, and humble. Rather than relying on institutions to help them bring their visions to life, Generation Xers work through alternative, grassroots means. And if they don't agree with rules or established ways of doing things, then they do things their own way. Because Generation Xers see elected officials as acting self-interestedly rather than in the best interests of the collective, they have record low levels of voter turnout. Headington talks about Generation X's approach to public service through community activism rather than elective office.

Generation Xers Need Support and Encouragement

While Generation Xers want to do things their own way, they still want and need support from today's leaders. They want role models who can inspire them to work toward their full potential. They want mentors to teach them the skills of leadership and help them overcome hurdles in their path. Church's mentor was her mother. Headington talks repeatedly of the inspiration of Robert Kennedy. Church provides some particularly insightful advice about the kind of support Generation Xers need: inspire and empower them—share, don't patronize; coach, don't teach. Provide youth with opportunities, and then let them loose.

Looking across the sorts of things that Generation Xers crave, we see a lot of similarity to what Handy referred to when he talked about entrepreneurial "fleas." These are the kind of environments that Generation Xers will thrive in. Now the challenge becomes how to create that kind of context even in traditional "elephants."

Unanswered Questions

The leading thinkers in the volume provide answers to many of twelve questions that keep gurus like Bennis up at night. The next generation of leaders will find comfort in the lessons provided by them. Yet four of Bennis's questions were not addressed in this volume and are ripe for exploration in future research. They are the most sensitive and politically hot issues of the bunch.

Disparities in Talent

Bennis asked what can be done about the unavoidable disparities in talent—surely capability is not distributed equally across the human population? Most of the authors of this book agree that leaders are made, not born—that everyone has some leadership potential. But that potential may be far from developed for many with little education, motivation, or natural talent. So this raises the question, Should everyone be a leader? Don't we need some followers too? In the "winner-take-all society" that is becoming increasingly prevalent in the West, where the best thrive and the rest subsist, there are important unanswered questions about equity and justice in organizations and society.

Unethical Ends and Means of Leadership

Leadership can bring greatness to organizations and society. Witness the "great society" programs championed by Franklin

Roosevelt and the individualization of the computer by Steve Jobs. Leadership can also devastate people and societies. Witness the horror of Hitler's "final solution" or the tragedy of Jim Jones and his religious cult. Are there ways to ensure that strong leadership contributes to the common good, not self-interest, that the leader works toward ethical ends, that leadership makes the world a better place to live? And even when leaders have worthy goals in mind, it is critical that they use ethical means to achieve them.

Work-Life Balance

Though this issue was touched on in the book, we do not have clear answers about how to create appropriate life balance. It's almost macho for leaders to say they work a hundred-hour week, that they cut vacations short or don't take them at all, that their frequent flier accounts are bulging. Many executives pay the price with poor family relationships, broken marriages, and poor health. In Japan, there is even a term for death by overwork. We have a long way to go before we understand how to create balance amid our 24/7 work norms.

Leader Education

Though many of the contributors in this volume are academics, surprisingly no one really attempted to tackle the role of business education for the next generation of leaders. We can speculate that for tomorrow's leaders, education will look less like formal degree programs and more like informal, on-the-job training and management development programs. A lifelong approach will dominate leadership development. Moreover, given advances in technology, it is likely that leaders will be educated through distance learning, where students will take classes when and where it is convenient for them. This should make management education more accessible to everyone who wants it.

While not answering all questions, the thought leaders in this volume go a long way in helping us to understand leadership in the new millennium. Hopefully, their wisdom can increase the "shelf life" of future leaders.

An Intellectual Memoir

Warren Bennis

> *Language, and thought like the wind*
> *and the feelings that make the town;*
> *[man] has taught himself, and shelter against the cold*
> *refuge from the rain. He can always help himself,*
> *He faces no future helpless.*
> —SOPHOCLES, *ANTIGONE*

The arc of events that have shaped my intellectual passions, all of which Sophocles describes: language, thought, feelings, community, change, human advancement, and a promising future—still remain obscure to me, perhaps easier to describe than understand. I remain as confused as my students when we argue the age-old dispute between those who think history is determined by events—that we are all, a la Tolstoy, "slaves of history"—or those who favor Carlyle and believe that history is simply a succession of biographies, that every great institution, in his words, is "the lengthened shadow of a Great Man." (It never occurred to Carlyle that there could be a Great Woman.) On the face of it, my path has seemed more Tolstoyan than Carlylian. It's as if I've stumbled, literally *careered,* into one zone of intellectual opportunity after the other, sort of an academic slalom, what I suppose many years later, Karl Weick would have referred to as a set of "eccentric precursors." The only thing I am certain about at this point is that history has favored my career.

There was a young soldier I got to know in Germany in late 1944 who had his mind set on attending Antioch College (in Yellow

Springs, Ohio) after the war because of its co-op program where students divided their time between the classroom and a job. That sounded appealing to me, too, because it was affordable. (Word of the G.I. Bill had not reached me.) Yellow Springs did sound a bit rural to a city boy; on the map, the two closest "metropolises" were Xenia and Springfield. But it still sounded attractive because of some vague idea that the life of the mind should have some connection to the so-called real life I had been experiencing in the Army. So, in 1947, at the advanced age of twenty-two and after four years in the Army, I ventured to Yellow Springs, Ohio.

At the beginning of my sophomore year there, in 1948, a new president was appointed, a forty-something, rather dashing professor from M.I.T., Douglas McGregor. He announced at his first student faculty "assembly" that he found his four years of psychoanalysis more important than his entire undergraduate education. This explosive and unexpected admission was taken in a variety of ways. Most of the faculty were disapproving and cynical and wondered, "What have we got ourselves into?" There were a few, at the other extreme, who thought, "Gosh, what a candid and brave thing to say!" There were no opinions in the middle, a rather common Antioch response to just about anything. McGregor brought along with him a brilliant and fascinating Merlin, one Irving Knickerbocker, an early pioneer at Black Mountain College—an institution perhaps even more supremely radical than Antioch. Their main interest was what appeared to be a new field of study, group dynamics.

In the first year of his tenure at Antioch, McGregor, along with his sidekick, Knickerbocker, decided to suspend all classes on successive Fridays (for the full academic year) for community-wide discussion groups that were to come up with a set of "goals" for the college, what nowadays we would refer to as a mission statement. There were "trained facilitators" and "process observers" and panelists and position papers and *rapporteurs* and spokespersons and God knows what else to coordinate this campuswide creative bedlam. Most of the faculty were either disapproving and cynical about what they bitterly referred to as "examining our own navels" or worse, and the students were somewhat stupefied but also somewhat excited about getting "Fridays off." For any number of reasons, it turned out to be something of a "learning experience," as we Antiochians learned to call virtually anything. And it was one heluva lot of fun.

Another ridiculously creative idea McGregor floated (and for which he raised a million dollars from the Kettering Foundation) was for Antioch faculty to take advantage of the co-op program by taking a year off to do real work in a nonacademic setting. Like a mini-co-op program for faculty. The faculty once again were disapproving and cynical. (I learned later that being disapproving and cynical is in our blood.) One hapless assistant professor, an art historian I seem to recall, did take advantage of this opportunity, opting for a job at what was then called Standard Oil of New Jersey. Nothing's been heard from him since.

Without any critical hesitation, I was enthralled with McGregor and his ideas—especially his concern with integrating theory and practice and his belief that the behavioral sciences could lead to a better understanding of organizational and group life, which in turn could lead to more enriching lives. After all, the motto of Antioch's founder, Horace Mann—burned into the limbic zone of our brains—was *Be ashamed to die until you have won some victory for humanity!* So, Candide-like, innocent and wondrous, I started on my academic odyssey, totally unaware that the career I was about to enter would turn out to be one long, adventurous co-op program.

Act I: The Academic Journey (1951–1967)

This entire act is set in Cambridge, Massachusetts, in three locations: M.I.T., Boston University, and Harvard. All of the action takes place within W.B.'s memory. He is twenty-six.

Keep in mind the *zeitgeist* of the 1950s and 1960s. World War II had ended only six years before the beginning of the period and remained deep in our collective memory. Between the ghost of Hitler and the victory of democracy and its close relative, science, there was hope in the air. Everywhere. Science and technology made us supremely confident that we were entering a new age. The shadow of Hitler's ghost dominated our thinking.[1] Those of us interested in social and political research were committed to the idea of democratic leadership and had an urgent need to understand more about the horror of collective pathology of groups and organizations such as those we witnessed in Germany, Russia, and the other Axis powers.

Keep in mind also that the behavioral sciences came of age during World War II. The Office of Strategic Service (OSS, the precursor to the CIA), the Office of War Information (OWI), the U.S. Army statistical branch, the Operations Research Group, plus hundreds of intellectuals who escaped Hitler's wrath developed a hugely successful behavioral science. The four volumes of *The American Soldier,* edited by S. Stouffer and F. A. Mosteller; *The Authoritarian Personality,* by Adorno, Frenkel-Brunswik and others, which purported to measure the "authoritarian personality" with its F-scale (for Fascist); the robust statistical and experimental methods created by the Operations Research Group, led by the likes of P. Morse, G. Kimble, R. Ackoff, and C. W. Churchman; the seminal work of the Tavistock Institute in the United Kingdom, directed by A.T.M. Wilson, working with E. Trist, F. E. Emery, E. Jaques, and others; the psychological testing of the OSS, with at least two future presidents of the American Psychological Association, D. Katz and J. G. Miller (as well as the inventor of the Likert Scale); the work of C. Hovland and I. Janis on persuasion and influence and Margaret Mead on propaganda at the OWI, all led to the creation of a truly scientific ethos for social research. Wars are a golden opportunity to restructure societies and to this extent, World War II was a Good War.

Scene 1 (1951–1955): Beginnings

On McGregor's advice, I went to the mecca of the scientific studies of group dynamics, M.I.T. By the time I got there, alas, most of the researchers I came to study with had gone; Lewin had died and many of his students—who would shape a fair amount of social psychological research for the latter part of this century, researchers such as H. J. Leavitt, M. Horwitz, L. Festinger, H. A. Kelley, K. Bach, M. Deutsch, and S. Schacter—had spread out at university centers all over the country to set up laboratories for social research. A good many joined Rensis Likert to establish the new Institute for Social Research at the University of Michigan. A few remained at M.I.T., Alex Bavelas and Herb Shepard being the most important for me; with them I managed to create a wild mosaic of a curriculum, with half of my studies at Harvard's Social Relations department, a lot of seminars with Bavelas and Shepard, and more courses than I would have liked in economic theory at M.I.T.

My department predated what is now called the Sloan School. It was simply called Course XIV, the Department of Economics and Social Science, numbered that way as are all departments and schools at M.I.T. in a more-or-less hierarchical scientific order, starting with math as Course I, physics as Course II, and so on. The buildings are also named thusly as in the famous domed Building 10, the seat of administrative power. (As far as I know the Sloan School is now Course XV.)

By the time I got there in 1951, economic theory—under the leadership of Paul Samuelson, Bob Solow, and Charles Kindleberger—was clearly the dominant emphasis and I found myself leaning ever more determinedly away from that and toward the social psychology of human institutions. When I told Paul Samuelson that I had decided not to do my dissertation in economics but in organizational theory, his face was a study of blissful, palpable relief.

Scene 2 (1956–1959): "Sperm in the Air"

Cambridge and Boston were alive with talent and ideas. How *incredibly* lucky I thought I was to end up here, not having the slightest idea of what I was getting into and what becoming an academic was all about, and feeling culturally inferior to everyone I met. (I realized later that I wasn't alone in feeling that, but we were all too insecure to come clean about it.) The atmosphere was electrifying, intense, competitive, challenging, animating, intimidating, incandescent, almost oppressively "hot." Many years later I wrote a book about Great Groups inspired by that era; and just last year my colleagues and friends, Jean Lipman-Blumen and Hal Leavitt, wrote an outstanding book with a similar theme, *Hot Groups*. Even today, when I think back to those times, they still, to use the words of the Doors, light my fire.

Perhaps the best way to describe the intellectual excitement in the air is an anecdote about Sigmund Freud. He was one of the last Jews to escape from Vienna in 1938. After a short stay in Paris, he settled in London. One day he accidentally met a fellow Viennese, the novelist Stefan Zweig, and asked him how he liked London. "London," Zweig spat, "London . . . how can you even mention London and Vienna in the same breath! In Vienna, there was sperm in the air." Politically incorrect or not, when I arrived in Cambridge in 1951, there *was* sperm in the air.

That's what I meant earlier when I said that history favored my career. Perhaps it's another of those imponderable "eccentric precursors," I don't know, but I can't exaggerate the importance of place and time in one's intellectual development.

In 1955 my thesis was completed and I stayed on that academic year as an assistant professor at M.I.T. Aside from teaching I worked very hard publishing pieces of my thesis in sociological and psychological journals.[2] But what I'm most proud of is an article I coauthored with my mentor, Herb Shepard, published in *Human Relations,* "A Theory of Group Development." It was based primarily on our experiences in leading T-Groups at M.I.T. and at Bethel, Maine. In a neo-Hegelian and perhaps overly formalistic way, Herb and I tried to make sense out of the two basic issues all groups have to confront, the issue of power and authority and the issue of intimacy. How those issues were addressed and resolved pretty much determined, in our view, whether or not groups could accomplish creative and productive work.

Between 1956 and 1959, I was awash with ideas and exciting colleagues, in fact *way* over my head. With that portentous headiness of youth and promise, reflecting and basking in the zeitgeist of that time, we thought our research and writing could change the world. Ken Benne and Bob Chin asked me to join them at Boston University. I held four positions there: teaching six hours of undergraduate social psychology at the school of business, coteaching the introductory general psychology course to the Ph.D. students in the Department of Psychology with the department chair, Nathan Maccoby, and teaching what was then called the Pro-Seminar with Ken and Bob in the Human Relations Center. My fourth job was directing a research project on the role of the Out-Patient Department nurse in nine major Boston hospitals, a study sponsored by the American Nursing Foundation that was later turned into a small book. That was twelve hours of teaching plus leading a research team composed of two doctoral students, both gifted social psychologists—Malcolm Klein, who retired recently as chair of USC's Sociology Department, and Norm Berkowitz, who migrated over to Boston College in the 1970s. We were also helped by the head of nursing at Peter Bent Brigham Hospital, Molly Malone, who provided the knowledge of nursing that we sorely needed.

BU also had an active evening school, so to augment my salary, I taught a course there. Not a bad "load," I thought, for my annual salary (including summer teaching) of $6,500.

That was my day job. I also accepted an appointment at Harvard's Social Relations Department teaching a section of a group course that met three days a week. The other "section men" were Freed Bales, Phil Slater, and Ted Mills. I also spent a lot of time at Harvard with two other researchers whose future paths went in somewhat parallel directions. Will Schutz was working at Harvard on a quantitative study of compatibility in small groups with the instrument that later became known as FIRO-B. The other was Timothy Leary, who was developing an observational scale based on Harry Stack Sullivan's interpersonal theories to elucidate the dynamics of groups. That was in Leary's antediluvian (pre-LSD) days, when he could accurately be described as a brass-instrument empiricist. Schutz became a guru and pioneer at Esalen and now leads a management consulting business. About Leary, well, I'm not really sure.

They were all my teachers and a wildly diverse lot. My "boss" at BU's school of business was a proper Bostonian with a name that bespeaks his Brahmin status, Lowell Trowbridge; Ken Benne, a Columbia-trained philosopher and one of John Dewey's last students, who could talk and always did so on any topic with cosmic virtuosity; Bob Chin, also a Columbia-trained social psychologist who worked with all the Greats there but especially with Gardner Murphy and Otto Klineberg plus the philosopher Morris Cohen, then at CCNY, where Bob did his undergraduate work. Then there was Nathan Maccoby, the redoubtable and crusty chairman of BU's psych department. I asked him many years later why he asked me to coteach that Ph.D. course with him, that I knew so little at that time. He said, "I know. That's why I asked you. I thought that everyone in the psych department should know at least a *little* general psychology." There was also Mikki Ritvo, later to become a high-flying management consultant, who deserves more than a sentence and who turned me into a feminist. And the young Ph.D. candidates I mentioned earlier, Klein and Berkowitz, along with the wildly bright and funny Barry Oshry and the deadly serious and saturnine Arthur M. Cohen, provided the acid antidotes to any and all pomposities that were in the air. They never lacked for material.

Those three years swarmed with Great Groups, perhaps the most lasting of which was the troika of Benne, Chin, and myself. Together we coauthored and edited *The Planning of Change,* my first book, published in 1961, an attempt to encompass in one volume the most seminal and original essays in the yet unborn field of organizational change. The book is still in print after forty years and was in its way and in its day influential. In that volume, Ken coined the phrase "change agent" and Bob's essay on system change still sets the standard on that topic. Of course, the very title, *The* Planning *of Change,* betrays our hubris, I suppose, but says far more about the optimistic climate of the time—that we could actually *plan* change. A humorous sidenote to all of this is that my mother, forever proud and innocent of my work, was convinced that a "change agent" was the person who made change for New York's subways.

On the other side of the Charles River, Schutz, Slater, Mills, and I did a massive amount of research on group psychotherapy, specifically developing measures of group interaction by observing the groups of the preternaturally gifted and amiably naive psychoanalyst and chief of clinical psychiatry at Harvard, Elvin Semrad. He wanted us to help him figure out why his clinical interventions seemed to be so effective. So for three years we observed his groups, composed of about fifteen first-year psychiatric residents, which met every Saturday morning. The following Wednesday afternoon, we would meet with Semrad and would spend between three and four hours poring over the protocols of the preceding Saturday morning's meeting, sharing our observations and ideas about groups and leadership. They were often riveting discussions and we learned a lot—and every once in a while, we thought we were on the bleeding edge of discovery. But we never did fathom the mystery of Semrad's magic.

Also during that time, I spent a fair amount of time with Mills at his small group research lab at Harvard. He was taken with

Georg Simmel's work on the effect of numbers on group decision making, especially three-person groups since that number is uniquely vulnerable to isolation and coalition building. Aside from helping him analyze the data, he got me to play the stooge in one of his ingenious experiments. Later on I got even with Ted by recruiting him to SUNY-Buffalo (from Yale, where he was chairing the Sociology Department) something for which he's not completely forgiven me.

Scene 3 (1959–1967): M.I.T.

It wasn't the salary that brought me back to M.I.T. in 1959. The $9,500 was only $500 more than what I was making at BU and the academic marketplace was booming with opportunities. Leaving BU and its sunny collegiality wasn't easy. From Ken Benne, especially, I learned what it was like to be an intellectual; on my next "co-op job," I learned how to be an academic.

What lured me to M.I.T. was my Antioch role model, Doug McGregor, who returned to establish a new "area"—there were no departments in the Sloan School—to focus on the study of human organizations. He was in the process of assembling a remarkable group of people including Ed Schein, Don Marquis, Dave Berlew, Per Soelberg, Bill Evan, and later on—with either visiting or adjunct status—Dick Beckhard, Bob Kahn, Harry Levinson, and Bob Greenleaf. Doug, among other things, taught me everything I needed to know about recruiting, which served me well later on during my administrative years. *Any* offer Doug made would be one I couldn't refuse.

Looking back, those seven years at M.I.T. were unquestionably the most intense and *academically* productive of my career. Back in those days (for reasons that still remain obscure to me), M.I.T. didn't grant tenure until you were thirty-six. To my knowledge, the only exception to this rule was made for the future Nobelist Bob Solow. It has often been said that academics should have remained the unmarried clerics they once had been and it was true enough. Life on the M.I.T. faculty was the academic fast track. The competition was from the start unbearably intense. So what else is an under-thirty-six-year-old, untenured associate professor to do but publish? I published like a madman, like there was no tomorrow.

Checking over an old vitae, I saw that there that I had written something like eight books (some coedited or coauthored), twenty-seven academic articles in referred journals (including my first article on leadership, published in *Administrative Science Quarterly,* "Leadership Theory and Administrative Behavior: The Problem of Authority," December 1959), my first major article on organizational change, also in the *ASQ* ("A New Role for the Behavioral Sciences: Effecting Organizational Change," September 1963), and a slew of other articles in journals such as *Sociometry, American Psychologist,* and *American Sociological Review.* You could tell I was a real academic. There wasn't an article I wrote that wasn't punctuated with a colon in the title.

Well, there were a few exceptions because somewhere in my bookbag, I came upon a "prophet's rod," and wrote several articles about the future. The future has fascinated me since my bar mitzvah, when I based the traditional "Today-I-Am-a-Man" speech—something I slaved over for months—on the prophet Jeremiah, an interesting choice for me since few have come to my lips since.

For me *the future* is a portmanteau word. It embraces several notions. It is an exercise in imagination that allows us to compete with and try to outwit future events. Controlling the anticipated future is, in addition, a social invention that legitimizes the process of forward planning. There is no other way I know of to resist the "tyranny of blind forces" than by looking facts in the face (as we experience them in the present) and extrapolating to the future—nor is there any other sure way to detect compromise. More important, the future is a conscious dream, a set of imaginative hypotheses groping toward whatever vivid utopias lie at the heart of our consciousness. "In dreams begin responsibilities," wrote Yeats, and it is to our future responsibilities as educators, researchers, practitioners that these dreams are dedicated.

Anyway, that's what fascinated me about the future—and still does. So with my prophet rod in hand and Phil Slater's genius at my side, we wrote an article that was published in the March/April 1964 issue of the *Harvard Business Review* forecasting the demise of the Soviet Union and the triumph of democratic capitalism. We based our 1968 book, *The Temporary Society,* on those ideas, a book that later won *HBR*'s McKinsey Award for the best business book for its year. It was, I have to say, a *succes d'estime* with mostly glowing reviews in places like the *New York Times* as well as academic periodicals. It was also a total flop commercially, remaindered scarcely eighteen months after publication, never to be heard from again until Jossey-Bass republished it in 1998.

I wrote several "more academic" papers around that time as well. My favorite was actually a keynote speech given at the American Psychological Association meeting in Los Angeles in 1964. I titled it "Organizational Developments and the Fate of Bureaucracy," at which time I took aim at the Weberian classic work on bureaucracy and predicted its demise. Of course, I always took careful academic refuge behind such terms as "between now and the next fifty years or so," just to be on the safe side. In any case, I redrafted that speech into a paper that only the IBM house organ, *THINK* (November/December 1966), thought well enough of to publish. It was titled, "The Coming Death of Bureaucracy." That was one article they should have taken seriously—they soon became victims of that scourge. As I peruse that same old vitae I see that for reasons still mysterious to me the *Junior League Magazine* reprinted it in 1968. My readership was becoming strangely eclectic—especially when I removed the colon.

My argument was based on a number of factors that I developed in a reprise of the 1964 APA speech, "A Funny Thing Happened on the Way to the Future" (*American Psychologist*, July 1970), from which I will now quote:

1. The growing influence of intellectual technology, and the growth of research and development.
2. The growing confluence between men of knowledge and men of power. [Or as I wrote about it in 1964, "a growing affinity between those who make history and those who write it."]
3. A fundamental change in the basic philosophy which underlies managerial behavior, reflected most of all in the following three areas: (a) a new concept of man, based on increased knowledge of his complex and shifting needs, which replaces the simplistic, innocent push-button concept of man; (b) a new concept of power, based on collaboration and reason, which replaces a model of power based on coercion and fear; and (c) a new concept of organizational values, based on humanistic-democratic ideals, which replaces the depersonalized mechanistic value system of bureaucracy.

4. A turbulent environment which would hold relative uncertainty due to the increase of R & D activities. The environment would become increasingly differentiated, interdependent, and more salient to the organization embedded in it. There would be greater inter-penetration of the legal policy and economic features of an oligopolistic and government-business controlled economy. Three main features of the human organizations would be interdependence rather than competition, turbulence, rather than a steady, predictable state, and large rather than small enterprises.

5. A population characterized by a younger, more mobile, and better educated workforce.

These conditions [I argued] would lead to significant organizational changes. First of all, the key word would be *temporary:* organizations will become adaptive, rapidly changing temporary systems. Second, they will be organized around problems-to-be-solved. Third, these problems will be solved by people who represent a diverse set of professional skills. Fourth, the groups will be conducted on organic rather than on mechanical lines; they will emerge and adapt to the problems, and leadership and influence will fall to those who seem most able to solve the problems rather to programmed role expectations.

Those words, written about thirty-five years ago, no longer seem quirky or outrageous. Certainly in the new, wired economy, we'll behave more like a biological community: growing, evolving, merging, developing, adapting organically without the necessity of centralized control.

I've left for last my work with Ed Schein. First of all, we authored a book Wiley published in 1965, *Personal and Organizational Change Through Group Methods,* wherein we took a hard look at the successful and unsuccessful examples of changing social systems via behavioral science interventions. Many of our colleagues protested because we included some examples of woebegone failures and pointed to some of the adamantine qualities of bureaucratic systems. Before undertaking that, we were the senior partners of a compendium of readings and essays, *Interpersonal Dynamics: Essays and Readings on Human Dynamics* (Irwin-Dorsey, 1963). Working with us as coeditors were Dave Berlew and Fritz Steele, the latter an M.I.T. Ph.D. and as bright as they come, and the former one of the most elegant minds and writers, who, with Dave McClelland, his Harvard Ph.D. thesis adviser, started the hugely successful firm, McBer. John van Maanen was senior editor of the fifth and final volume of *Interpersonal Dynamics.*

On top of all that publishing, Ed Schein, Dick Beckhard, and I were able to interest Addison-Wesley in a series of paperbacks on the nascent and inchoate field of organizational development. I dropped out of the editing and left it in the able hands of my two colleagues and, as of now, it's fair to say that the series has proved to be extremely successful with at least forty titles in print.

Two other events must be mentioned, having nothing to do with publishing, before I move beyond the colon and into Act II, my administrative saga. The first has to do with two international adventures. Serving in Germany in World War II was not exactly an experience that would develop one's understanding of the global economy. You got dog tags, not passports. So when overseas opportunities presented themselves at M.I.T.—and because of its being M.I.T., there were many such opportunities—I jumped at them. And the encouragement of Dean Howard Johnson, later to become M.I.T.'s president, provided the support I needed to take advantage of overseas activities.

The first was anything but a hardship post. I was invited to spend a year (1961–62) teaching at IMEDE in Lausanne, Switzerland, now known as IMD, one of Europe's leading business schools. At that time, IMEDE was primarily an executive finishing school for Nestlé's high potentials and primarily supported by that company. There were fifty senior executives in the class, about a third of them from Nestlé, the rest from all over the world. The modal age of the class was thirty-six, the same as mine. IMEDE then drew its faculty from the Harvard Business School. I was one of the few exceptions. The year was memorable for two quite different things. First, because IMEDE was an HBS satellite where the case study method was king, I learned—again, with the faculty tic of disapproval and cynicism—how powerful and subtly nuanced the case method can be. I was a novice at it but my officemate, Ed Learned (one of the founders of the policy area at Harvard), Frank Aguilar (then a DBA candidate and Baker Scholar), and Dave Leighton (who taught me all about marketing) were among my many mentors.

Far more cosmic was my introduction to the global economy. The European Economic Community (EEC) was just getting its sea legs. What with the student mix at IMEDE and global business cases, plus writing a case with my students on a French company in Annecy, my eyebrows were continually raised about both the future of globalism and its discontents.

When the possibility of another global adventure came up, this time as faculty director of the Indian Institute of Management at Calcutta, I went for it. Just as IMEDE was an HBS proxy in its early days, the IIM-Calcutta was initially staffed by Sloan School professors conjointly with an outstanding, primarily Bengali, faculty. When I left IMEDE, I thought I understood perhaps at most 40 percent of what was going on in my students' heads; at IIM-C I figured a max of 10 percent—but that 10 percent was far more provocative and interesting than the cultural knowledge I picked up in Europe.

I loved working with the Bengali faculty. Intellectually, they were world-class, argumentative, brilliant, and ferociously articulate on any number of matters. Just to give you a little idea of what I was facing there, a playwright (who is also the home minister for the state's Communist government) recently said, "Intellectually, I humbly proclaim we are more advanced than anyone else. We discuss the great questions: What is post-modernism? What does Noam Chomsky have to say about this or that? The Bengali may have no food on the table, but he's off arguing somewhere about the Vietnam War or the last book he has read or whether it is a good idea to change every signboard in the city from Calcutta to Kolkata."

In addition to codirecting the school (our own Arvind Bhambri is one of IIM-C's distinguished MBA graduates), I helped to establish an international organization on OD known as INCOD. My cohorts on that project were my Indian colleagues, Suresh Srivastva, Ishwar Dayal, and Nitish De; a social psychologist from the University of Michigan and the director of our sister institute at Ahmadabad (IIM-A), Kamala Chowdhury; Allen Cohen, on leave from HBS and that year at IIM-A; John Thomas from M.I.T.; Barry Richman from UCLA; and Howard Baumgartel from the University of Kansas were all U.S. representatives. Two others joyfully contributed in translating our dreams into reality, one an Indian, Udai Pareek, and his U.S. counterpart, Rolf Lynton. These stalwarts, working at the very soul of social change, ridiculously ahead of its time, established the Aloka Institute to train Indian change agents.

The other event I referred to earlier is a sad one for me to recall now, let alone write about. Doug McGregor suffered a massive heart attack and died at the tragically early age of fifty-eight. He was the emotional and intellectual center of our group. I was—we all were—very dependent on him: his brio, his informed optimism, and most of all, his unbridled capacity for joy. No one could light up a room the way Doug could after two martinis, smoking his pipe and telling an off-color joke. He was a thoroughly engaged man and totally supportive. Doug was, in the finest sense of that phrase, a "change agent," able to change an entire concept of the hollow Organization Man and replace it with a theory that stressed our human potential, our capacity for growth, and a theory that elevated man's role in an industrial society. The truth is that a large segment of our professional lives now operate in an environment he created.

He was also a close personal friend. I remember the time in 1960 when I wanted to buy a small townhouse in a mews on Beacon Hill and asked him whether he thought it was a sound investment for someone without tenure. In a heartbeat, he said, "I'll lend you the money for the down payment. And don't worry about tenure." His word was always good. I still worried.

I was his reluctant successor at M.I.T. and in a way I don't think it's too fanciful to think that my next career move was a way to incarnate his dreams along with my own.

Act II: Just Do It (1967–1978)

This entire act takes place at two universities, SUNY-Buffalo and the University of Cincinnati. Our protagonist served as provost at the former for four years and president of the latter for seven.

University campuses, throughout the world but especially in the United States, were roiling with conflict and riots and to someone whose own education—at least that part of it that led to degrees—was completed when campus was synonymous with a certain degree of detachment, even civility, the late 1960s and early 1970s were a nightmare. It was first of all baffling and unreal. One could not believe that a campus could be dangerous, that a student could firebomb an office or a policeman beat up a faculty member. But all those things were happening on campuses in those days. Sometimes the mist in the early evenings was smog and sometimes it was tear gas. Fear and violence, states we had only recently come to identify with the American urban experience, became part of the university climate as well.

The moments of horror were captured in gut-rending photographs, rows of police and guardsmen behind masks, a shattered science building in Wisconsin, the Bank of America in flames in Santa Barbara, a dying student sprawled in the grass at Kent State. Universities had moments of horror during that period and they also had moments of almost frantic joy. The atmosphere was that of wartime. Between the terrible reality of the battles were the stretches characterized by boredom, sometimes by enormous freedom as if one were relieved by the special circumstances of all normal duties and responsibilities. When the students weren't denouncing their ideological enemies or confronting (and often being beaten by) the police, they seemed to be having a wonderful time. In this ambivalent emotional climate, the mundane business of going to class, teaching and learning, often went on uninterrupted.

It was the worst of times . . . and it was the worst of times, "So why," an M.I.T. colleague asked, "did you choose the period of greatest campus upheaval in history and leave a full professorship, with a corner office overlooking the Charles River, and go to *Buffalo* as provost?" He spat out "Buffalo" with the same sort of contempt that Stefan Zweig spoke of London. I suspect that he gave up on me completely when I accepted the presidency of the University of Cincinnati in 1971, because I've not heard from him since.

I needn't go on at length here about my eleven years as an administrator because I've written a great deal about it in the past. In fact, three of my books dwell on this period in detail. (*The Leaning Ivory Tower,* Jossey-Bass, 1973, *Why Leaders Can't Lead,* Jossey-Bass, 1989, and *An Invented Life,* Perseus, 1994.) Things have become clearer to me with the passage of time. One thing that's become clear is that why I chose to go into administration and what I learned were two quite separate things. Whoever knows all the "why's" of one's own motivation, but here are some of them:

Ever since my days at Antioch, I wanted to follow in McGregor's footsteps and become a college or university president. I won't argue that that's rational, but it was a strong factor.

I was tired of being Montaigne in the bleachers. He once said, "If it were my due to be believed I wouldn't be bold." Easy to be bold for someone in the bleachers, a detached analyst and objective observer, several terrain features away from the action. I wanted to be bold in the arena, to see if my written words could be embodied in the practitioners' world where deeds more than words counted. I recalled the words of Robert Graves's poem:

> Experts ranked in seried rows
> Fill the enormous plaza full;
> But only one is there who knows
> And he's the man who fights the bull.

Well, it wasn't quite fighting the bulls that I had intended but it turned out to be a terrific eleven-year validity check on my ideas.

Related to that, I suppose, is what all composers or playwrights must desperately want, getting their work performed, realized. How would a composer know how the music sounds without hearing it; how would a playwright know how the scenes actually play without seeing and hearing them. How would I know if my words had resonance, practical consequence for the world of management?

I had ideas—ideas about higher education—and I wanted an opportunity to see if I could be a champion of higher education reform.

I had an epiphany (I don't use that word lightly) visiting Michael Murphy in his San Francisco apartment in 1966 or so. He was the founder of Esalen and a brilliant expositor of New Age philosophy. He was lamenting a recent story about Esalen in *Life* magazine. Before the magazine issue was published, Michael was thrilled at the visibility a story in *Life* would mean. That kind of coverage was what every entrepreneur would die for. But he was, for good reason, appalled by the story when it appeared—featuring not the intellectually challenging ideas of Esalen but only the hot tubs and massage and the one nude group. (Hey, this was the 1960s!) What made matters worse, Michael felt, and again for good reason, was the cover of that same issue of *Life*. It was a different kind of nude group: dead, naked Biafran children, stacked grotesquely like cordwood, the result of a brutal tribal war. I was appalled by the juxtaposition of those two stories and wanted to get beyond disembodied analysis, beyond disengagement and detachment, and yes, beyond the colon: *to do something!*[3]

Then I suppose there were a whole lot of ineffables that even when I look back through the shining ether of time, I'm unclear about. When I try to express them, they sound tritely jumbled. . . . As John Cage once said, "I have nothing more to say but I'm going to say it anyway." So I won't.

What I learned was far more important than these ruminations about the *why's:*

• About *power:* In my academic writings, I underplayed most forms of power while emphasizing the role of the leader as "facilitator" and stressed, to use McGregor's famous metaphor, an "agricultural model" of seeding, nurturance, and climate building. I utilized a domesticated version of power, emphasizing the process by which authorities attempt to achieve collective goals and to maintain legitimacy and compliance with their decisions, rather than the perspective of potential partisans, which involves diverse interest groups' attempting to influence the choices of authorities. Put differently, I realized that an organization was as much a political model (that is, allocating scarce resources) as a human-relationship model.

• About *change:* Similarly, my writings had implied a rather simple model of change, based on gentle nudges from the environment coupled with a truth-love strategy; that is, with sufficient trust and collaboration, along with knowledge, organizations would progress monotonically upwards and onwards along a democratic continuum. In short, the organization of the future I had envisaged would most certainly be, along with a Bach chorale and Chartres Cathedral, the epitome of Western civilization.

One other thing about change I learned was that to be an effective leader qua change agent, you had to adhere simultaneously to the symbols of tradition and stability and to the symbols of revision and change. I was seen by many constituents as emphasizing the latter and tone-deaf to the former. I think there is more than a little validity to that perception. I should have learned more about the City of Cincinnati and its proud traditions and some of my interventions appeared to slight faculty sensibilities.

- About *bureaucracy:* A lot more stubborn and obdurate than I had thought. Not a bad lesson for someone who was called the "Buck Rogers of Organizational Change."[4] Perhaps universities are more resistant than most. The old saw about universities being harder to move than cemeteries has a ring of truth about it. The clogged cartography of stakeholders in a modern university is both breathtakingly confusing and filled with conflict. Much like internal stakeholders, interests vary and that brings up another old saw, that the way to success for a university president is to provide sex for students, a winning football team for alumni, and a parking place for the faculty.

When I was at Cincinnati I would hold "Open Hours" every Wednesday afternoon where anyone could come in and surface their problems, complaints, ideas, or whatever. It was an expedient move, I thought; so many people wanted a hearing that this was a way I could manage to squeeze everyone into a 2–5 P.M. time slot. At first, I would see students, faculty, or administrators—or for that matter, anyone from the community—one on one. Then word got around and more and more people wanted an "audience with the president." Both to keep order and have a decent place to wait, I opened up the adjacent boardroom and stocked it with soft drinks and cookies. Finally, it got so jammed with supplicants that the boardroom was no longer adequate to contain all comers, at which point I invited everyone to sit in my office. Open Hours began to resemble something like a fifteenth-century Persian court, supplicants of various kinds crowded into my office. Most of the problems were bureaucratic glitches and upsets. I didn't want to make decisions that department chairs, deans, and vice presidents should make, so university officers were invited to attend. The university ombudsman was always present to take notes and follow up. The sessions often went into the evening hours and it was not unusual for me to leave the office after seeing the last person out at eight or nine at night. Often, people came in groups to lobby me—townies with complaints about unruly students, parents unhappy with their children's grades. Many of the sessions were also hilarious and, if they accomplished nothing else, they exposed to me the DNA of the university. I noticed one elderly woman, perhaps in her sixties, who seemed to have no relationship with the university, who came every week and sat quietly observant, knitting and looking on quite contentedly. One Wednesday I asked her if she had an issue she'd like to raise or a question she'd like to ask. "No," she replied, "I'm here because it's the best show in town."

I held these Open Hours for two years and then decided to stop. I had hoped, naively, that I would set a model that other university administrators would emulate. Even more naively, I had the unrequited wish that somehow or another these sessions, along with other administrative interventions, would de-burcaucratize the campus, make it more responsive to faculty and students. Perhaps I should have kept at it longer, I'm not sure, but it was a painfully revealing—going back to my Antioch roots—"learning experience."

It wasn't fatalism that gripped me, only realism.

• About *leadership* (and about *me*): Those eleven years at Buffalo and Cincinnati were arduous, difficult, and enormously important. Doing it is remarkably different from writing about it. Business professors are especially vulnerable to a dangerous chasm between the practice of management and the study of management. In most professions, professors are practitioners as well as teachers and researchers. Take medicine—the professors are clinicians. Of course, there are a few who only conduct research, usually those who hold dual Ph.D. and MD degrees. But for the most part, medical school teachers and researchers also practice; they not only chair departments but also maintain a practice. Consulting, as many management professors do, is not the same as doing management. Faculty who teach direction and production at USC's top-ranked Cinema and TV School also direct and produce films; faculty teaching screenwriting also write screenplays. I don't think it's possible to understand a profession, as compared to an academic discipline such as physics or English literature, without practicing it. There is a profound difference, it seems to me, between reading up on something and performing it, between observed truth and participative truth. Eleven years of actually "running something" provided an understanding of the thick texture of leadership, the sweaty complexity of it, the triumphs and tragedies of it, the personal underworld that leaders experience. It's not for everyone, I know, but those years on the ground grounded me in an understanding of management that, speaking as an experiential freak, I couldn't have gotten any other way.

In many ways, I have to add quickly, it wasn't for me either. Not for the long run, anyway. The truth is that I wouldn't have missed it for the world and I wouldn't want to do it again. It's no false modesty to say that although I had a curious admixture of shortcomings and competencies as an academic leader, I knew in my heart that there were others who could do it as well or better. It simply wasn't my calling. There was a definite turning point, a glistening moment in time, when that realization crystallized.

I was delivering an evening lecture to the faculty and students of Harvard's School of Education, sometime in 1976. They invited me to speak on the topic of academic leadership and I spent a fair amount of time writing for the event. The auditorium was full and I thought I was at my best, enjoying myself enormously as I described wittily and ironically the existential groaning, the ups and downs, the backstage gossip of governing a large urban university. As I think back to that evening I was part social anthropologist and part standup comic. The audience seemed to enjoy it as much as I did. And then came a question from the dean of the school, Paul Ylvisaker, one of the most respected figures in all of higher education, a consultant to the Ford Foundation and a man whose wisdom was sought after by everyone from the U.S. president to Harvard's. He was the uncontested Clark Clifford of higher ed.

Now I thought that my experience responding to questions was sharpened to a fine point after so many years of teaching as well as spending a lot of time with the media, who loved asking embarrassing and difficult questions. My singular conceit, shortly to end, was that there wasn't a question I couldn't respond to in a convincing (and winning) way. At the least, I thought I was beyond being stumped. He was sitting near the back of the room and the question came out me like a long, high lob, floating lazily over the audience and masking its astuteness in that self-effacing (and deceptive) Midwestern drawl of his. It was short. "Warren," he asked, "do you *love* being president of the University of Cincinnati?" I don't know how many seconds passed before I responded. The room was suddenly so quiet that I could hear my heart beating. Finally, I looked up at Paul and haltingly said, "I don't know." Actually, that was the moment I knew the answer but hadn't yet told myself.

The truth is that I didn't love it and didn't have the passion for it and that what I was doing wasn't my own voice. I wanted to *be* a university president. I didn't want to *do* university president. Now that was a huge lesson for me because if there is one single thing I have found out about leaders is that, by and large if not every day, they seem to love what they're doing. C. Michael Armstrong, the exemplary CEO and chairman of AT&T, told me recently that his favorite day of the week is Monday. I told him that he should have his license plate read TGIM (Thank God, It's Monday).[5] It won't be Jack Welch's strategic genius that will be remembered as the signature of his almost twenty years of GE's leadership. It will be the way he has mobilized and energized hundreds of thousands of workers across many types of businesses into constructive activity that will mark his place in business history. And when I coteach a course on leadership to undergraduates with USC's president, Steve Sample, I realize how much he loves what he's doing. I felt that fundraising was an unnatural act; that guy loves it. He loves dealing with the daily conflicts, the numbing daily interactions, being always on the phone in his car, trying his best to keep his Sundays "free" but not always successfully, and dealing with the countless other responsibilities that go with leading a major research university. No one can be a great leader without that passion and love.

Ylvisaker's question made me aware that administration wasn't for me. I didn't have the passion and love for it. That epiphanic moment I had was later confirmed over the following twenty years' researching the qualities of exemplary leaders. The simple fact is that all exemplary leaders have found their unique voice, their trademark. They know who they are and that what they do, no one else can quite do it their way. The late Jerry Garcia, the great, gray presence of the Grateful Dead, said it better than I just did. He once observed, "You do not merely want to be considered just the best of the best. You want to be considered the only one who can do what you do."

To this day I don't know what Ylvisaker was picking up in my delivery or my body language that informed his question. It may have been my casual, detached delivery or something in my eyes. Perhaps he had read the W. H. Auden poem I recently came upon:

> You need not see what someone is doing
> To know if it is his vocation,
> You have only to watch his eyes:
> A cook mixing a sauce, a surgeon
> Making a primary incision,
> A clerk completing a bill of lading
> Wear the same rapt expression,
> forgetting themselves in a function.

He must have known that I couldn't forget myself in that function.

Act III: USC (1979)

In 1978 I resigned from UC and received a Twentieth Century Fund grant to write a book on leadership. Shortly after, in April 1979, I found myself in a London hospital recovering from what my British doctors called a "moderately roughish" heart attack. I had been attending a conference at St. George's House in Windsor Castle. It so happened that my longtime friend from M.I.T. days, Charles Handy, was provost of St. George's House, the newly established continuing education center for the Church of England. Charles was also chairing the conference I was attending when I collapsed. I was recuperating in improbable quarters, the flat of Elizabeth and Charles Handy, compressed into the ancient wall of Henry the Third's wing of Windsor Castle. The Handys graciously and generously looked after me for three long months as I wobbled back to health.

An important, almost Dickensian, coincidence occurred during my convalescence at Windsor. Jim O'Toole called, out of the blue, and invited me to join him on the faculty of the University of Southern California. It was a godsend. I was out of work. Literally. I was considering a number of professorships, but they all paled in comparison with going West and working with Jim, Ian Mitroff, Ed Lawler, Larry Greiner, Steve Kerr, Tom Cummings, and Dick Mason—and the all-star cast being assembled by the business school dean, Jack Steele, an intellectual outlaw who broke all the rules of the game and built the best management department in the world. I thought, oh yes, oh yes, here was a chance to really make a dent in the universe and make some useful mischief.[6]

I felt like Rip Van Winkle when I joined USC, or to be more current, like Austin Powers. It wasn't twenty or thirty years, only eleven since I left the world of scholarship, but the field I left in 1967 was unrecognizable. It hadn't just blossomed, it had become a heavy industry. I felt that the tiny municipality I had known was now Brobdingnag. Virtually every business school and other professional schools as well had their own version of an Organization Behavior Department, parading under a variety of names such as Management and Organization (our version at USC) or just Management sometimes commingled with Strategy and other combinations. There were to my astonishment a number of hugely successful, best-selling business books, mega-hits like Peters and Waterman's *In Search of Excellence*, Naisbitt's *Megatrends*, Blanchard and Johnson's *The One Minute Manager*, Covey's *The Seven Habits*, and anything Drucker wrote.

To put this in perspective, Doug McGregor's book on management, *The Human Side of Enterprise*, sold at its peak year (1965) thirty thousand copies and Abe Maslow's book on management—sure it had a weird title, *Eupsychian Management*—sold only three thousand copies when it was published. Last year, when it was republished by Wiley, it sold three thousand copies in its first week on the market.

I suspect that one of two factors, or probably both, may have caused this explosive interest: one was the unexpected and reluctantly accepted notion that maybe the attitudes, perceptions, and feelings of the workforce and the social architecture they worked under could have something to do with productivity. The other factor may have been the unprecedented competition that American industry was facing from Japan and Germany, which was occurring most dramatically in the late 1970s and the 1980s. In many industrial sectors such as automobiles and consumer electronics they were—to put it politely—eating our lunch. Tom Peters credits the multimillion-book sales of his best-seller primarily to the latter. Whatever explanation you prefer, one thing was clear: the United States was no longer Numero Uno and

enlightened business leaders were no longer as supremely confident as they had been for the four decades following World War
II. They opened their minds to our ideas.

It's also been one long boom for business schools. The last statistic I saw showed that eighty-five thousand MBAs graduated in
1998. A concomitant of that is the widespread growth of Ph.D. programs. In 1959 I chaired the Sloan School's committee to design
its first Ph.D. program. Up to that point, most business schools did
not offer Ph.D.'s. In fact, business schools were not thought to be
an integral part of the intellectual life of the modern university.
Most professors of business did not have doctorates. Those who
did were either DBAs or had came out of industrial engineering or
held an advanced degree in accounting.

What drastically changed the intellectual landscape of business
education was the influence of two major foundation reports, both
published in 1959. The Gordon/Howell report (sponsored by the
Ford Foundation) and the Pierson study (funded by the Carnegie
Foundation) were enormously influential and had a formidable
impact on how business education was done. They led to the flow
of vast amounts of dollars to a new breed of business professors
and to a new type of business school. So we observed the new
schools such as Carnegie-Mellon's Graduate School of Industrial
Administration, the already mentioned Sloan School, the Stanford
School of Management, and too many others to mention here
carving out new curricula and new research agendas, and in the
process shedding their Rodney Dangerfield syndrome.

If I could put important findings of these two foundation
reports into one pithy statement (doing a grave injustice to both),
it would be this: business schools had to get away from their almost
exclusive reliance on "clinical experience" and develop a more
rigorous and scientifically based canon. The tension between em-
pirical experience and codified, systematic knowledge is still a live-
wire issue, regularly contested in all professional schools. The
extent to which schools of management learn how to make this a
creative rather than a divisive tension will determine whether or
not they can accomplish their academic purposes successfully.

USC, for me—emerging after eleven years of fairly grueling
administrative duties—was like joining an intellectual spa, an
"Intellectual Fitness Center."[7] This was *Home*, writing and teaching

again; finding my own voice. To paraphrase Jerry Garcia, I was back to being the only one doing what I can do.

These past twenty years may not have been as intense as those Cambridge and Boston ones, but I've never been happier or enjoyed so many significant intellectual partnerships. I could fill a complete book if I were to mention all of them, but here goes with a few:

With the partnership of Jim O'Toole and others from the Management and Organization Department, we founded the Leadership Institute, one of the first such centers in the country.

Again with Jim as editor, we created a radically different formatted management periodical, *New Management,* a magazine that foreshadowed the very popular, hip 'zine, *FAST COMPANY.* With Dean Steele's support and Richard Wurman's design, we made the business of business interesting.

Working with Ian Mitroff and Dick Mason, we inaugurated a series of management books under the Jossey-Bass label.

I coauthored a number of books with colleagues: with Burt Nanus, *Leaders;* with Ian Mitroff, *The Unreality Industry;* with Pat Biederman, *Organizing Genius;* and with Dave Heenan, *Co-Leaders.*

The most intense and exciting collaboration going on at the present time is coteaching an undergraduate course on leadership with USC's president, Steve Sample. We recruit fifty of USC's best and brightest students and introduce these sharp twenty-year-olds to leadership through the Great Books, novels, movies, Socratic-like discussions, weekly essays, and a wide selection of guest speakers, from Michael Dukakis to former governor Pete Wilson, from the Reverend Cecil Murray to Mayor Richard Riordan.

Great cities and great institutions have the Spirit of Place. Certainly, the Boston area had it when I was there earlier in the century. I would argue that now Southern California and the university that is most emblematic of this region, USC, has that spirit.

We do know that cities that have remained great and glorious over long periods of time are those with a rich variety of population, economic enterprise, and social functions. Diversity endows them with resilience and the gift of maintaining identity in the midst of endless changes. Perhaps this is all an elegant justification for why these past twenty years have been, for me, so alive, so absorbing, and so invigorating, who knows. But I want to add something to what I said earlier—it isn't only history that favored my career, it's also geography, the spirit of the *place*.

Notes and References

Chapter One: Note

1. Peter Capelli, *The New Deal at Work: Managing in the Market-Driven Workforce.* Cambridge, Mass.: Harvard Business School Press, 1999.

Chapter Two: References

Lawler, E. E. *From the Ground Up: Six Principles for Creating the New Logic Corporation.* San Francisco: Jossey-Bass, 1996.

Lawler, E. E., with Mohrman, S. A., and Ledford, G. E., Jr. *Strategies for High Performance Organizations: The CEO Report.* San Francisco: Jossey-Bass, 1998.

Lawler, E. E. *Rewarding Excellence: Strategies for the New Economy.* San Francisco: Jossey-Bass, 2000.

Prahalad, C. K., and Hamel, G. "The Core Competence of the Corporation." *Harvard Business Review,* 1990, *68*(3), 79–91.

Chapter Four: References

American Management Association, 1997. "Corporate Job Creation, Elimination, and Downsizing: Summary of Key Findings." Washington, D.C.: American Management Association.

Bennis, W., and Biederman, P. W., 1997. *Organizing Genius.* Reading, Mass.: Addison-Wesley.

Cortada, J., 1998. "Where Did Knowledge Workers Come From," in J. Cortada (ed.), *Rise of the Knowledge Worker.* Portsmouth, N.H.: Butterworth-Heinemann.

Davenport, T., Jarvenpaa, S., and Beers, M., 1996. "Improving Knowledge Work Processes," *Sloan Management Review,* Summer, pp. 53–65.

Drucker, P., 1969. "Management's New Role," *Harvard Business Review,* Nov.-Dec. Reprinted in *Harvard Business Review Leadership Series,* Part II, pp. 64–69.

Kanter, R., 1997. "Restoring People to the Heart of the Organization," in F. Hesselbein, M. Goldsmith, and R. Beckhard (eds.), *The Organization of the Future.* San Francisco: Jossey-Bass.

Leonard, D., 1995. *Wellsprings of Knowledge.* Cambridge, Mass.: Harvard Business School Press.

Machlup, F., 1992. *The Production and Distribution of Knowledge in the United States.* Princeton, N.J.: Princeton University Press.

Pfeffer, J., 1998. *The Human Equation.* Cambridge, Mass.: Harvard Business School Press.

Quinn, J. B., 1992. *Intelligent Enterprise: A Knowledge and Service-Based Paradigm for Industry.* New York: Free Press.

Wenger, E., 1998. *Communities of Practice: Learning, Meaning, and Identity.* Cambridge, England: Cambridge University Press.

Chapter Six: Notes

1. William H. Whyte Jr., *The Organization Man* (New York: Touchstone, 1956), pp. 14ff.
2. Gary Heil, Warren Bennis, and Deborah C. Stephens, *Douglas McGregor, Revisited: Managing the Human Side of the Enterprise* (New York: Wiley, 2000), p. 6.
3. Etienne Wenger, *Communities of Practice: Learning, Meaning, and Identity* (Cambridge, England: Cambridge University Press, 1998), p. xiii.
4. Thomas A. Stewart, "See Jack. See Jack Run Europe," *Fortune,* September 27, 1999, pp. 124ff.
5. Rick Levine, Christopher Locke, Doc Searls, and David Weinberger, *The Cluetrain Manifesto: The End of Business as Usual* (Reading, Mass.: Perseus Books, 2000), pp. xii–xvii.

Chapter Seven: Notes

1. "Where Are We on the Web? *FAST COMPANY* (October 1999): 306.
2. Public Allies, *New Leadership for a New Century* (Washington, D.C.: Public Allies, 1998).
3. PriceWaterhouseCoopers, *Innovation Survey* (London: PriceWaterhouseCoopers, 1999), p. 3.
4. Frederick F. Reichheld and Phil Schefter, "E-Loyalty: Your Secret Weapon on the Web," *Harvard Business Review* (July-August 2000): 107.
5. Barry Z. Posner, "What It Means to Act with Integrity." Paper presented at the 6th International Meeting of the Western Academy of Management Conference (Shizuoka, Japan), July 2000.

6. Warren Bennis, *Managing People Is Like Herding Cats* (Provo, Utah: Executive Excellence Publishing, 1997), p. 86.
7. Warren Bennis, *On Becoming a Leader* (Reading, Mass.: Addison-Wesley, 1989), p. 40.
8. Diane Dreher, *The Tao of Personal Leadership* (New York: Harper-Business, 1997).
9. Anne Lamott, *Bird by Bird: Some Instructions on Writing and Life* (New York: Pantheon, 1994).
10. Richard P. Farson, *Management of the Absurd: Paradoxes of Leadership* (New York: Simon & Schuster, 1996).
11. Dreher, *The Tao of Personal Leadership.*

Chapter Eight: References

Allinson, R. E. (1993). *Global disasters.* Upper Saddle River, N.J.: Prentice-Hall.

Berliner, P. F. (1994). *Thinking in jazz: The infinite art of improvisation.* Chicago: University of Chicago Press.

Campbell, D. T. (1990). Asch's moral epistemology for socially shared knowledge. In I. Rock (Ed.), *The legacy of Solomon Asch: Essays in cognition and social psychology* (pp. 39–52). Hillsdale, N.J.: Erlbaum.

Hurst, D. K. (1995). *Crisis and renewal.* Boston: Harvard Business School Press.

Isenberg, D. (1985). Some hows and whats of managerial thinking: Implications for future army leaders. In J. G. Hunt & J. D. Blair (Eds.), *Leadership on the future battlefield* (pp. 168–181). Dulles, Va.: Pergamon-Brassey's.

Kellman, S. G. (1999). Swan songs. *American Scholar, 68*(4), 111–120.

McDaniel, R. R., Jr. (1997). Strategic leadership: A view from quantum and chaos theories. *Health Care Management Review, 22*(1), 21–37.

Muller, W. (1999). *Sabbath: Restoring the sacred rhythm of rest.* New York: Bantam.

Roethlisberger, F. J. (1977). *The elusive phenomena.* Cambridge, Mass.: Harvard University Press.

Ryle, G. (1979). Improvisation. In G. Ryle, *On thinking* (pp. 121–130). London: Blackwell.

Schön, D. A. (1987). *Educating the reflective practitioner.* San Francisco: Jossey-Bass.

Weick, K. E. (1995). *Sensemaking in organizations.* Thousand Oaks, Calif.: Sage.

Chapter Nine: References

Bennis, W., and Biederman, P. W. *Organizing Genius.* Reading, Mass.: Addison-Wesley, 1997.

Bennis, W., and Nanus, B. *Leaders.* New York: HarperCollins, 1985.

Bennis, W., and Slater, P. *The Temporary Society.* San Francisco: Jossey-Bass, 1999.

Davis, S., and Meyer, C. *Blur: The Speed of Change in the Connected Economy.* Reading, Mass.: Perseus Books, 1998.

Friedman, T. L. *The Lexus and the Olive Tree.* New York: Farrar, Straus & Giroux, 1999.

Jackson, M. "Women's Business Thriving," *Santa Cruz Sentinel,* Apr. 28, 1999, p. B5.

Kelly, K. *New Rules for the New Economy.* New York: Viking, 1998.

Knoke, W. *Bold New World.* Kodansha International, 1996.

Margulis, L., and Sagan, D. *Microcosmos.* New York: Summit Books, 1990.

Metcalf, H. C., and Urwick, L. (eds.). *Dynamic Administration: The Collected Papers of Mary Parker Follett.* New York: HarperCollins, 1942.

Naisbitt, J., and Aburdene, P. *Megatrends 2000.* New York: Morrow, 1990.

Postrel, V. *The Future and Its Enemies.* New York: Free Press, 1998.

Sahtouris, E. *Earthdance.* Lincoln, Nebr.: iUniverse.com, 2000. Available online: http://www.ratical.org/LifeWeb/Erthdnce/chapter6.html.

Tannen, D. *The Argument Culture.* New York: Random House, 1998.

Chapter Ten: References

Bennis, W., and Biederman, P. (1997). *Organizing genius.* Reading, Mass.: Perseus Books.

Csikszentmihalyi, M. (1996). *Creativity: Flow and the psychology of discovery and invention.* New York: HarperCollins.

Csikszentmihalyi, M. (1999a). Implications of the systems perspective for the study of creativity. In R. J. Sternberg (Ed.), *Handbook of human creativity,* pp. 313–338. New York: Cambridge University Press.

Csikszentmihalyi, M. (1999b). Kreativität und die Evolution Komplex Systeme (Creativity and the evolution of complex systems). In M. Sauer-Sachtleben (Ed.), *Kooperation mit der Evolution* (Cooperation with evolution), pp. 415–438. München: Eugen Diederich Verlag.

Csikszentmihalyi, M. (2000). Creativity. *Encyclopedia of psychology.* New York: Oxford University Press.

Drucker, P. F. (1985). *Innovation and entrepreneurship.* Oxford, England: Butterworth-Heinemann.

Hauser, A. (1951). *The social history of art.* New York: Vintage.

Heydenreich, L. H. (1974). *Il primo Rinascimento* (Early Renaissance). Milano: Rizzoli.

Chapter Eleven: Notes

1. Admittedly, all ages have their uncertainties, and every era experiences change. Besides, both the nature of the uncertainties and the rate of change differ from one era to the next.
2. Tom Peters, *Thriving on Chaos: Handbook for a Management Revolution* (New York: Random House, 1987).
3. We are ineluctably interconnected on every level—economically, environmentally, organizationally, politically, sociologically, and psychologically. In large technical systems, interdependence and tight coupling lead to unforeseen interactions that, in turn, cause normal accidents, according to C. Perrow, in *Normal Accidents: Living with High-Risk Technologies* (New York: Basic Books, 1984). Interdependence has similar consequences for the organizational world. A downturn on the New York Stock Exchange ripples through financial markets around the globe. Events witnessed on television have worldwide reverberations.
4. Max Weber noted that charismatic leaders are "born of distress." (See his "The Sociology of Charismatic Authority," in H. H. Gerth and C. Wright Mills (eds.), *From Max Weber: Essays in Sociology*, pp. 245–252 (New York: Oxford University Press, 1946). For a discussion of connective leaders, see Jean Lipman-Blumen, *Connective Leadership: Managing in a Changing World* (New York: Oxford University Press, 2000).
5. Sigmund Freud, *Group Psychology and the Analysis of the Ego* (New York: Bantam Books, 1965), p. 16. (Originally published 1921.)
6. Ernest Becker, *The Denial of Death* (New York: Free Press, 1973), p. 133.
7. Albert Camus, *The Fall* (New York: Knopf, 1957), p. 133.
8. John A. Byrne, *Chainsaw: The Notorious Career of Al Dunlap in the Era of Profit-at-Any-Price* (New York: HarperBusiness, 1999).
9. This occurs through the familiar psychological process we know as "transference," as described by Freud, Rank, Becker, and others. For an interesting contemporary discussion of transference, see Daniel Liechty, *Transference and Transcendence: Ernest Becker's Contribution to Psychotherapy* (Northvale, N.J.: Aronson, 1995).
10. Erich Fromm, *Escape from Freedom* (New York: Avon Books, 1941).
11. For a more in-depth explanation of the working of control myths, see Jean Lipman-Blumen, *Gender Roles and Power* (Upper Saddle River, N.J.: Prentice-Hall, 1984).
12. F. G. Bailey, *Humbuggery and Manipulation: The Art of Leadership* (Ithaca, N.Y.: Cornell University Press, 1988).

13. Clifford Geertz, "Centers, Kings, and Charisma: Reflections on the Symbolics of Power." Chapter 6 in *Local Knowledge: Further Essays in Interpretive Anthropology* (New York: Basic Books, 1983).

14. Ernest Becker, *Escape from Evil* (New York: Free Press, 1976), p. 109.

15. Søren Kierkegaard, *The Concept of Dread,* trans. Walter Lowrie (Princeton, N.J.: Princeton University Press, 1957), p. 144. (Originally published 1844.)

16. James Campbell Quick and Joanne H. Gavin, "The Next Frontier: Edgar Schein on Organizational Therapy." *Academy of Management Executive* 14, no. 1 (2000): 31–44, see p. 37.

17. Kierkegaard, *The Concept of Dread.*

18. That is what Schein calls "survival anxiety."

19. Schein calls this "learning anxiety." See Quick and Gavin, "The Next Frontier."

20. Kurt Lewin's well-known notion of freezing, unfreezing, and refreezing is relevant here. When we are in a frozen state, we feel a sense of certitude, false or otherwise, but a sense of assurance, nonetheless. As we move into an unfrozen state, we feel anxious because the certainties have been removed, and we are not quite sure what will happen next. It is in this unfrozen state, this state of anxiety, that we are open to change, to newness, to experimentation, to learning, to testing ourselves. See Kurt Lewin, "Group Decision and Social Change," in T. M. Newcomb and E. L. Hartley (eds.), *Readings in Social Psychology* (New York: Henry Holt, 1947).

21. Harold J. Leavitt, *Managerial Psychology* (4th ed.) (Chicago: University of Chicago Press, 1978), p. 131.

22. Warren Bennis, "Followership," Chapter 20 in *Managing the Dream* (Reading, Mass.: Perseus Books, 2000), p. 270.

23. Lipman-Blumen, *Connective Leadership.*

24. Chester Barnard, *The Functions of the Executive* (Cambridge, Mass.: Harvard University Press, 1938).

25. This point has been explored by many, including Kierkegaard, Freud, Rank, and Becker. There is a particularly useful discussion in Viktor E. Frankl, *Man's Search for Meaning: An Introduction to Logotheraphy* (4th ed.) (Boston, Mass.: Beacon Press, 1992). (Originally published 1959.)

26. For an extended discussion of this point, see Jean Lipman-Blumen, "Ideology, Social Structure, and Crisis." Paper presented at the American Sociological Association annual meeting, August 25–27, 1974, Quebec, Canada.

27. This point has been articulated by Sheldon Solomon in a set of superb taped lectures on Kierkegaard, Rank, and Becker. (Available from the Ernest Becker Foundation, Seattle, Washington.)

28. Ron Leifer, "The Legacy of Ernest Becker," Part I, *Psychnews International* 2, no. 4 (July-September 1997).

29. For an expanded discussion of symbolic immortality, see Robert J. Lifton, *The Broken Connection: On Death and the Continuity of Life* (New York: Simon & Schuster, 1979).

30. This point is further elaborated in Lipman-Blumen, *Connective Leadership*, Chapter 12.

31. Clifford Geertz, "Thick Description: Toward an Interpretive Theory of Culture." Chapter 1 in *The Interpretation of Cultures* (New York: Basic Books, 1973).

32. For detailed discussions of the nature, role, and pitfalls of immortality projects, see Becker, *The Denial of Death.*

33. Mihaly Csikszentmihalyi, *Flow: The Psychology of Optimal Experience* (New York: HarperCollins, 1990), pp. 222, 240.

34. Warren Bennis, "An Invented Life: Shoe Polish, Milli Vanilli, and Sapiential Circles." Chapter 16 in *Managing the Dream,* pp. 199–200.

35. The immortality project has been discussed by Freud, Rank, Becker, and others.

36. Anthropological and historical research provides ample evidence that in the earliest societies hero status could not be achieved without confronting fear and death in war and other rituals. The hero was the individual who faced death, "who could go into the spirit world, the world of the dead, and return alive. He had descendants in the mystery cults of the Eastern Mediterranean, which were cults of death and resurrection. The divine hero of each of these cults was one who had come back from the dead." Becker, *The Denial of Death,* p. 12. Christians also believe that the central figure in Christianity rose from the dead.

37. I am indebted to Neil Elgee for refining my definition of courage.

38. Becker described this as "reaching out by [our] whole being toward life." Becker, *The Denial of Death,* pp. 152–153.

39. See Becker, *The Denial of Death.*

Chapter Twelve: References

Bennis, Warren, and Goldsmith, Joan. *Learning to Lead* (Reading, Mass.: Addison-Wesley, 1997).

Deiss, Kathryn J., and Soete, George. "Developing Shared Leadership: A Note for a New Year." *ARL Newsletter,* December 1997.

Forum Corporation. *Leadership—A Forum Issues Special Report.* Boston: Forum Corporation, 1990.

Groves, Martha. "Careers/Leadership: Cream Rises to the Top, but From a Small Group." *Los Angeles Times,* June 8, 1998.

Joyce, Amy. "Young Leaders Sidestepping Old Rules of Management: As Ranks Grow, Twentysomethings Find Ways Around Age Gap." *Washington Post,* July 19, 1998.

Lewis, Diane E. "Generation X's Rapid Rise in Workplace Leaves Elders Feeling Threatened." *Boston Globe,* June 24, 1998.

"The Region: Not a Pretty Picture," *Boston Globe,* October 18, 1998.

Chapter Fifteen: References

Alexander, Keith, "CEO Leaving Tarnished Legacy," *USA Today,* March 14, 2000, p. 6-1.

Bannon, Lisa, and Deogun, Nikhul, "How Times Mirror Official Won Chandler's Trust," *Wall Street Journal,* March 16, 2000, p. 17.

Barrett, Amy, "The Comeback of Henry Silverman," *Business Week,* March 13, 2000, pp. 128–150.

Barringer, Felicity, "A General Whose Time Ran Out," *New York Times,* March 15, 2000, pp. C-1, C-7.

Bennis, Warren, *An Invented Life,* Reading, Mass.: Addison-Wesley, 1993.

Bennis, Warren, and O'Toole, James, "Choosing the Right CEO," *Harvard Business Review,* May-June 2000, pp. 170–175.

Benoit, William L., *Accounts, Excuses, and Apologies: A Theory of Image Restoration Strategies,* Albany: State University of New York Press, 1997.

Bloomberg, Michael, *Bloomberg on Bloomberg,* New York: Wiley, 1997.

Braudy, Leo, *The Frenzy of Renown: A History of Fame,* New York: Oxford University Press, 1986.

Burrows, Peter, and Elstrom, Peter, "The Boss: Carly Fiorina's Challenge Will Be to Propel Staid Hewlett-Packard into the Internet Age Without Sacrificing the Very Things That Made It Great," *Business Week,* August 2, 1999, pp. 76–80.

Campbell, Joseph, *The Hero with a Thousand Faces,* Princeton, N.J.: Princeton University Press, 1949.

Carlton, Jim, *Apple: The Inside Story of Intrigue, Egomania, and Business Blunders,* New York: New York Times Books, 1997.

Coleman, Calmetta, "Kmart Lures Bozic away from Levitz to Be Vice Chairman, CEO Contender," *Wall Street Journal,* November 18, 1998, p. B-10.

Cooper, Cary L., *Stress Research: Issues for the Eighties,* New York: Wiley, 1983.

Cooper, Cary L., and Payne, R., *Causes, Coping, and Consequences of Stress at Work,* New York: Wiley, 1988.

Elsbach, Kimberly D., and Sutton, Robert, "Acquiring Organizational Legitimacy, Through Illegitimate Actions," *Academy of Management Journal,* 35, 1992, pp. 699–738.

Fisher, Lawrence, "H-P Chairman David Packard Will Retire," *New York Times,* September 15, 1993, p. B-15.

Fombrun, Charles, and Shanley, M., "What's in a Name? Reputation Building and Corporate Strategy," *Academy of Management Journal,* 33, 1990, pp. 233–258.

Freedman, Samuel G., "Alan Jay Lerner, the Lyricist and Playwright Is Dead at 67," *New York Times,* June 15, 1986, pp. 1, 36.

Gardener, Howard, *Extraordinary Minds,* New York: Basic Books, 1998.

Golembiewski, Robert T., Menzenrider, Robert F., and Stevenson, Jerry G., *Stress in Organizations,* New York: Praeger, 1986.

Henahan, Donal, "Leonard Bernstein, 72, Music's Monarch, Dies," *New York Times,* October 15, 1990, A-1.

Holmes, T. H., and Rahe, R. N., "The Social Adjustment Rating Scale," *Journal of Psychosomatic Research,* 11, 1967, pp. 213–218.

Hurwitz, Johanna, *Leonard Bernstein: A Passion for Music,* New York: Morrow, 1989.

Jones, Edward E., and Nesbitt, Robert E., "The Actor and the Observer: Divergent Perceptions of Cause and Behavior," in E. E. Jones, D. E. Kanouse, Kelly H. H. Weiner, R. E. Nesbitt, S. Valines, and B. Weiner, eds., *Attribution: Perceiving the Causes,* Morristown, N.J.: General Learning Press, 1971.

Kobassa, Susan, "Stressful Life Events, Personality, and Health: An Inquiry into Hardiness," *Journal of Personality and Social Psychology,* 37, 1979, pp. 1–11.

Laurents, Arthur, *Original Story by Arthur Laurents,* New York: Knopf, 2000.

Leonhardt, David, "Afterlife of a Powerful Chief," *New York Times,* March 15, 2000, pp. C-1, C-10.

Marcus, Bernard, and Blank, Arthur, *Built from Scratch,* New York: New York Times Books, 1999.

Matheny, Kenneth B., and Riordan, Richard J., *Stress and Strategies for Lifestyle Management,* Atlanta: Georgia State University Press, 1992.

Palmeri, Christopher, "Radio Shack Redux," *Forbes,* March 23, 1998, p. 54.

Pollack, Andrew, "Can Steve Jobs Do It Again?" *New York Times,* November 8, 1997.

Pulley, Brett, "Strained Family: Culture of Racial Bias at Shoney's Underlies Chairman's Departure," *Wall Street Journal,* December 21, 1992, p. A-1.

Rank, Otto, *Art and Artist,* New York: Knopf, 1932, pp. 214–216.

Romeo, Peter, "What Really Happened at Shoney's?" *Restaurant Business,* May 1, 1993, pp. 116–120.

Rouvalis, Christina, "A Wild Ride," *Pittsburgh Post Gazette,* July 2, 1995, pp. C-1, C-6.

Rutenberg, James, "Towering Comeback for Trump," *New York Daily News,* April 7, 1996, p. 10.

Schiesel, Seth, "The Numbers Don't Explain the Woes of AT&T," *New York Times,* May 3, 2000, pp. C-1, C-13.

Schuler, Randall, "Organizational and Occupational Stress and Coping: A Model and Overview," in Mary Dean Lee and Rabinara Kanungo, eds., *The Management of Work and Personal Life,* New York: Prager, 1984, pp. 169–172.

Scott, Marcus B., and Lyman, Stanford, "Accounts," *American Sociological Review,* 33, 1968, pp. 46–60.

Sonnenfeld, Jeffrey, *The Hero's Farewell: What Happens When CEOs Retire,* New York: Oxford University Press, 1988.

Staw, Barry M., McKechnie, Pamela, and Puffer, Sheila, "The Justification of Organizational Performance," *Administrative Sciences Quarterly,* 28, 1983, pp. 582–600.

Thomkins, Richard, "Casinos Deal Trump a Fistful of Aces," *Financial Times,* June 31, 1994, p. 14.

Chapter Sixteen: References

Warren Bennis, *Managing People Is Like Herding Cats,* Provo, UT: Executive Excellence Publishing, 1999, p. 25.

Disney Institute, Lake Buena Vista, FL, May 10, 2000; poll group of 2,000 youth from ninety countries distinguished by their good deeds in communities. Available online: http://www.mcdonalds.com/corporate/press/corporate/2000/05102000/index.html.

James M. Kouzes and Barry Z. Posner, *The Leadership Challenge: How to Get Extraordinary Things Done in Organizations,* San Francisco: Jossey-Bass, 1987.

Thomas J. Peters, "Foreword," in James M. Kouzes and Barry Z. Posner, *The Leadership Challenge: How to Get Extraordinary Things Done in Organizations,* San Francisco: Jossey-Bass, 1987, p. xiii.

Robert D. Putnam, *Bowling Alone: The Collapse and Revival of American Community,* New York: Simon & Schuster, 2000.

Search Institute, "Five Fundamental Resources for Children and Youth: Search Commissioned and Published by America's Promise," survey of 254,000 6th to 12th grade youth in 460 communities across

America, Minneapolis, MN: Search Institute, 1997. Available online: http://www.search-institute.org.

Susan J. Tolchin, *The Angry American: How Voter Rage Is Changing the Nation,* Boulder, CO: Westview Press, 1996.

Chapter Seventeen: References

Bagby, Meredith. (April 25, 2000). "Neglection 2000 Report: Don't Ask, Don't Vote: Young Adults in the Presidential Primary." *Third Millennium.*

Bennis, Warren G. (1994). *On Becoming a Leader.* Reading, MA: Perseus Books.

Brinkerhoff, Noel. (December 1999). "Gen X: The Unknown Quantity." *California Journal.*

Burns, James MacGregor. (May 14, 2000). "Dive In Gents. Boldness Is No Vice." *Washington Post.*

Dionne, E. J., Jr. (August 26, 1998). "Reform Generation?" *Washington Post.*

Halstead, Ted. (August 1999). "A Politics for Generation X." *Atlantic Monthly.*

Hart, Peter. (August 28, 1998). "New Leadership for a New Century: Key Findings from a Study on Youth, Leadership, and Community Service." Washington, DC: Peter D. Hart Research Associates.

Light, Paul C. (1999). *The New Public Service.* Washington, DC: Brookings Institution Press.

McGrory, Mary. (February 6, 2000). "Gen X Marks the Ballot." *Washington Post.*

Panetta, Leon. (January 13, 2000). "Institute Poll Shows College Students Turned Off by Politics, Turned On by Other Public Service." Monterey Bay, CA: Panetta Institute.

Shore, Bill. (1999). *The Cathedral Within: Transforming Your Life by Giving Something Back.* New York: Random House.

Thornburgh, Ron. (February 10, 1999). "New Millennium Project: Why Young People Don't Vote." Washington, DC: National Association of Secretaries of State.

Postlude: Notes

1. I've taken the phrase "Hitler's ghost" from Barbara Kellerman's seminal essay on this topic.
2. Actually, the very first academic article I wrote was published in 1953 by the *M.I.T. Graduate Magazine,* "*Antigone, Billy Budd,* and *The Caine Mutiny:* The Individual vs. Society."
3. My school motto at Westwood High (in New Jersey) was *Res non Verba,* Deeds not Words.

4. The title appeared in a review of my book *Changing Organizations,* McGraw-Hill, 1966.

5. Incidentally, this is the title of a splendid book by Ken Cloke and Joan Goldsmith, Irwin Press, 1997.

6. I lifted most of this paragraph from my epilogue to Jim's book, an uncommonly masterful one, *Leadership A to Z,* Jossey-Bass, 1999.

7. I stole this phrase from Mort Meyerson. When he was CEO of Perot Systems, he would on occasion take a group of diverse and different executives through brainstorming sessions. He called these "Intellectual Fitness Centers."

Index

The Authors

Warren Bennis is university professor and founding chairman of the Leadership Institute at the University of Southern California. He is the author or editor of over twenty-six books on such topics as leadership, change management, and creative collaboration. About two million copies of his books are in print.

He consults with a number of global corporations as well as political leaders. His book *Leaders* was recently designated as one of the top fifty business books of all time by the *Financial Times*. *Forbes* magazine refers to him as the "Dean of Leadership Gurus." His latest books, *Organizing Genius*, 1997, *Co-Leaders*, 1999, and *Managing the Dream*, 2000, summarize his major concerns: leadership, change, and creative collaboration.

Tara Church cofounded Tree Musketeers at age eight as a neighborhood tree-planting project, and has grown it into a national nonprofit organization with a network of millions. She is a tireless activist in tree planting and other "in the trenches" kinds of projects, but her greatest love is empowering and mentoring other young people. She coordinated two national conferences, launched the national One In A Million campaign to empower a million kids to plant a million trees by the end of 2000, and currently promotes youth volunteerism as a partner on the White House Millennium Council.

Church's work has been widely recognized with honors such as the 1994 President's Volunteer Action Award from President Clinton, the 1996 BRICK Award for community building efforts, John Denver's Windstar Youth Award, and the United Nations/Earth Day International "Youth & Environment Award." In a tremendous honor, she was also named one of fifty nonprofit delegates to the

President's Summit For America's Future, and was recently selected as a Daily Point of Light.

Her academic achievements earned her membership in Phi Kappa Phi and Phi Beta Kappa; she was also a finalist for the Harry Truman Award and the Rhodes Scholarship. She graduated from the University of Southern California in 2000 with highest honors in political science and history. She is currently pursuing a JD at Harvard Law School.

Mihaly Csikszentmihalyi is the C. S. and D. J. Davidson Professor of Psychology at the Peter F. Drucker Graduate School of Management at Claremont Graduate University and director of the Quality of Life Research Center. He is also emeritus professor of human development at the University of Chicago, where he chaired the department of psychology. His life's work has been to study what makes people truly happy. Drawing upon years of systematic research, he invented the concept of "flow" as a metaphorical description of the rare mental state associated with feelings of optimal satisfaction and fulfillment. His analysis of the internal and external conditions giving rise to "flow" show that it is almost always linked to circumstances of high challenge when personal skills are used to the utmost. The Hungarian-born social scientist, a graduate of the classical gymnasium Torquato Tasso in Rome, completed his undergraduate studies at the University of Chicago and earned a Ph.D. in psychology there in 1965. He is a fellow of the American Academy of Arts and Sciences, the American Psychological Society, the National Academy of Education, and the National Academy of Leisure Studies and is a foreign member of the Hungarian Academy of Sciences.

Serving on the editorial boards of numerous professional journals, he has been a consultant to business, government organizations, educational associations, and cultural institutions and has given invited lectures throughout the world. In addition to the hugely influential *Flow: The Psychology of Optimal Experience* (1990), which was translated into fifteen languages, he is the author of thirteen other books and some two hundred research articles. His latest volume is titled *Becoming Adult* (2000).

Thomas G. Cummings is a professor, chair of the Department of Management and Organization at the University of Southern California, and executive director of the Leadership Institute. He received his B.S. and MBA degrees from Cornell University, and his Ph.D. in sociotechnical systems from the University of California at Los Angeles. He was previously on the faculty at Case-Western Reserve University. He has authored thirteen books and over forty scholarly articles, and has given numerous invited papers at national and international conferences. He is associate editor of the *Journal of Organizational Behavior* and former editor-in-chief of the *Journal of Management Inquiry,* chairman of the Organizational Development and Change Division of the Academy of Management, and president of the Western Academy of Management.

His major research and consulting interests include designing high-performing organizations and strategic change management. He has conducted several large-scale organization design and change projects, and has consulted to a variety of private and public sector organizations in the United States, Europe, and Mexico.

Thomas H. Davenport is director of the Accenture Institute for Strategic Change, a visiting professor at the Amos Tuck School at Dartmouth College, and a distinguished scholar in residence at Babson College. He is a widely published author and acclaimed speaker on the topics of information and knowledge management, reengineering, enterprise systems, and the use of information technology in business. He has a Ph.D. from Harvard University in organizational behavior and has taught at the Harvard Business School, the University of Chicago, and the University of Texas at Austin Graduate School of Business. He has also directed research at Ernst & Young, McKinsey & Company, and CSC Index.

Davenport wrote the first article on reengineering and the first book—*Process Innovation: Reengineering Work Through Information Technology* (Harvard Business School Press, 1993). He has recently published two well-received books on new approaches to information and knowledge management, *Information Ecology: Mastering the Information and Knowledge Environment* (Oxford University Press, 1997) and the best-seller *Working Knowledge: Managing What Your Organization Knows* (Harvard Business School Press, 1998). His book on enterprise systems, *Mission Critical,* was published by Harvard Business School Press in March 2000. His latest work on attention management will appear in *The Attention Economy* in Spring

2001. His articles have appeared in *Harvard Business Review, Sloan Management Review, California Management Review,* and many other publications. Tom also writes a monthly column created expressly for him by *CIO Magazine* called "Davenport on . . . ," is one of the founding editors of *Knowledge, Inc.,* and is a board member for a variety of organizations.

Cathy L. Greenberg-Walt is a partner with Accenture, Organization and Human Performance. In 1996, Greenberg-Walt founded the Executive Leadership Theme Team at the Institute for Strategic Change, with Alastair Robertson as co-lead. For more than two decades, Greenberg-Walt has used her academic training and professional expertise to assist companies with the successful management and integration of business strategy, process, technology, and people. She has consulted in numerous fields including finance, utilities and regulated industry, manufacturing, transportation, consumer goods, and government. Her expertise in transformational and transitional business change includes process reengineering, executive coaching, cultural and organizational assessment, and journey management during enterprise-wide change programs. With an interdisciplinary doctorate in the behavioral sciences from the Department of Anthropology at Rutgers University, Greenberg-Walt is a frequent keynote speaker and an adjunct professor at Rutgers University.

Charles Handy was, for many years, a professor at the London Business School. He is now an independent writer and broadcaster, and describes himself, these days, as a social philosopher. Handy's main concern is the implications for society, and for individuals, of the dramatic changes that technology and economics are bringing to the workplace and to all our lives. His book *The Empty Raincoat* (published in the United States as *The Age of Paradox*) is a sequel to his earlier best-selling *The Age of Unreason,* which first explored these changes.

Handy graduated from Oriel College, Oxford, with first class honors in "Greats," an intellectual study of classics, history, and philosophy. After college, Handy worked for Shell International before entering the Sloan School of Management at M.I.T. After only one week at Sloan, Handy had already met Warren Bennis, Chris Argyris, Ed Schein, and Mason Haire, among others—

people who fired his fascination with organizations and how they work. When he received his MBA from Sloan in 1967, he returned to England to design and manage the only Sloan Program outside the United States, at Britain's first Graduate Business School, in London. In 1972 Handy became a full professor at the school, specializing in managerial psychology. From 1977 to 1981, he served as warden of St. George's House in Windsor Castle, a private conference and study center concerned with ethics and values in society. He was chairman of the Royal Society of Arts in London from 1987 to 1989, and holds honorary doctorates from seven British universities. Handy lives and works in London, with his wife and business partner, the photographer Elizabeth Handy.

Edward W. Headington serves as a staff assistant to the Political Operations Department, Government Affairs Division, for the National Association of Home Builders. Headington is also a student at George Washington University's Graduate School of Political Management—leadership tract. In addition to his work responsibilities and academic studies, he also served as a graduate senator in GWU's Student Association.

Prior to joining the NAHB and attending GWU's GSPM, he served as an aide to California Assemblymember Scott Wildman and Los Angeles Mayor Richard Riordan. He has also founded the Robert F. Kennedy Forum, an education forum on the life and legacy of RFK, self-published a book of quotes and phrases titled *The Speaker's Bible,* and currently releases a quarterly newsletter called the *Headington Cabal.*

His campaign experience includes fieldwork done at the state, local, and presidential level. He holds a B.A. in political science from the University of Southern California and is a charter student of Warren Bennis and Steven Sample's USC leadership course.

Steven Kerr is vice president of corporate leadership development and chief learning officer for General Electric, including responsibility for GE's renowned leadership education center at Crotonville. He was previously on the faculties of Ohio State University, the University of Southern California, and the University of Michigan and was dean of the faculty of the USC business school from 1985 through 1989.

Kerr is a past president of the Academy of Management, the world's largest association of academicians in management. His writings on leadership, substitutes for leadership, and "The folly of rewarding A, while hoping for B" are among the most cited and reprinted in the management sciences. Among his recent publications are *The Boundaryless Organization* (Jossey-Bass, 1995; coauthor); "Risky Business: The New Pay Game" (*Fortune,* July 22, 1996), and *Ultimate Rewards* (Harvard Business School Press, 1997; editor).

James M. Kouzes is the coauthor, along with Barry Posner, of several award-winning books on leadership, including *The Leadership Challenge: How to Keep Getting Extraordinary Things Done in Organizations; Credibility: How Leaders Gain and Lose It, Why People Demand It; Encouraging the Heart: A Leader's Guide to Rewarding and Recognizing Others;* and *The Leadership Challenge Planner: An Action Guide to Achieving Your Personal Best.* He also codeveloped the widely used and highly acclaimed "Leadership Practices Inventory," a 360-degree questionnaire assessing leadership behavior. Kouzes is chairman emeritus of tompeters!company, a professional services firm that specializes in developing leaders at all levels. He's also an executive fellow in the Center for Innovation and Entrepreneurship, Leavey School of Business, Santa Clara University. A popular seminar and conference speaker, in 1993 Kouzes was cited by the *Wall Street Journal* as one of the twelve most-requested "nonuniversity executive-education providers" to U.S. companies. Among his clients have been AT&T, Arthur Anderson, Bank of America, Boeing, Charles Schwab, Consumers Energy, Dell Computer, Federal Express, Johnson & Johnson, 3M, Motorola, Pacific Telesis, and the YMCA.

Edward E. Lawler III joined the faculty of Yale University as assistant professor of industrial administration and psychology after graduating from the University of California at Berkeley in 1964. In 1978, he became a professor in the Marshall School of Business at the University of Southern California. During 1979, he founded and became director of the University's Center for Effective Organization. In 1982, he was named professor of research at the University of Southern California. In 1999, he was named Distinguished Professor of Business.

Lawler has been honored as a major contributor to theory, research, and practice in the fields of human resources management, compensation, organizational development, and organizational effectiveness. He is the author or coauthor of over two hundred articles and thirty books. His most recent books include *Tomorrow's Organization* (Jossey-Bass, 1998), *Strategies for High-Performance Organizations: The CEO Report* (Jossey-Bass, 1998), *The Leadership Challenge Handbook* (Jossey-Bass, 1999), and *Rewarding Excellence* (Jossey-Bass, 2000).

Jean Lipman-Blumen is an organizational sociologist who received her Ph.D. from Harvard University and both A.B. and A.M. degrees from Wellesley College. She spent two postdoctoral years of study in mathematics, statistics, and computer science, the first at Carnegie-Mellon University and the second at Stanford University. In addition to her professorial roles at Claremont Graduate University, she is cofounding director of the Institute for Advanced Studies in Leadership at the Peter F. Drucker Graduate School of Management. She also is director of the Achieving Styles Institute, a Pasadena-based consulting group.

Before coming to Claremont, Lipman-Blumen held appointments as visiting professor of sociology and organizational behavior at the universities of Connecticut and Maryland. Prior to that, she served on the Domestic Policy Staff under President Carter. Lipman-Blumen spent 1978–79 as a fellow at the Center for Advanced Study in the Behavioral Sciences. From 1973 to 1978, she was an assistant director of the National Institute of Education (NIE), where she directed the Women's Research Program. Subsequent to her NIE appointment, she served as a special assistant in the Office of the Assistant Secretary for Education. From 1979 to 1984, she served as president of LBS International, Ltd., a Washington-based policy analysis and management consulting firm.

James O'Toole is research professor in the Center for Effective Organizations at the University of Southern California. In 1994, he retired after a career of over twenty years on the faculty of USC's Graduate School of Business, where he held the University Associates' Chair of Management. At USC he served as executive director of the Leadership Institute, editor of *New Management* magazine, and director of the Twenty-Year Forecast Project (where from 1973 through 1983 he interpreted social, political, and economic change for the top management of thirty of the largest U.S. corporations). O'Toole's research and writings have been in the areas of political philosophy, planning, corporate culture, and leadership. He has published over seventy articles and thirteen books. His most recent books, *Leading Change* and *Leadership A TO Z: A Guide for the Appropriately Ambitious,* are both published by Jossey-Bass.

O'Toole received his doctorate in Social Anthropology from Oxford University, where he was a Rhodes Scholar. He has served as a special assistant to Secretary of Health, Education and Welfare Elliot Richardson, as chairman of the Secretary's Task Force on Work in America, and as director of field investigations for President Nixon's Commission on Campus Unrest. He has won a coveted Mitchell Prize for a paper on economic growth policy, has served on the prestigious Board of Editors of the *Encyclopaedia Britannica,* and has served as editor of the *American Oxonian* magazine.

From 1994 through 1997 O'Toole was executive vice president of the Aspen Institute. Most recently, he has been managing director of the Booz•Allen & Hamilton Strategic Leadership Center, where he currently serves as chair of the center's academic Board of Advisors.

Tom Peters followed *In Search of Excellence* (1982, with Robert H. Waterman Jr., and named by NPR as one of the three most influential management books of the century) with four more best-selling hardback books: *A Passion for Excellence* (1985, with Nancy Austin), *Thriving on Chaos* (1987), *Liberation Management* (1992, and recently acclaimed as the "Management Book of the Decade" for the 1990s), *The Circle of Innovation: You Can't Shrink Your Way to Greatness* (1997); and a pair of best-selling paperback originals, *The Tom Peters Seminar: Crazy Times Call for Crazy Organizations* (1993) and *The Pursuit of WOW!: Every Person's Guide to Topsy-Turvy Times* (1994). The first three of his new series of books on reinventing work were released in September 1999.

Peters is a graduate of Cornell (B.C.E., M.C.E.) and Stanford (MBA, Ph.D.). He served on active duty in the U.S. Navy in Vietnam (a Navy Seabee) and Washington from 1966 to 1970, was a senior White House drug abuse adviser in 1973–74, and worked at McKinsey & Co. from 1974 to 1981, becoming a partner in 1977. He is a fellow of the International Academy of Management, the World Productivity Association, the International Customer Service Association, and the Society for Quality and Participation.

Barry Z. Posner is dean and professor of leadership at the Leavey School of Business, Santa Clara University. He coauthored (with Jim Kouzes) several award-winning books on leadership, along with two other books in the area of project management, and is the author of more than ninety academic and practitioner-oriented articles on leadership, organizational culture, managerial values, and teamwork. He serves on the editorial review board of three journals and is on the board of directors of several organizations. He is a widely renowned leadership speaker, and has conducted leadership development programs for organizations around the globe, including Applied Materials, Ciba-Geigy, Conference Board of Canada, Hewlett-Packard, Kaiser Permanente Health Care, Levi Strauss & Co., Merck, Network Appliance, and the U.S. Postal Service.

Alastair G. Robertson heads up Accenture's Worldwide Leadership Development Practice. He is also a partner in the Organizational and Human Performance Competency, providing in-depth expertise in strategic change, leadership, and organizational performance. He has worked extensively with clients on the development of leadership behaviors specifically linked to the building of enhanced performance, tailored to the context of an organization's business strategy. He is a specialist in individual, team, and organization leadership assessment and behavior development, building on personal motivational strengths, and is an adviser and coach to many European and U.S.-based executives. His clients include many Fortune 500 companies across all industry sectors. In addition to consulting and coaching, Robertson conducts research in leadership on an ongoing basis and is regularly interviewed by the media on this topic.

Robertson has also published extensively in books and professional journals; recent publications include "The Leader Within" (June 1999), "Leadership Under Stress" (February 1999),

"Leadership's New Convergence" (October 1998), "E-Leadership" (November 1999), and "Leadership: One Size Does Not Fit All" (March 2000), as well as a chapter in the book *Coaching for Leadership* published in May 2000 (Wiley). Robertson has an M.S. from the University of Glasgow, United Kingdom, and spent a total of twelve years with the Pillsbury Corporation, PepsiCo, and Mars Inc. before joining PA Consulting in London in 1994. He joined Accenture in 1995.

Philip Slater was a professor of sociology and department chair at Brandeis University in 1971 when he decided to leave academia. He cofounded Greenhouse, Inc., a growth center, then moved to Santa Cruz to study theater and write plays. He is the author of ten books of nonfiction and a novel, *How I Saved the World.* His nonfiction includes *The Pursuit of Loneliness, Wealth Addiction,* and *A Dream Deferred,* and he is coauthor with Warren Bennis of *The Temporary Society.* His articles have appeared in the *Washington Post, Newsday, Psychology Today, Ms.,* and various professional journals. He is currently at work on a new nonfiction book, tentatively titled *The Gun and the Web.*

Jeffrey Sonnenfeld is chairman and president of the Chief Executive Leadership Institute, a nonprofit organization dedicated to the advancement of management education through scholarly research and peer-driven educational programs. He is also an adjunct professor at Yale University's School of Management. Previously, he was a professor at the Goizueta Business School of Emory University. There he founded the Center for Leadership & Career Studies, which he ran for eight years. Prior to this, Sonnenfeld spent ten years as a professor at the Harvard Business School. His research, publications, and consulting address issues of top leadership development, executive succession, and board governance.

Sonnenfeld received his A.B., MBA, and doctorate from Harvard University. He has been the recipient of the Irwin Award for Social Research in Industry, AT&T's Hawthorne Fellowship for Social Research in Industry, the John P. Whitehead Faculty Fellowship, and—on two occasions—Emory's Outstanding Educator Award. He was awarded another Outstanding Educator Award in 1996 from the American Society for Training and Development, the nation's professional association for corporate educators. Sonnenfeld has published five books and numerous articles in the areas of career management, executive training and development, and the management of corporate social performance. He has served as a member of the board of governors of the Academy of Management, and recently chaired the Blue Ribbon Commission on CEO Succession for the National Association of Corporate Directors. Sonnenfeld has served on several boards of directors.

Gretchen M. Spreitzer is a faculty member at the University of Southern California's Marshall School of Business and a faculty affiliate of both the Center for Effective Organizations and the Leadership Institute. She focuses her research in the areas of employee empowerment and managerial development, particularly in a context of organizational change and decline. Based on extensive field research, she has authored numerous articles on contemporary issues in organizational behavior. Her recent books include *A Company of Leaders: Five Disciplines for Unleashing the Power in Your Workforce* (2001, with Robert Quinn) and *The Leader's Change Handbook: An Essential Guide to Setting Direction and Taking Action* (1999, edited with Jay Conger and Edward Lawler). She completed her doctoral work and continues to teach in executive education programs at the University of Michigan School of Business. She is an editor of the *Journal of Management Inquiry* and on the Editorial Board of the *Journal of Organizational Behavior.* She is also a member of the Academy of Management (where she serves on the Executive Board of the Organization Development and Change Division), the Western Academy of Management (where she serves on the Executive Board as well). She was recognized as an Ascendant Scholar by the Western Academy of Management in 1997.

Thomas A. Stewart is a member of the Board of Editors of *Fortune* and the author of the monthly management column, "The Leading Edge," as well as other articles. His book, *Intellectual Capital: The New Wealth of Organizations,* was a finalist for the Financial Times/Booz•Allen & Hamilton award for the best business book of the year in 1997. In 1999, the American Society for Training and

Development gave him its second Champion of Workplace Learning and Performance Award—won the previous year by General Electric CEO Jack Welch. In 1996, *Business Intelligence* awarded Stewart its inaugural Knowledge Management Awareness Award. In 1993, the *Journal of Financial Reporting* named him to its "Blue Chip Newsroom" of best business journalists. The previous year, he received the Gay and Lesbian Alliance Against Defamation Media Award for his December 1991 cover story, "Gay in Corporate America."

Prior to joining *Fortune,* Stewart worked in the book publishing business for eighteen years, serving as editor-in-chief, president, and publisher of Atheneum Publishers. He held editorial jobs at Harcourt Brace Jovanovich and Farrar, Straus & Giroux. He has written articles that were published in *Manhattan, Inc., 7 Days, Town and Country,* the *New York Times,* and *Harvard Magazine.* His areas of expertise include intellectual capital, the management of change, human resources, business sociology, global competitiveness, and information technology. Stewart is a fellow of the World Economic Forum and served as an adviser to the World Bank's 1998 World Development Report. He graduated summa cum laude from Harvard College in 1970.

Karl E. Weick is the Rensis Likert Collegiate Professor of Organizational Behavior and Psychology and professor of psychology at the University of Michigan. His Ph.D. is from Ohio State University in social and organizational psychology. He is a former editor of the journal *Administrative Science Quarterly* (1977–1985), former associate editor of the journal *Organizational Behavior and Human Performance* (1971–1977), and current topic editor for human factors at the journal *Wildfire.* Weick's research interests include collective sensemaking under pressure, medical errors, handoffs and transitions in dynamic events, high-reliability performance, improvisation, and continuous change. His book *The Social Psychology of Organizing* was named by *Inc.* magazine as one of the "nine best business books ever written."